Y0-BQR-684

Scientific Journals: Issues in Library Selection and Management

About the Author

Tony Stankus graduated from Holy Cross College in 1973. He took his Master of Library Science degree from the University of Rhode Island, and in 1974 returned to Holy Cross as Science Librarian. In 1982, members of Sigma XI, the national honors society for the promotion of science, awarded Tony a certificate of recognition for his efforts on behalf of research at the school. In that year, he also became Adjunct Professor for Special Libraries in the U.R.I. librarianship program. In 1983, after the acceptance of three of his papers in *Science & Technology Libraries*, editor Ellis Mount of Columbia University invited him to become a member of the editorial board. In 1984, he was assigned his own column.

Tony gardens and fishes when not working or writing. Along with his wife, a public health nurse, he is active at St. Paul's Cathedral, an inner city church of the local Catholic Diocese.

Scientific Journals: Issues in Library Selection and Management

Tony Stankus, MLS
Editor

The Haworth Press
New York • London

Scientific Journals: Issues in Library Selection and Management is monographic supplement #3 to *The Serials Librarian*. It is not supplied as part of the subscription to the journal, but is available from the publisher at an additional charge.

The Haworth Press, Inc., 12 West 32 Street, New York, NY 10001
EUROSPAN/Haworth, 3 Henrietta Street, London WC2E 8LU England

Library of Congress Cataloging-in-Publication

Scientific journals.

(Monographic supplement #3 to the Serials librarian)
Includes bibliographical references and index.
1. Libraries – Special collections – Scientific literature. 2. Serials control systems. 3. Acquisition of scientific publications. 4. Acquisition of serial publications. 5. Science – Periodicals – Bibliography – Methodology. 6. Scientific libraries – Collection development. I. Stankus, Tony. II. Series: Monographic supplement . . . to the Serials librarian; #3.
Z688.S3S35 1987 025.2′832 87-7047
ISBN 0-86656-616-3

Dedication

This book is dedicated to my wife, Mary Frances Stankus, RN, who has thankfully persevered with a patient whose fever for writing is probably beyond treatment. This work also serves as a remembrance of my late infant son, Andrew Francis Stankus.

CONTENTS

Acknowledgements

Many of these papers could not have been written without exceptionally capable and understanding coauthors. I thank them all:

BARBARA A. LOCKETT, the former Barbara A. Rice, now Director of Libraries, Rensselaer Polytechnic Institute.

RASHELLE KARP, the former Rashelle Schlessinger, now Assistant Professor, College of Library Science, Clarion University of Pennsylvania.

BERNARD S. SCHLESSINGER, now Professor and Associate Dean, School of Library Science, Texas Woman's University.

VIRGIL P. DIODATO, now Reference Librarian, Governor's State University.

KEVIN ROSSEEL, now a student at the Indiana University Graduate School of Library and Information Science.

WILLIAM LITTLEFIELD, Assistant to the Science Librarian, Science Library, College of the Holy Cross.

I wish to especially thank Ellis Mount, Editor, *Science & Technology Libraries*, faculty member, Columbia University School of Library Service, and winner of the John Cotton Dana Award of the Special Libraries Association, for both writing the introduction and for sustained encouragement of my work.

Finally, I wish to thank the following publishers and copyright holders, not of The Haworth Press family, who allowed the reprinting of papers from their journals for this collection:

The College of Information Studies, Drexel University, for the paper "The Serials Librarian as a Shaper of Scholars and Scholarship" from the *Drexel Library Quarterly*, volume 21, number 1, pages 112-119, Winter, 1985.

Pergamon Press for the paper "New Specialized Journals, Mature Scientists, and Shifting Loyalties" from *Library Acquisitions: Practice and Theory*, volume 9, pages 99-104, 1985.

The Graduate School of Library and Information Science, acting for the Board of Trustees of the University of Illinois, for the paper

"Looking for Tutors and Brokers: Comparing the Expectations of Book and Journal Evaluators" from *Library Trends*, volume 33, number 3, pages 349-365, Winter, 1985.

The Office of Rights and Permissions, the American Library Association, for the paper "Publication Quality Indicators for Tenure or Promotion Decisions: What Can the Librarian Ethically Report? from *College and Research Libraries*, volume 44, number 2, pages 173-178.

Introduction

Anyone with only a slight knowledge of sci-tech libraries is likely to realize soon after working in and with them that journals are the backbone of most libraries devoted to science and technology. The reasons are many—the ability of journals to present current information, the fact that articles are often written on very specific topics, the great variety of topics covered, etc. Scientists and engineers would be lost if the supply of journals suddenly disappeared through some disastrous set of circumstances.

It is thus appropriate for a supplement to this journal to be devoted to the nature and problems of collecting science journals. It is also appropriate that this supplement has been prepared by Tony Stankus. I know of no other librarian in recent years who has written so many articles on science and engineering journals. His research has taken him from citation analysis to faculty output of papers to the relation of foreign language journals to those in English. Not only has his output been voluminous, it has also been original and carefully researched.

Readers of this supplement should find examination of its contents a worthwhile experience.

Ellis Mount, Research Scholar
School of Library Service
Columbia University

THEME ONE

The Life-Long Affair: Scientific Careers and Science Journals

This section is founded on two assumptions: that scientists are not born knowing about science journals and that once they find out about them, they can't live without them. The essential tension is in deciding how many are needed to keep both the scientists who use them and the librarians who pay for them reasonably happy. The key to striking good deals lies in frank communication between the two groups. Each initiates the exchange of information at different times during their careers. When the scientist is a student, the librarian must take the lead. The knowledgeable librarian has much to teach the neophyte scientist at a time when he or she is very likely to need help. Librarians who fail in this opportunity make it difficult for all the other librarians farther down the line. Without a sharp, well-versed librarian to shape his or her thinking, the scientist may well have developed a sense of assurance about journals that is based more on glands than sound information. As the scientist matures, on the other hand, the librarian must listen at least as much as speak. It is a common mistake to assume that since the scientist is not talkative, he or she is not telling us anything. Every time he or she uses a journal in the collection, assigns students a reading from a journal, cites one journal in a manuscript and then sends that manuscript to yet another journal, he or she is talking about journals. And when the scientist stops doing all these things, the librarian must once again be bold. While the librarians instinct is usually that there is something wrong with the collection, it is equally probable that there is something wrong with the scientist. Libraries are filled with journal holdings for scientists who are no longer active. The librarian should perhaps be redirecting time and attention to that young science major now coming through the door.

The Serials Librarian as a Shaper of Scholars and Scholarship

Tony Stankus

INTRODUCTION

Between the ages of eighteen and thirty, the serials librarian's customers go from a position of almost total ignorance of scholarly journals to being contributors within them. Customer service to students, often seen by serials librarians as being disruptive and apart from the more serious duties of their working life, is in fact, an opportunity for those librarians to participate in one of the central rites of passage of a young scholar. Students, who may well begin their awareness of journals with a mixture of annoyance and confusion, should be viewed as young voyagers. They are about to undertake an odyssey, which with the librarian's help, can be made a little less frightening, and a little more rational. The end result will be increasingly confident adventures, in whose triumphs the librarian has a share.

INTO THE LABYRINTH

The initial encounters of students and scholarly journals may be many and varied, but are rarely of themselves a well-rounded introduction to the relative importance of scholarly journals in serious research. An encounter may come as part of a vague assignment to find and read some current papers on a topic discussed in class. They can arise from textbook references. They can come from the student's own browsing of displayed current periodicals. They can be stimulated by pathfinders or specialized bibliographies worked up by reference librarians. Curiosity can be piqued by commercially prepared reprint

Reprinted with permission from the *Drexel Library Quarterly*, volume 21, number 1, pages 112-119, Winter, 1985.

packages, or books of readings from the journal literature designed to supplement texts and lectures.

And yet, each possible introduction involves as much potential for confusion as for orientation. (See Table 1.) Getting the title right is often an immediate difficulty. Both the lack of a widely accepted uniform system of title abbreviations and the similarity of many titles pose problems. There is a bewildering variety of journals in terms of subjects, scope (multiscience, entire discipline, specialty, subspecialty, single topic), functions (preliminary accounts of research, fully described research papers, extended reviews of published research, capsule reviews of relevant papers in other journals, book reviews, personnel news, announcements of conferences, etc.), formats (thin typescript journals, fat typeset journals, journals that come hardbound, journals that come apart, journals in English, journals in foreign languages) and publishing schedules (journals that come weekly,

Table 1
Journal World View

Journal World View from Frequency of Textbook References	Journal World View from Frequency of Citations by Researchers
Books 134	*Journal of Biological Chemistry* 131,922
Scientific American 91	*Nature* 110,923
Science 30	*Proceedings of the National Academy of Sciences* 110,436
Annual Review of Biochemistry 8	*Biochimica et Biophysica Acta* 71,656
Nature 8	*Science* 70,867
Trends in Biochemical Science 7	*Biochemistry* 46,682
Federal Procurement 5	*Biochemical Journal* 38,440
FEBS Letters 4	*Biochemical and Biophysical Research Communications* 35,407
Advances in Enzymology 3	*Cell* 29,150
Essays in Biochemistry 3	*European Journal of Biochemistry* 26,223
Current Topics in Cellular Regulation 3	*FEBS Letters* 23,224
Journal of Biological Chemistry 2	*Analytical Biochemistry* 22,737
Perspectives in Biology and Medicine 2	*Archives of Biochemistry and Biophysics* 19,883
Proceedings of the National Academy of Sciences 2	Perhaps 50 others
Others 17	

Note: Contrasting the relative importance of books and given journals as seen by the student through references in a widely adopted textbook versus the actual citations of researchers in 1982, a student might well surmise that an assortment of books and a subscription to *Scientific American* were what mattered in biochemistry, and that the *Journal of Biological Chemistry* and the *Proceedings of the National Academy of Sciences* were relatively minor titles! Sources: Albert L. Lehninger. *Principles of Biochemistry*. New York: Worth, 1982, and Eugene Garfield, ed. and comp. *Journal Citation Reports*, Philadelphia: Institute for Scientific Information, 1982.

monthly, quarterly, annually, journals that come whenever the publisher feels like publishing them). Added to this is the problem of the differing locations of journals within the library, making their physical retrieval a problem. Most libraries shelve current periodicals, bound periodicals, and indexing-abstracting tools all separately.

As if all of this were not a problem, students trying to read articles in scholarly journals find further bewilderment. They are often aggravated to find that articles are not written at their level of comprehension, much as textbooks are. Article structure is often fragmented into parts with unfamiliar names and often differing typefaces, with sizes ranging down to miniprint. Gone, in many cases, is familiar illustrative material; in its place may be spectra, graphs, equations, and schematics. In many cases the promise of a subject entry in a searching tool does not seem fulfilled when the article itself is examined. In initial contacts with journal literature, students may simply complain that they cannot read the article and walk away.

The librarian must understand that the students' frustrations are due in part to justified exasperation with the eccentric world of journals, and in part due to the students' personal immaturity. The librarian can do much to ameliorate the first situation and should not give in to the second.

In this rite of journal passage there are many arbitrary difficulties in which the librarian can reasonably help a searcher. And each occasion can provide an opportunity to fill in the gaps in a student's journal world view, as well as to correct misconceptions. While deciphering an abbreviation, for example, the librarian can tell the student a little bit about other journals which had their origins as "Proceedings." Instruction in the use of an indexing-abstracting tool can directly help the student understand the magnitude and importance of the journal literature, as well as locate a current paper on a topic. Examining the bibliography of an annual reviews type publication provides an opening for a discussion of this genre as compared to, say, a preliminary communications journal, while providing some legitimate savings in search time. A little creativity in demonstrating the use of a citation index helps to settle doubts in the mind of a student about whether or not people actually pay attention to given articles, or given journals. One service provided at the author's Science Library is the checking of citations in term papers and lab reports for style. Since many students now compose their papers via remote terminals connected to the campus' mainframe, the librarian and customer can call up the draft at the librarian's desk terminal, and make changes before a hard copy is printed offline. Not only does this reasonably reduce student anxiety over what is essentially an arbitrary detail, it provides the librarian with a good feel for the increasing extent and maturing nature of journal use by the subject. It is important to tell the student that in many cases, questions cannot be answered with a simple rule. Sometimes *ann.* stands for *annals* and sometimes for *annual*. Sometimes a "quarterly review" will come trimestrally and contain neither survey articles nor book reports. The wise librarians promotes further confidence-building experiences for the young explorer, but also hopes to develop within him or her a certain tolerance of persistent ambiguity and to encourage inventiveness in the face of complexity.

Above all, the librarian must guard against commiseration ("Yes, isn't his awful. I know I hated it!"), a tendency to do the substantive reading of the text for the student ("The author means that *x* is greater than *y*, and that . . . "), or dubious shortcut suggestions ("You'll never have to plow through all this; just read the abstract, and fake it"). The correct responses to tough situations are positive reinforcement that suggest that the goal is important and worth the effort: "This paper is by a Nobel Prizewinner"; "This journal is the most cited in its field"; "Important cancer research is often found here"; "Members of your department had six papers in these two journals already this year." The serials librarian should develop an ability to flesh out scholarly journals in terms of some of the people and achievements associated with them. The serials librarian who is an uninformed, uninventive, dispassionate dispenser of photocopies will readily be replaced by a full-text, online journal article dispenser. The serials librarian who participates eagerly, even provocatively, in the development of new research and researchers will be around for some time to come.

THE SORCERER'S APPRENTICE

Both encouragement and the sophistication of assistance must increase as the young scholar begins research for publication, and that can occur as early as the junior undergraduate year. (See Figure 1.) Not only does routine journal and article finding take on a new seriousness, but new considerations must be addressed. Will the paper be a preliminary communication, or a fully reported article, or will it be broken up into several articles? Is it a paper in an existing series? (What were its predecessors like?) Which style does this journal adhere to? Given a choice of journals, what can you tell the student about their relative prestige, citedness, society affiliations, rejection rates,

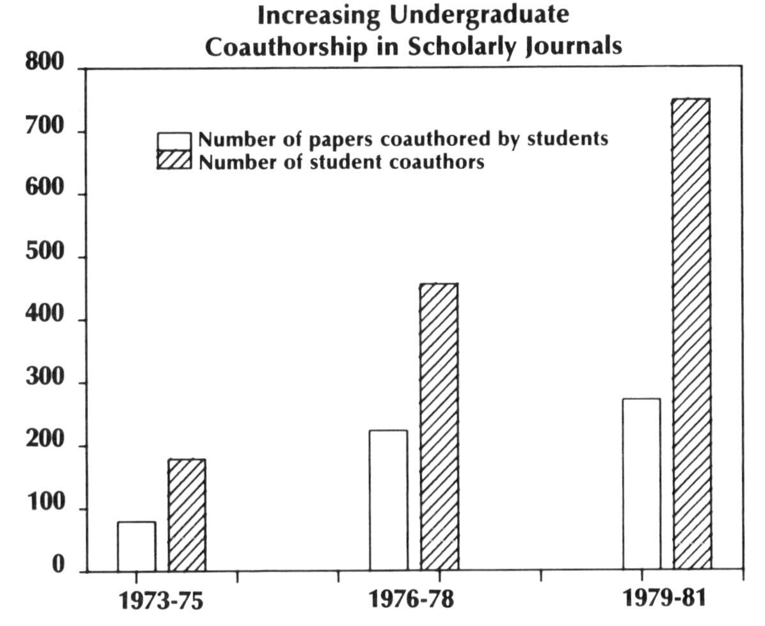

Figure 1. While the graduate school years are probably the principal time for young scholars to begin coauthoring articles in serious journals, an increasing number of undergraduates in small, competitive liberal arts colleges are getting an early start. Yet the number of students per article is increasing even more rapidly. Is each student still given an adequate explanation of journal background? Data derived from Brian Andreen, Editor, *Research in Chemistry at Private Undergraduate Colleges*. Council on Undergraduate Research, 1979, and Eugene Garfield, Editor and Compiler, Corporate Source Index, v. 7, *Science Citation Index Annuals 1979–1981*. Philadelphia: Institute for Scientific Information.

manuscript turnaround times? What can you tell the student about the journal's editors or reviewers? While some critics will suggest that all of this is the business of the faculty member directing the research, the young scholar has a special stake that could easily be overlooked. The research director is typically more interested in getting the bench work done and the manuscript out in time than in explaining details such as these to the student. Yet, without discussion of these details, an opportunity to educate the students on a higher plane is lost. They are treated as technicians. Their view of the world of journals, research, and manuscript preparation reverts to confusion or mindless conformism. The serials librarian can make sense of some of the ritual to the students and bring them beyond mere "task fulfillment" to an understanding of fundamental rationale and overall strategy of research and publication. This becomes increasingly important as students pursue graduate research. Without this sense of broad vision, they may well pursue projects that are ultimately unpublishable.

LIKE JANUS, LOOKING BACKWARD AND FORWARD

The consultative relationship between the serials librarian and young scientists does not end when they complete their doctorate, for in many cases they gradually lose their other advisor, the dissertation director. While newly emancipated scholars will likely follow their advisors' footsteps in choices of journals for publication for three to five years, they are faced with setting up new scholarly contacts, choosing new research problems, and identifying the journals which favor them. (See Table 2.) New postdoctorate scholars particularly need intelligence work from the serials librarian on the journals favored by their new immediate colleagues or the industrial firm which has hired them. In many instances they will need help in readjusting their sights after early manuscript rejections (a situation which almost certainly happened to the advisor, but which the advisor was unlikely to have discussed with them). The proper response from the serials librarian in such cases is a packet of "Instructions for Authors" of competitive journals, chosen perhaps from a combination of experience and the citation interactions in the field as seen in *Journal Citation Reports*. In some settings the postdoctorate student will need to deal with the stylistic distinctions among writing technical reports for

Table 2
Advisor/Student Publication Patterns

Journal Type	Publications of Advisor Before Young Scholar	Publications in Which Advisor & Young Scholar Coauthor	Publications of Young Scholar After Advisor
Multidisciplinary	88 (11%)	20 (8%)	71 (9%)
Core Discipline	296 (36%)	114 (46%)	209 (26%)
Subspecialty, neighboring discipline, applied specialty	448 (54%)	114 (46%)	539 (66%)
Totals	832	248	819

Note: Thesis advisors seem to pass on two stronger journal preferences: one for core journals that integrate young scholars among others in their discipline; the other for subspecialty, neighboring discipline or the applied specialty titles that set them apart. There tends to be a tension at this stage of a young scholar's career between maintaining the pattern suggested by the advisor and establishing one's own way, with the latter approach favored after 3–5 years. Source: Tony Stankus, "Negotiating Journal Demands with Young Scientists Using Thesis Advisor Records," *Collection Management* 5 (Fall/Winter 1983):185–98.

internal distribution, grant requests, and patent applications. All of these are likely to require extensive serials work.

FACING THE HYDRA

Even when the scholar is no longer young, the serials librarian can still offer insights at two junctures.

The first is field-switching. While some scholars will make barely perceptible moves from their original areas of study, the worlds of granting and the marketplace continue to force changes in the need for journals information even among mature scholars. An advantage here is that the scholars will often have parallels in their old field to go by. New items may include publishers that have unique prominence in the new field, and unfamiliar stylistic conventions in journal format or manuscript preparation. Some fields will also have their own specialized indexing/abstracting/altering systems.

The second instance for aid from the serials librarian is tied in with the appearance of new journals. Aggressive librarians will obtain information on the editors, early contributors, early citation records, early records of manuscript turnaround time, supposed-versus-actual dates of publication and distribution, cost comparisons. The underlying questions include both subscription need from the librarian's viewpoint and suitability for manuscript submission in terms of the scholar. The serials librarian should develop an instinct as well for the response of the old journals to the new competitor. Will they improve their format, schedules, or conditions for acceptance? In this day of exploding numbers of journals and imploding library budgets, few publishers can stand still in the face of challenges to their turf. (See Table 3.) The serials librarian is facing a lively new age of bare knuckles competition among print publishers, and will increasingly see this as involving electronic publisher as well. The alert serials librarian will continue to be of value as advisor as long as publishing remains in flux, research continues, and young scholars need shaping.

Table 3
A Test

A
Journal of Comparative Physiological Psychology 1921
Physiology and Behavior 1966
Physiological Psychology 1973
B
Journal of Organometallic Chemistry 1963

TABLE 3 (continued)

Polyhedron 1982
Organometallics 1982

C

Journal of Cellular Physiology 1932
Experimental Cell Research 1950
Journal of Cell Biology 1955
Journal of Cell Science 1966
Cytobios 1969
Cell 1974

Note: The endless introduction of new competitors for roughly the same pool of scholarly journal contributors requires the serials librarian to be ready with much more sophisticated information than price, frequency, and bibliographic description for even the mature scholars. How many readers could answer the following questions of importance to a customer with a manuscript: In which group has the oldest journal maintained the highest impact factors? In which is it the youngest? Which journal in group B seems to be attracting the highest proportion of papers from highly rated US graduate programs in its field? Answers are A, C, and *Organometallics*.

Negotiating Journal Demands With Young Scientists Using Lists Derived From Thesis Advisor Records

Tony Stankus

ABSTRACT. This paper combines insights from the Sociology of Science concerning the strong role of thesis advisors in shaping the attitudes of young scientists with an appreciation of *Journal Citation Reports* in identifying families of related journals. The result is a series of tools for the librarian to use in anticipating or confirming the journal purchase request of this particular clientele. It is shown that checklists based on the individual master/apprentice relationship can be prepared prior to the first meeting of librarian and young scientist, can be used with confidence in negotiations, and are often superior to lists based on more generalized data. A successful test involving the case studies of 231 young biochemists and their advisors is offered as tentative validation of these procedures.

INTRODUCTION

A journal needs interview may well set the tone for the working relationship between a librarian and a newly appointed, typically recently graduated, science faculty member. While the librarian often has a somewhat vague authorization from the top administration to go along with "appropriate" requests within "budgetary reason," he or she may still feel some uncertainty about the course of initial interviews with such scientists. The librarian may well lack subject expertise.[1] He or she cannot guess the costs involved when it is not known which journals are likely to be requested. The interview can well degenerate into a professorial lecture with the young scientist making a

Reprinted from *Collection Management*, volume 5, numbers 3/4, pages 185-198, 1983.

series of requests that seem impossible to respond to, while the librarian docilely takes notes for what amounts to a "take-home exam." In such a circumstance, the new scientist can well leave the interview with no firm answers but with a firm impression of the librarian as an order clerk with little sophistication and authority.

Other course, the librarian has reason to be cautious. The money involved for science journal subscriptions is usually serious. He or she is unlikely to have a report on the young scientist's journal use during graduate school. The few publications that the young scientist has on his *vita* may be too little evidence upon which to base purchase requests. Moreover, these journals probably reflect the preferences of his dissertation advisor.

Ironically, too quick an abandonment of this last point can cause the librarian to miss an important opportunity. This paper suggests that an advisor's publication list offers clues to the young scientist's journal wants and early pattern of publication – and does so prior to the interview, giving the librarian a basis for an advance investigation of the possibilities. Particularly when the advisor's list is augmented by adding other journals that these original journals cite, it becomes what this paper will define as an anticipatory checklist. When information on current holdings and prices for unheld journals is entered as well, the librarian can advise his or her higher-ups of the range of costs involved and often get the kind of meaningful clearance in advance that will permit an immediate response, even as the new scientist enumerates his or her requests. When unanticipated requests crop up, a variant of the anticipatory procedure, which this paper will define as confirmatory checklisting, enables the librarian to momentarily confirm or query them.

The young scientist is likely to respect his more thorough preparation on the part of the librarian, and appreciate the sense of active interest implied by the brisk give-and-take that ensues. It is important that the librarian be in a good position to contradict a request on either budgetary grounds (through prior discussion of parameters with his or her superiors) or subject appropriateness (by arguing from data that this paper will show to have predictive power), and thereby avoid any suggestion that a negative reply is some sort of prejudice directed at the young scientist personally. The validity of this paper's approach is demonstrated by showing that journals that might have been cleared for purchase for members of a group of young scientists at the time of their hiring often turned out to be the actual journals in which these scientists appeared in following years.

METHODS FOR THE HISTORICAL STUDY AND CURRENT APPLICATIONS

Biochemistry was chosen as a test discipline for the study, as it had both sufficient journals to ensure randomness[2] and entailed sufficient costliness[3] to make the procedure worthwhile. A list of 231 matched pairs of dissertation advisors and PhD recipients was drawn up from the classes of 1974 and 1975 as reported in *Dissertation Abstracts*.[4] Using *Biological Abstracts*,[5] the journal outlets of the advisors were recorded for the years 1970-75, and those of the young scientists from 1974-82, with any coauthorship noted and credited to the advisor, for reasons noted later. The advisors' direct lists were individually augmented by adding the journals that were cited in them according to the "Citing Journal Package" of the 1975 *Journal Citation Reports*.[6-7] It should be noted that it was not then, or now, necessary to include obviously inappropriate titles cited in any multiscience journals on the advisor's list (e.g., when dealing with biochemists it is clearly not necessary to include citations made by the journal *Science to Astrophysical Journal* or *Deep Sea Research*). When the entry in *Journal Citation Reports* lists more than 50 items, the author's experience suggests that the top half yields 80% of the predictive power, and as a practical matter, is all that needs to be recorded. Finally, the librarian should not be daunted by what at first appears to be an overwhelming task involving several original journals and many cited journals as a "commonality-of-citations" effect occurs. When the librarian actually tallies the unique occurrence of titles, an anticipatory checklist based on four core disciplinary journals, each having 30 cited journals, will boil down to perhaps 40 journals, not 120. Moreover, experience will show that drawing up the lists is actually an assignable clerical task. The use of a word processor with sorting and alphabetizing routines further reduces the tedium.

Figure 1 is a composite but typical example drawn from the historical study. The direct list of the advisor and the subsequent list of the young scientist represent the average number of journals published in, and their variety of scope (multiscience, core disciplinary, subspecialty, neighboring discipline, applied discipline). There were between four and five journals for the 231 advisors (1081 overall), and between three and four journals for the 231 young scientists (819 overall). In Figure 1 the highlighted items correspond to titles in the advisor's list that subsequently appeared in that of the young scientist.

Figure 2 shows how an unanticipated request that came out during

ADVISOR'S DIRECT LIST . . . .

Science Biochemistry J. BIOL. CHEM.* Lipids J. Bact.

JOURNALS AUGMENTING THE ADVISOR'S DIRECT LIST . . . .

Am. J. Physiol.

Anal. Biochem.

Anal. Chem.

Ann. N.Y. Acad. Sci.

Annu. Rev. Biochem.

Arch. Biochem. Biophys.

Bacteriol. Revs.

Biochem. Biophys. Res. Commun.

Biochem. J.

Biochim. Biophys. Acta

Biopolymers

Brain Res.

Can. J. Biochem.

Can. J. Micro.

Cancer Res.

Chem. Phys. Lipids

Cold Spring Harb. Symp.

Comp. Biochem. Physiol.

Endocrinology

Eur. J. Biochem.

Experientia

Exp. Cell Res.

FEBS Lett.

Fed. Proc.

Gastroenterology

J. Am. Chem. Soc.

J. Cell Biol.

J. Chem. Phys.

J. Chromatogr.

J. Clin. Invest.

J. Dairy Sci.

J. Exp. Med.

J. Gen. Micro.

J. Immunol.

J. LIPID RES.*

J. Mol. Biol.

J. Nat. Canc. Inst.

J. NUTR.*

J. Org. Chem.

J. Pharm. Exp. Therap.

J. Physiol. (London)

Methods Enzymol.

Mol. Gen. Genet.

Nature

New England J. Med.

Phytochem.

Proc. Nat. Acad. Sci.

Proc. Soc. Exp. Med. Biol.

Steroids

YOUNG SCIENTIST'S LIST . . . .

J. BIOL. CHEM.* J. LIPID RES.* J. NUTR.*

J. SCI. FOOD AGRIC.

FIGURE 1. An anticipatory checklist for the example in the text, minus current holdings or price information as would be appropriate in a real application. Journals are arranged alphabetically for quick referral during the interview. Highlighted journals in the advisor's lists match those of the young scientist. One journal, the *J. Sci. Food Agric.*, remained unanticipated.

UNANTICIPATED JOURNAL TO BE CONFIRMED USING THE CITED JOURNAL PACKAGE AND THE ADVISOR'S LIST . . . .

J. Sci. Food Agric.

ADVISOR'S DIRECT LIST . . . .

Science Biochemistry J. Biol. Chem. LIPIDS* J. Bact.

JOURNALS THAT CITE THE UNANTICIPATED JOURNAL . . . .

J. Sci. Food Agric.

J. Agric. Food Chem.

J. Food Sci.

Brit J. Nutr.

Phytochem.

Cereal Chem.

J. Sci. Industr. Res. India

Z. Lebensmittel. Untersuch.

Brit. Poultry Sci.

Adv. Chem. Series

Can. J. Anim. Sci.

Can. J. Food Sci. Tech.

Qual. Plant

J. Anim. Sci.

J. Agric. Sci.

Bull. Jap. Soc. Sci. Fish.

J. Chromatogr.

Plant & Soil

Chem. Industr. London

Pesticide Sci.

J. Inst. Brew.

World Poult. Sci. J.

Irish J. Agric. Res.

J. Dairy Sci.

Poultry Sci.

Process. Biochem.

Biochem. J.

Comp. Biochem.

J. Am. Oil Chem. Soc.

Agric. Biol. Chem. Tokyo

Agrochimica

Agron. J.

Analyst

Biochem. Physiol. Pflanzen

J. Soil. Sci.

LIPIDS*

Anal. Chem.

Can. J. Plant Sci.

Commun. Soil Sci. Plant.

J. Am. Soc. Hort. Sci.

Carbohydr. Res.

J. Nutr.

Lancet

Tropical Agric.

Ann. Zootech.

Austral. J. Agric. Res.

Crop. Sci.

J. Fish Res. Bd. Can.

Marine Biol.

Plant Sci Lett.

Z. Ernahrungwiss.

Anim. Prod.

Ann. Technol.

Appl. Microbiol.

Bull. Environ. Contamin.

Feedstuffs

J. Assoc. Off. Anal. Chem.

Physiol. Plant.

Zbl. Bakt. Parasit.

FIGURE 2. The unanticipated journal of the young scientist can be confirmed through the "Cited Journal Package" of *Journal Citation Reports*, with the list reproduced here in the order it appears. Highlighting indicates *Lipids*, a journal on the advisor's direct list.

the interview might be quickly confirmed using a reverse procedure. While *Journal Citation Reports* is still used, it is the "Cited Journal Package" that is consulted. Here the journal is analyzed in terms of which journals cite it. Confirmation is suggested by finding one or more of the journals on the advisor's list. Here again, the correspondence is highlighted in the figure.

It is important to understand, as one looks at these figures, that anticipatory lists can be expected to have many journals that will not be requested by the young scientist, and that confirmatory lists will show many links to journals other than those of the advisor, and that this does not compromise their validity or utility.

This paper is based on the assumption that an advisor can transmit, through his papers, a real interest in some of the subjects covered by a journal to a young scientist, and make him or her aware of other journals in the field through citations in those papers, without requiring him or her to absorb all the subjects of journals wholly. In particular, this paper argues that its methods are not so much invalidated by this young scientist's failure to follow through on clues provided by the advisor's *Journal of Bacteriology*, as much as validated by his following through along lines suggested by *Science, Biochemistry,* the *Journal of Biological Chemistry*, and *Lipids*.

It must be emphasized that anticipatory and confirmatory lists are not themselves the buying lists. These are hammered out in negotiations concerning only a small part of the longer lists. And as long as some of these are, they are generally much shorter than the list of holdings of most libraries or the entries in a jobber's catalog, and certainly more convenient to consult during an interview.

STEP-BY-STEP RESULTS

Figure 3 shows which steps in the procedure accounted for given shares of prediction or confirmation in the historical group study. The top tier shows step-by-step cumulative results. The lower tier shows the make up of the journals predicted or confirmed for the first time at any given step.

Approximately one journal in the average group of four (25%) for a young scientist could be anticipated directly from the advisor's direct, unaugmented list. This journal was most often one of the core disciplinary titles (e.g. the *Journal of Biological Chemistry*).

Use of an augmented list anticipated one or two more journals (63%). These were typically subspecialty journals (e.g. the *Journal of*

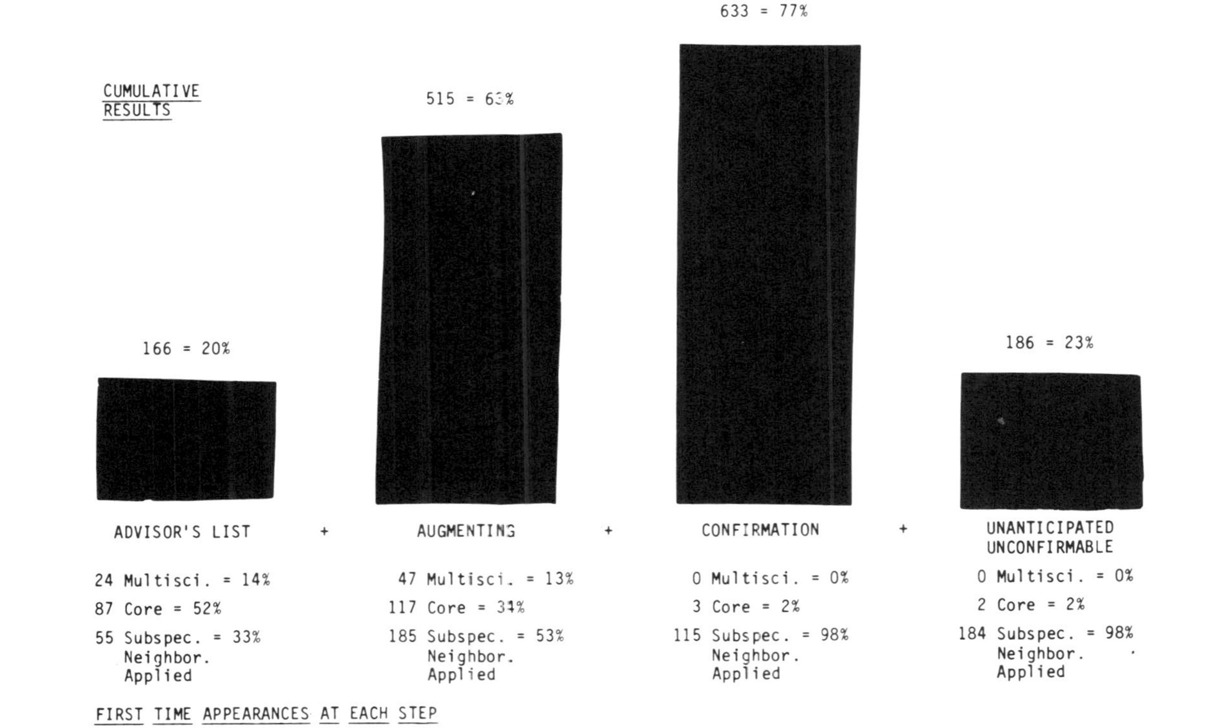

FIGURE 3. The top tier shows the mounting success after each step in the procedure: the lower tier, what types of journals are encountered at each step.

Lipid Research) or those of a neighboring discipline (e.g. the *Journal of Nutrition*).

When the study showed a journal that remained unanticipated, its entry in the "Cited Journal Package" was checked for a title on the advisor's own list for confirmation, much as the *Journal of the Science of Food and Agriculture* was confirmed by *Lipids*. It is at this confirmatory step that the more obviously applied journals are first encountered in any substantial numbers. They tend to be unanticipated because advisors tend to publish in pure journals, which cite other pure journals more often than they do applied titles. Nonetheless, enough interaction remains to boost the success rate an additional 14% to a final 77% of the total journals in which the young scientists actually appeared in subsequent years.

It should be noted here that multiscience journals are more important than their weak numerical showing indicates. Publication in journals like *Science* is prestigious partly because it is so rarely achieved. As a practical matter, many multiscience journals will be taken automatically in most libraries, obviating a need for anticipatory or confirmatory procedures to justify them.

ANSWERING AN IMPORTANT TECHNICAL OBJECTION

Would any list of roughly similar length anticipate as well as these individually tailored lists? What if, for example, the librarian were to consult a list based on the citation interactions of the best or biggest core disciplinary core journals, arguing that the discipline is best defined by its leading exclusively dedicated journals. This method has been successfully used by Garfield[8] to survey this very discipline. Such a list could be commercially published annually along with price information and blanks for current holdings, standardizing this anticipatory step in our procedure, and presumably saving the individual librarian a good deal of time.

As a test, just such a list was made by combining the citations to other journals made by arguably the best journal from the bio-medical community, the *Journal of Biological Chemistry*; the best journal from the chemistry community, *Biochemistry*; the most voluminous journal, *Biochimica et Biophysica Acta*, as well as seven other major Western-alliance English-language titles. See Figure 4.

As it turns out, this generalized core-based list anticipated the same number of journals in 159 cases (68% total cases). It even improved upon the individualized list four times (2%), usually in anticipating

DIRECT LIST OF CORE JOURNALS . . . .

Arch. Biochem. Biophys., Biochem. Biophys. Res. Commun., Biochem. J., Biochemistry, Biochim. Biophys. Acta, Can. J. Biochem., Eur. J. Biochem., FEBS Lett., J. Biochem. Tokyo, J. BIOL. CHEM.*

JOURNALS AUGMENTING THE CORE LIST . . . .

Acta Chem. Scand.
Advan. Enzymol.
Agric. Biol. Chem. Tokyo
Am. J. Physiol.
Anal. Biochem.
Anal. Chem.
Ann. N.Y. Acad. Sci.
Annu. Rev. Biochem.
Biochem. Pharmacol.
Biochem. Soc. Trans.
Biochimie
Biophys. J.
Biopolymers
Cancer Res.
Cold Spring Harbor Symposia
Endocrinology
Exp. Cell Res.
Fed. Proc.
Hoppe-Seylers Z. Physiol. Chemie.
J. Am. Chem. Soc.
J. Bacteriol.
J. Cell Biol.
J. Clin. Invest.
J. Exp. Med.
J. Gen. Micro.
J. LIPID RES.*
J. Mol. Biol.
J. Membrane Biol.
J. Nat. Canc. Inst.
J. Neurochem.
J. Pharm. Exp. Therap.
J. Virol.
Meth. Enzymol.
Mol. Gen. Genet
Nature
Photochem. Photobiol.
Phytochem.
Plant Physiol.
Proc. Nat. Acad. Scis.
Proc. Roy. Soc. Lond. B.
Proc. Soc. Exp. Med. Biol.
Science
Seikagaku
Steroids
Virology
Z. Naturforsch. B.

YOUNG SCIENTIST'S LIST . . . .

J. BIOL. CHEM.* J. LIPID RES.* J. NUTR.

J. Sci. Food Agric.

FIGURE 4. An anticipatory checklist based on a core list. Note its similarity to the individualized list in Figure 1, since it too had some core journals. Nonetheless it fails to anticipate one title, the *Journal of Nutrition*, identified in the earlier list.

one more journal, but in a surprising 68 cases (30%), the individualized lists remained superior, usually by the margin of one journal.

The equal performance in 68% of the cases is understandable. Virtually all the advisors in this study published in one or more of the core journals, and so their direct and augmented lists could be expected to be somewhat similar. Indeed, as Figure 5 shows, the generalized list actually does a slightly better job of telling the librarian what scholars of a given discipline have in common: core journals, of which five more were anticipated. The superiority of the individualized lists lies in telling the librarian what sets the particular scholar seated in front of him or her apart from others in the same general discipline: subspecialty, neighboring discipline, and more applied journals, of which 68 more were anticipated. By way of analogy, it appears wiser to anticipate the particular features of a "child-in-the-making" from a study of the most appropriate individualized information – his parents – as opposed to studying even good generalized data, like the Census, although both will often agree.

A proposal for the temporary reliance on this limited form of citation data might find acceptance even from the most eminent critic of the more general use of citation data in practical library journal collection management, Maurice Line. He allows for the use of citation data to identify pertinent journals in neighboring disciplines that are not yet taken in an otherwise satisfactory collection of core journals.[9] This, of course, is the special strength of the procedures outlined in the present study, except that it treats the new scientist as the variable to be considered in an otherwise presumably satisfied set of customers, whose well-established record of use guides the librarian.

Comparing the Success Rate of Two Approaches To Anticipatory Checklist Composition

	INDIVIDUALIZED ADVISOR-BASED	GENERALIZED CORE-BASED
Multiscience	71	71
Core	204	209
Subspecialty Neighboring Applied	240	167
Totals	515	447

FIGURE 5. In the historical study group, more journals could be anticipated by the individualized, advisor-based lists than by generalized, core-based lists. The key to their success lies in being more closely attuned to the subspecialty, neighboring discipline, and more applied journals that set individual scientists in the same discipline apart.

WHY DOES IT WORK? AN ANSWER FROM THE SOCIOLOGY OF SCIENCE

There is a seriously researched basis underlying the success of these anticipatory and confirmatory procedures. Recent work by Zuckerman[10] strongly suggests that it is in graduate school, and often from a thesis advisor, that a young apprentice is socialized in what it means to become a scientist. Apart from much factual information and many technical skills, the advisor imparts a set of critical thinking and transmits a sense of what research problems are worthwhile. It would be surprising if some notion of what journals were best or most appropriate for given kinds of work were not included.

One can imagine, for example, that a graduate student signs on with his advisor knowing what journals the advisor has published in.[11] (This is often publicized in graduate program announcements and catalogs, and reprints are often plastered all over departmental bulletin boards.) Porter[12] notes that apprentice scientists generally hold a very high opinion of their advisors' contributions to science, and presumably of the journals that publish them. Porter particulary stresses the role of the dissertation, and the papers derived from it, in setting the pace and tone of the young scientist's career. He reports that the young biochemist will write up to three papers, usually coauthored with the advisor after the dissertation, on topics related to it. In this study, 71% of the advisors and young scientists coauthored at least one paper (248 overall, 2.67 on average). What suggests that it is the advisor who chooses the journal of publication is that, in 70% of the cases, at least one of the journals is already represented in his list of recent publications.

This sense of direction, from advisor to apprentice, underlies the success of the individualized anticipation lists. There is particular emphasis on the less obvious journal choices: subspecialty, neighboring discipline, and the more applied title. At this impressionable juncture of coauthorship, journals of this kind share the lead with the more obvious core disciplinary outlets (46% each, 8% multiscience). See Figure 6.

One can still consider alternative time spans for an apprentice's development of journal preferences, but will most likely discard them as unreliable. This author[13] has demonstrated elsewhere that the undergraduate degree years are an unlikely time for this, despite at least two possible, plausible, influences. References in the most widely adopted textbooks stress a type of article and categories of journals that did not figure prominently in our study. These were survey articles in hard-

	ADVISOR BEFORE YOUNG SCIENTIST	ADVISOR & YOUNG SCIENTIST COAUTHOR	YOUNG SCIENTIST AFTER ADVISOR
Multisci	88(11%)	20(8%)	71(9%)
Core	296(36%)	114(46%)	209(26%)
Subspec Neighbor Applied	448(54%)	114(46%)	539(66%)
Totals	832	248	819

FIGURE 6. Advisors seem to pass on two stronger journal preferences: one for core journals that integrate the young scientist among others in his discipline; the other for subspecialty, neighboring, or the more applied journals that set him apart.

bound continuing serials (e.g. the *Annual Review of Biochemistry*), or in the major multiscience journals (e.g. *Science*), or in popular titles (e.g. *Scientific American*). Neither did the publication practices of those most closely involved in teaching undergraduates, liberal arts college biochemists, appear obviously influential. This group published primarily in a preliminary communications journal that features short papers, *Biochemical and Biophysical Research Communications*, and in a journal with a strong zoologist's orientation, *Comparative Biochemistry and Physiology*. Again, neither of these titles figures prominently in this study.

At least two interrelated questions remain. First, if the thesis advisor's role, and the thesis itself, are so important, why not focus on the journal's cited in the thesis alone? Earlier the reader was told it was not necessary for the young scientist to absorb all of the advisor's subjects and journals in order for proof of a strong influence to be accepted. Now the reader is asked to pull back from too extreme a stance on selectivity. The thesis itself may focus only a small portion of the subjects to which the advisor has exposed his young apprentice and of itself be less representative than the view suggested by the advisor's list of papers during the young scientist's training. This may be particularly true when the advisor heads a large group of young scientists who pursue several interrelated investigations, most of which are familiar to all members. As a practical matter, and indeed to ensure the graduation of individual members, the "write-up" of given parts into dissertations is often assigned by the advisor.

A second question asks if the graduate school experience is the only, or most important, socialization process in the development of journal preferences. Do not other influences come into play with time? This objection has special merit in the long run. Many young scientists will undergo postdoctoral training, join in unforeseen collaborations, and make contacts at professional meetings. In light of the diminished government support of pure research, and the increase of industrial interest in some fields (biotechnology is a pertinent example) the young scientist may find himself stressing more applied research and using the journals in which the results of such research appears. All of those postgraduate influences will certainly be borne out in time, and eventually be noticeable in the individual's library use record. But the individualized, advisor-based list is effective immediately, in those initial years when that record is yet to be built.

FURTHER STUDY IS NEEDED

While this paper has sought to provide arguments for the use of individualized lists in preparing for initial science journal purchasing negotiations, and to answer a variety of foreseeable objections, its findings cannot be regarded as conclusive. More disciplines in which journals are both important and expensive need to be tested. More years of both classes of comparable young scientists and advisors, and of citation data need to be tried. A record of practical applications involving a wide range of institutions needs to be built up and analyzed. But even while waiting for uncontestable validity, the librarian who works through lists similar to those described in this paper, but derived from local circumstances, will go into negotiations more confident through better preparation. He or she will convey a more accurate impression of the professional level of insight and service of which librarians are capable.

NOTES

1. The inadvisability of relying on the librarian's personal subject expertise as a matter of course is succinctly discussed in a paper by Stephen E. Wiberley, Jr., "Journal Rankings From Citations Studies: A Comparison of National and Local Data From Social Work," *Library Quarterly* 52, no. 4(Winter 1982): 348-359. See the concluding paragraph on p. 358.

2. I. N. Sengupta, "Recent Growth of the Literature of Biochemistry and Changes in Ranking of Periodicals, "*Journal of Documentation* 29, no 2(June 1973): 192-211. One of several excellent survey articles on what has been called the central scientific literature of our times. This paper has the most extensive historical explanation of the plurality of journals. Other surveys of this literature will be cited later in this paper when a particular point they touch upon is emphasized.

3. F. F. Clasquin and Jackson B. Cohen, "Biochemistry and Molecular Biology Journal Prices," *The Serials Librarian* 4, no. 4(Summer 1980): 381-392.

4. *Dissertation Abstracts International B; The Sciences and Engineering* (Ann Arbor: University Microfilms, 1975-76) vol. 35, Only entries under "Chemistry, Biological" that included the names of both an advisor and recipient who had published were included.

5. *Biological Abstracts* (Philadelphia: BIOSIS, 1970-82) vols. 51-74, were used for this study.

6. Eugene Garfield, ed. and comp., *Journal Citation Reports: A Bibliometric Analysis of References Processed for the 1974 Science Citation Index* (Philadelphia: Institute for Scientific Information, 1975, © 1976) was used for the historical study.

7. The most recent discussion of this tool is by Eugene Garfield, "How to Use *Journal Citation Reports*, Including a Special Salute to the *Johns Hopkins Medical Journal*," *Current Contents* 26, no. 17(April 25, 1983): 5-12.

8. Eugene Garfield: "Trends in Biochemical Literature," *Trends in Biochemical Sciences* 4, no. 12(December 1979): 290-295.

9. Maurice B. Line, "Rank Lists Based on Citations and Library Uses as Indicators of Journal Usage in Individual Libraries," *Collection Management* 2, no. 4(Winter 1978): 313-316.

10. Harriet Zuckerman, *The Scientific Elite: Nobel Laureates in the United States* (New York: The Free Press, 1977), pp. 96-143, is especially pertinent.

11. A good example is the very widely distributed *Directory of Graduate Research* (Washington, DC: The American Chemical Society, biannually revised). Students observed by the author are using the "Corporate Index" of *Science Citation Index* in a similar manner.

12. Alan L. Porter et al., "The Role of the Dissertation in Scientific Careers," *American Scientist* 70, no. 5(Sept-Oct.): 475-481.

13. Tony Stankus, "Collection Development: Journals for Biochemists," *Special Collections* 1, no. 2(Winter 1981): 51-74.

New Specialized Journals, Mature Scientists, and Shifting Loyalties

Tony Stankus

ABSTRACT. A study was made of the level of sustained interest in 10 new specialized biomedical journals as indicated by a pattern of repeated publications. It was shown that a majority of the 265 mid-career scientists studied continued to publish within the journals after an initial paper and that the new journals became firmly embedded in their personal publication patterns. Loyalty to the new journals did not detract from established journals with a similar type and level of specialization, nor were the most prestigious multi-speciality journals of less immediate relevance to their ongoing interests were abandoned, and are suggested for cancellation. Scientists at this most prolific stage of their publishing careers seemed quite receptive to the flood of new, superspecialized titles being marketed by an increasingly sophisticated publishing industry.

INTRODUCTION

What happens to scholars' journal loyalties when a new journal appears in their specialties? How long will their interest be maintained after they publish there initially? Will they publish there again? Just how frequently will they use this new outlet? Will this new journal displace some of their former titles? What types of established journals are at risk? What does the situation suggest for librarians who must often finance the cost of the new subscription out of cancellation of some older titles?

This paper is part of an ongoing series on the career-long interactions of scientists and their journals, with emphasis on its meaning for subscription management. Earlier work delineated the strong role of these advisors in shaping the journal preferences of young scientists

---

Reprinted with permission from *Library Acquisitions: Practice and Theory*, volume 9, pages 99-104, 1985.

fresh from PhD training.[1] It demonstrated that librarians who had examined the advisors' publication patterns, as enhanced by the use of *Journal Citation Reports*,[2] could generally anticipate and confirm about 75% of the newly minted PhD's subscription requests for the first few years at their new institutions' library. After this period, any changes in the research direction and journal preferences of the now maturing scholars would became apparent through their own patterns of publication, and to the degree observable, through their use of titles within the library. This paper focuses on the more mature scholar, the type Sinderman calls Stage 3 Scientist: the Professional Team Leaders.[3] The laboratory groups they now direct are likely to be producing more manuscripts than ever before in their experience, and they are now responsible for placing the manuscripts. This paper explores their response in this situation to another event in their personal development of a journal worldview: the birth of a new title in their fields.

METHODS

Specialized biomedical journals were chosen because of their importance in a wide variety of libraries, their exceptional habit of giving birth to even more journals, and their continuing leadership in average price and rate of inflation.[4] Articles in 10 journals published for the first time between 1979 and 1980 (see Table 1) were examined to draw up a list of the principal investigators, usually the authors designated for correspondence. In light of the goal of studying the more mature scholar, it was gratifying to note that of 265 scientists thus identified, 97% had publications in the 3 years before the appearance of the new journal (the time allowed for drawing up their established pattern) and 98% continued to publish during the 3 years afterwards (the time allowed to observe changes in those patterns). This strongly suggests that neither newborn nor senescent careers, are, in fact, involved. The "Source Index" of annual cumulations of *Science Citation Index*[5] was used to follow both patterns.

LOYALTY TO THE NEW JOURNAL

One of the first concerns of this study – and for working librarians – is whether scholars maintain an interest in a journal after their initial paper is published there. Given the difficulties of direct observation of journal use, and the critical role of publication in given journals for tenure and grantsmanship,[6] a pattern of continuing publication in the

TABLE 1

JOURNALS EXAMINED FOR THIS STUDY

Environmental Mutagenesis, New York: Alan R. Liss, Inc., all papers in v. 1, 1979.

Journal of Andrology, Philadelphia: Lippincott, all papers in v. 1, 1980.

Journal of the Autonomic Nervous System, Amsterdam, Netherlands: Elsevier Science Publishers, all papers in v. 1, 1979.

Journal of Interferon Research, New York: Liebert, papers in the 1979 portion of v. 1, 1979-1980.

Journal of Muscle Research and Cell Motility, London: Chapman & Hall, all papers in v. 1, 1980.

Journal of Receptor Research, New York: Dekker, all papers in v. 1, 1980.

Placenta, Philadelphia: Saunders, all papers in v. 1, 1980.

Prostate, New York: Alan R. Liss, Inc., all papers in v. 1, 1980.

Thymus, Amsterdam, Netherlands: Elsevier Science Publishers, all papers in v. 1, 1979-1980.

Ultrasonic Imaging, New York: Academic Press, all papers in v. 1, 1979.

journal is one good sign.[7] In this study, 160 of the 265 scientists published subsequent papers in their new journals. (See Table 2 for a detailed listing of all results discussed.) Many mature scientists seem ready to give new journals a thorough trial.

A second concern was how relatively important the new journal had become to those who had published there repeatedly. At least one measure of this is the frequency the scientist publishes in the new journal as compared to publication within other outlets. Results show that a surprising 60% made the new title one of their favorites, with a more statistically expected 30% of choosing it at a rate roughly equal to most of their customary titles. Only 10% seemed to use it infrequently, although this statistic is itself misleading in that certain authors with enormous publication records can publish there annually and still rank in the bottom third.

LOYALTY TO ESTABLISHED JOURNALS

Does the new journal dislodge other journals, and if so, what types? In this study, 59% of the repeat publishers showed some drop-off of

TABLE 2

STATISTICAL SUMMARY OF RESULTS

Question	No. Cases	Percentage
Does the mature scientist publish in the new journal again?		
Yes	160	60
No	105	40
Total	265	100
Where does the new journal rank in the subsequent publication pattern of the mature scientist?		
Top third	101	60
Middle third	42	30
Bottom third	17	10
Total	160	100
How often does the new journal displace other journals in the author's publication pattern?		
Competitive specialized titles	10	11
Major multispecialty titles	12	13
Convention abstracts titles	4	4
Marginally related titles	68	72
Total	94	100

other journals. Surprisingly, the dropped title was rarely (11%) a direct specialized competitor of the new journal: *Environmental Mutagenesis* did not usually eliminate *Mutation Research*, not did the *Journal of Andrology* entirely displace *Andrologia*, and so on. While there may be some shifting of relative frequency of publication or priority of affections, it appears that scientists rarely divorce one spouse who is primarily devoted to their research specialty for another. Rather, they enlarge their harem, usually at library expense, a point not lost on journal publishers.

Neither did the scientist typically stop publishing in the major multispecialty journals (down 13%). Any drop-off in appearances in journals such as *Science* and *Nature*, or the *New England Journal of Medicine* and the *Journal of the American Medical Association* may well be attributable to the difficulty of getting a paper accepted there on a regular basis.

Neither did the scientists abandon the major convention abstracts journals (4% of the titles dropped). General journals of this type, such as *Federation Proceedings* and *Clinical Research*, continued to dominate this area, although there was some infiltration by the new journal when its publisher sponsored the meeting.

SHIFTS IN JOURNAL LOYALTY

The majority of drop-off (72%) occurred in the more general journals that were only marginally related to the scientist's ongoing special interests. An understanding of the possible reasons for having published in these journals in the past is required here. Motives may be enumerated and the depth of the loyalty engendered estimated.

1. The now out-of-place journal may be a remnant of a past research interest. Perhaps the paper was merely very long in press. Alternatively, scientists, rather than scrapping remaining unpublished data, had been publishing it at their leisure.
2. The paper may be an isolated, unanticipated, finding in a specialty other than their own. Often by co-opting an outside specialist, the scientist gets sufficient expertise and reassurance to handle a one-time publication in the journal of another specialist.
3. Scientists may themselves be co-opted to assist a large research group in another field. That group may well award them a coauthorship, which they will accept, even if in a journal that does not represent their personal continuing interest.

In the above cases, little journal loyalty is likely to be engendered. The librarian can approach the scientist with a confident recommendation for immediate cancellation.

1. The author may have had to publish in a less specialized journal because there was no unambiguously appropriate specialized journal. Many new specialized journals stress the notion that they gather together in one journal papers that otherwise would have been scattered over many journals. Moreover, the new journal may claim to offer the disaffected scholars a sense of "in-group" identity. Indeed, the current emphasis in journal marketing is on diligently identifying these new special library category clienteles rather than on pushing old titles.[8]
2. The author may have met a variety of editorial barriers in a seemingly more appropriate journal and may have turned to this vaguely related title. Barriers included outright rejection for reasons of suspect validity to rejection for details such as length, topic fashionability, poor grammar, too great a backlog of papers, personal animosity of editor or referees to the author, and so on.
3. The author may have met financial barriers. Many established journals assess page charges, some in an excess of $85 per page. In other cases, authors may question the wisdom of publishing in a journal that even their library cannot afford to take.
4. The author may have the curious American phobia for foreign titles, even when they seem to be more appropriately specialized. By way of reply, German publishers have in particular Americanized their language of publication and formats.[9]

Journals that fall into these categories may well be ripe for cancellation, but concerned scientists may have an intermediate level of loyalty to them. While the new journal may provide the right answer for them, they may not be sure that other scientists in their specialty agree and will follow their path. The librarian's strategy must be more gradual. While aiming for the eventual cancellation of all the irrelevant titles, the librarian must move first on those which show little citation interaction with current journals. Librarians must reassure scientists that by following their old journals through *Current Contents*[10] or similar alerting services, they will not miss important papers. Eventually, as scientists find themselves writing for fewer reprints or requesting fewer interlibrary loans, they will assent to further cancellations.

WHEN LOYALTY TO THE NEW JOURNAL FAILS

Discussion thus far has focused on those scientists who are apparently pleased and involved with their new journals, with the librarian cancelling other titles as they are abandoned. But 40% of the study group did not "repeat publish" after 3 years, and at least some of the 10% "bottom third frequency" publishers rarely reappear in the journal. It must be acknowledged that in these cases, publication in the new journal may have been itself a marginal affair, for reasons similar to those discussed in the previous sections. Little loyalty is likely to have been engendered. The question may well be whether a proposed cancellation should be immediately broached after a three-year trial or whether the approach should be gradual. A check with *Journal Citation Reports* should help determine whether the interest in reading the journal is as likely to be dead as the interest in publishing within it. Some special explanations are useful here:

1. Publication on the new journal may really have been a case of *noblesse oblige* in response to a direct invitation to contribute. Authors may not have ever wished to identify themselves on a continuing basis with the new title.
2. Publication int he new journal may well have been in the nature of a personal experiment that failed. Authors may well have been displeased with the actual treatment that their papers received in terms of production quality or timelessness. Or they may have felt that the other papers in the journal were not of suitable quality or from the best workers in their specialty.
3. The established journals that appeared to be threatened by the new journal may have altered their policies for format by way of response, with the author now finding them more acceptable.

There is one important exception to a strategy of cancellation, based on a special situation. The scientist may have been named an editor with the new journal. Some journals discourage editors from too frequently accepting their own papers, so as not to give the journal the tinge of a vanity publication.

This is not a cancellation opportunity. Loyalty may be assumed.

CONCLUSIONS

Many mature biomedical scientists, typically those with high manuscript production, seem quite willing to venture some papers in new journals in their specialties. They remain loyal to both equivalent specialty journals and to the major general multi-specialty and convention abstracts journals. They tend to drop journals of an intermediate level of specialization that no longer identify, or less exclusively identify, with their current research interests. Those journals may often be dropped from library holdings to help finance continuing subscriptions to the new titles. Monitoring of library use, publication patterns, *Journal Citation Reports*, and discussion with the concerned scientist are interacting tools in the subscription management of the new-title-adoption/old-title-suspension situation.

NOTES

1. Stankus, Tony, "Negotiating Journal Demands With Young Scientists Using Lists Derived From Thesis Advisor Records," *Collection Management* 5, 3/4(Fall/Winter, 1983): 185-198.

2. Garfield, Eugene. "How to Use *Journal Citation Reports*, Including a Special Salute to the *Johns Hopkins Medical Journal*," *Current Contents* 26, 17(April 25, 1983): 5-12.

3. Sinderman, Carl J. *Winning the Games That Scientists Play*. New York: Plenum, 1982, p. 140.

4. Brown, Norman B. and Phillips, Jane. "Price Indexes for 1984: U.S. Periodicals and Serials Services," *Library Journal*, 59, 13(August, 1984): 1422-1425, Biomedical titles are almost always near the top of any price or inflation rate listing. This latest study places them second on both counts in a fairly wide field.

5. The "Source Index" is that component of *Science Citation Index* that most closely resembles an entry-by-author bibliography.

6. Rice, Barbara A. and Stankus, Tony. "Publication Quality Indicators for Tenure or Promotion Decisions: What Can the Librarian Ethically Report?," *College and Research Libraries*, 44, 2(March, 1983): 173-178.

7. Stankus, Tony. "Collection Development: Journals for Biochemists," *Special Collections*, 1, 2(1982): 51-74.

8. Sabosik, Patricia. "Trends in Marketing Serials to Libraries," as reported by Schaplowsky, Alan. "Third Annual Serials Conference, November 3-4, 1983; the *LAPT* Report," *Library Acquisitions: Practice and Theory*, 8, 2(1984): 136-137.

9. Stankus, Tony, Schlessinger, Rashelle and Schlessinger, Bernard S. "English Language Trends in German Basic Science Journals: A Potential Collection Tool," *Science and Technology Libraries*, 1, 3(Spring, 1981): 55-66.

10. The most appropriate edition for this group as a whole is *Current Contents: Life Sciences*, although some of the titles are also carried in *Current Contents: Clinical Practice*.

Journal Weeding in Relation to Declining Faculty Member Publishing

Tony Stankus

ABSTRACT. In light of financial and housing constraints a new exclusionary budgeting alliance for expensive, space-consuming specialty journals may be forced between academic sci-tech librarians and only those faculty whose publications activity and grantsmanship help support the library. In stringent circumstances the needs of productive scholars for new titles and shelf space must often be met by the business-like reassignment of the funds and space given over to scientists whose research publishing careers are over. Reliable, unobtrusive methods of determining when a scientist's apparent cessation of publications is likely to be permanent are discussed. The human circumstances unobtrusive methods of determining when a scientist's apparent cessation of surrounding an individual's termination of publishable research are discussed in conjunction with findings from the Sociology of Science. A highly professional, nonjudgmental style of informing the faculty member of intent to proceed and negotiating the cancellations is outlined.

INTRODUCTION

Science librarians may well feel caught between the demands of tenured faculty for continued subscriptions to their favorite specialized journals even as new faculty in different specialties are hired. The situation has become particularly acute in the case of costly and voluminous science journals in small libraries, particularly those at competitive liberal arts colleges. At these institutions, prestige-and-cost-conscious top administrators may feel that the abundance of job-seeking PhDs allows for increased publication and grants-winning

---

Reprinted from *Science & Technology Libraries*, volume 6, number 3, pages 43-53, 1986.

expectations of their existing untenured faculty. Those faculty that do not produce can be readily replaced. Yet librarians seeking to give these younger scientists a fighting chance may not be able to get either the initial funding or added shelf space from these same administrators. This paper suggests that there can be a rational way out of this dilemma based on a reexamination of those tenured faculty whose research careers appear to be over, with a reassignment of "their" funds and shelf space to more productive scholars. Two premises underlie this approach:

- That in an increasing number of cases representation of a faculty member's specialty journals in the library collection can no longer be regarded as a perquisite of tenure or seniority. It must become a visible sign of an implicit understanding between the librarian and the individual faculty member. The librarian is doing his best to aid the faculty member in his research and the faculty member is doing his best to turn out the papers that bring in the grants dollars whose overhead deductions help support the library.
- That the advanced specialty journals targeted for cancellation are rarely intellectually accessible or of interest to faculty outside their specialties or to most students. Cancellation of this type of journal rarely involves "innocent victims" since most small colleges avoid closely duplicating subject specialists. Undergraduates moreover are rather closely directed int heir advanced reading by their research advisors, faculty reasonably assumed to be active.

BACKGROUND

This study is part of an ongoing series on the career-long interactions of scientists and their journals and its meaning for subscription management. The first work[1] dealt with the surprising predictability of the speciality journal preferences of young scientists when librarians took into account the journals favored by their PhD advisors and other journals frequently cited in those journals. A second study[2] dealt with highly prolific midcareer scientists and their propensity to invest some of their papers tentatively in brand new journals devoted to their specialties, with a majority of initial contributors eventually making the new journal a favorite outlet. This study deals with scientists, who for one reason or another, have disengaged from research and grantsmanship and whose journals are thereby ripe for cancellation. It contains both a search for reliable indicators of research death after which cancellations may be initiated, as well as quest for an understanding of why these professors are neither continuing on the journal paths of their advisors nor venturing into new journals to call their own.

METHODS

Fifty-three recipients of PhDs in Chemistry employed at 34 small, competitive liberal arts colleges were identified through a scan of the directory *Research in Chemistry at Private Undergraduate Colleges.*[3] Faculty identified had indicated no publications for at least a five-year span. Their earlier publication histories were then traced via a tabulation of entries in the author indexes of *Chemical Abstracts*. A few younger, but equally inactive faculty had their histories traced by the more convenient "Source Index" of *Science Citation Index*. All of the identified professors had earned their degrees after 1961, a time frame chosen to generally eliminate consideration of soon-to-be-replaced elderly faculty members. To a surprising degree the group were graduates of America's better-rated graduate programs and were employed at highly selective institutions, schools which, while emphasizing undergraduate instruction, encouraged publications for tenure and promotion. Virtually all had access to rather creditable journal holdings (a factor hearteningly and highly correlated to productivity[4]), many in separate science libraries on campus.

HOW CLOSELY RELATED IS AGE TO CESSATION OF PUBLICATION?

Professors in our study published their last paper sat a wide variety of ages: from 24 to 57 (see Figure 1). Two findings are immediately apparent. While there seems to be a significant number of cessations at ages 27-30, there seems to be no clear-cut chronological age at which, as a general rule, chemistry professors who will eventually quit publishing, in fact, do quit. A cancellation policy based purely on age then would not only be discriminatory, it would not be based on the collected experiences of this study group nor on any carefully drawn research of which this author is aware. Indeed it would have been rather easy to have identified from the same directory an equal number of chemists at matching ages or older with continuously productive

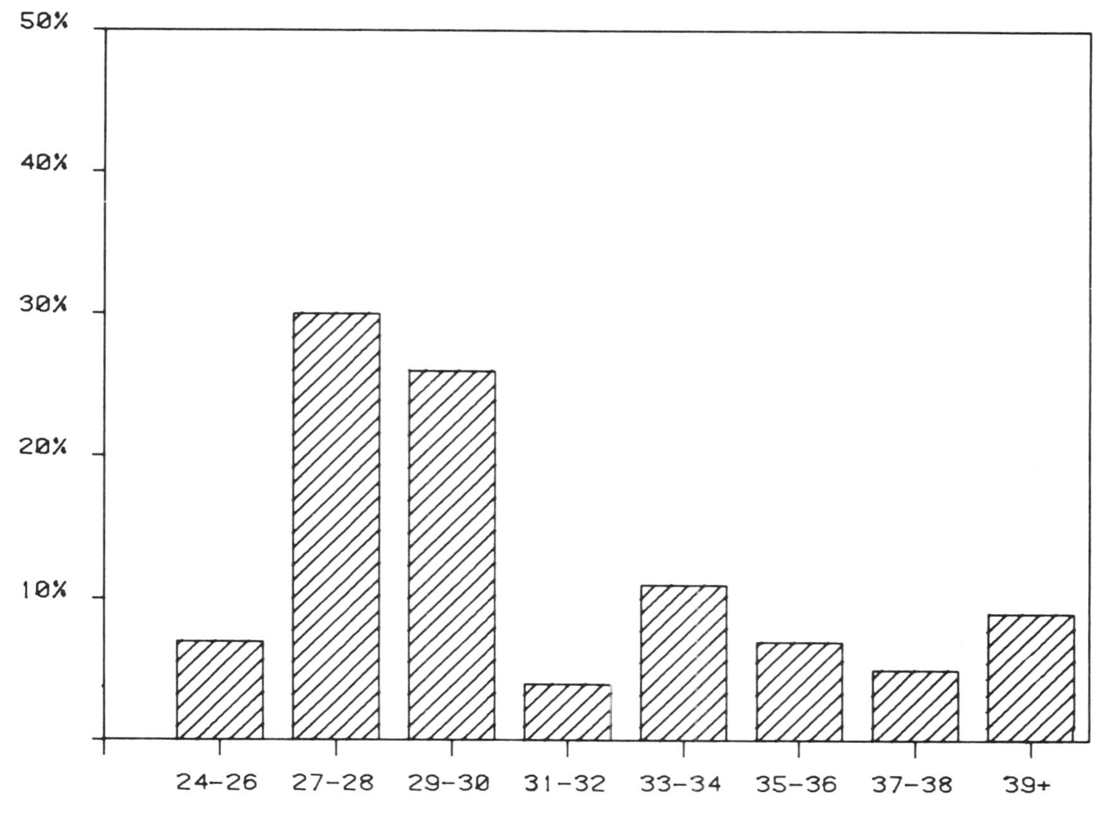

FIGURE 1. Age at last paper. While it is clear that many of our scientists cease publication between 27-30, there is no sure rule based on age alone that can guide cancellation policy.

records. Nonetheless, some explanation of the rise in publication cessation at ages 27-30 is warranted. What seems to be happening to these chemists at such early stages of their careers?

ARRESTED CAREER DEVELOPMENT AND CESSATION OF PUBLICATION

Figure 2 shows the year after receipt of the PhD within which those chemists who published had their last paper. Again, there are two significant findings. A large percentage of chemists seem to stop publishing within a few years of their PhD. A substantially smaller, but still noticeable group stops during their fifth and sixth post-PhD year. A few interpretations are likely. One is that some newly minted PhDs quickly use up the publishable material developed during their dissertation, and, either through a poverty of ideas, time or materials, never seem able to publish again. Some support for this explanation lies in the fact that the median number of publications of authors in this group (2-3) approximates the independent findings of both Porter[5] and Stankus[6] concerning the numbers of papers typically derived from the dissertations of two separate groups of biochemists (3 and 2.67, respectively).

An explanation of the somewhat larger number of chemists ending their research output in post-PhD years five and six might well center on a last effort to fulfill tenure requirements. By the end of year six, many of these chemists will have stood for tenure. Indeed, 86% of those who will have written their last paper had done so by then. This finding ties in with the somewhat larger numbers of chemists who stopped publishing between the ages 27 and 30.

THE WAKE

Figure 3 is a display based on hindsight. It is an attempt to answer the question of how long must a librarian wait to be sure the faculty member's career is dead, not just sleeping. It shows the percent of eventually correct cancellations assuming a cutoff of subscriptions after given waiting periods. It uses the gap between the next-to-last and last papers as a test period.

When the spacings between all of the faculty member's papers are examined an interesting finding comes to light. When a faculty member exceeds his own longest previous gap without a paper, he is likely

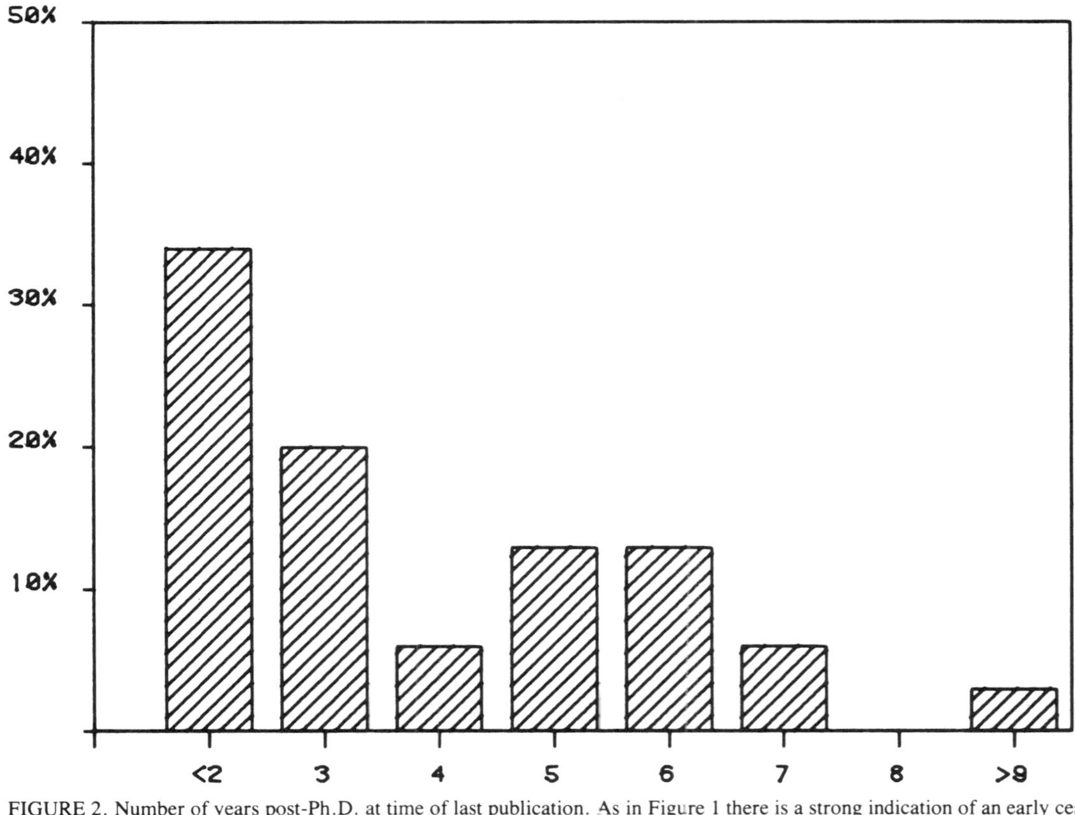

FIGURE 2. Number of years post-Ph.D. at time of last publication. As in Figure 1 there is a strong indication of an early cessation of publication, but note the "bump" in years 5 and 6, typically the time of tenure decisions. A certain security in having fulfilled research commitments may combine with increased administrative and family responsibilities in a way that discourages continued publications.

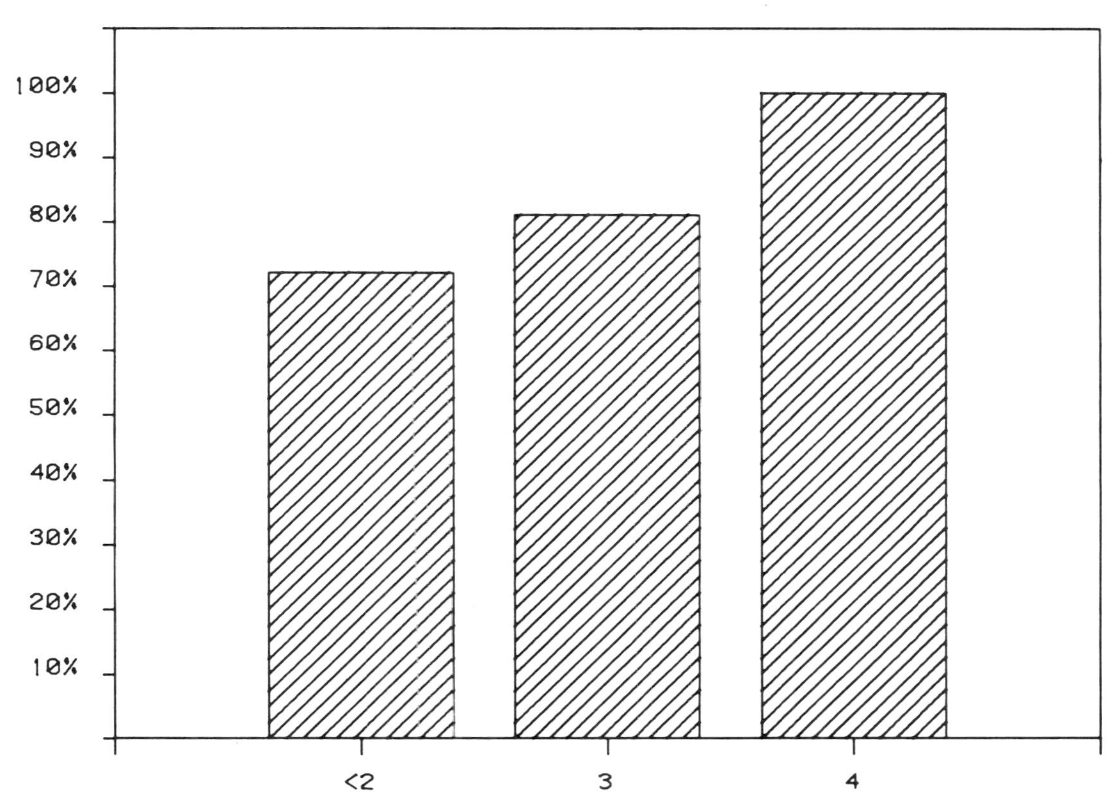

FIGURE 3. How long must the librarian wait? Using the gap times between the next-to-last and last papers of the authors in our group as a test for "premature burial", we found that there is virtually no chance for error after four years.

to have stopped altogether. It seems that a faculty member's publishing career rarely slows down and still continues successfully. Bensman has noted:[7] "Highly productive young scientists later maintained or increased their productivity, while young scientists who produced very little initially produced even less later . . . "

Two human circumstances provide a sympathetic explanation of how this situation can come about. The first deals with family responsibilities. The late twenties to mid-thirties represent the principal years of early childrearing for most college-educated couples. The second circumstance is the mixed blessing of being appointed to higher administrative duties. In a smaller institutions where this "promotion" does not greatly increase access to funds, instrumentation, or support personnel, it is both an obligatory "honor" and a research distraction to the appointed or elected chairman, premedical advisor, faculty senator, or chronic committeeman. The role of both family and administrative pressures has been discussed by Sinderman:[8] "Sooner or later many runners elect to get off the fast track voluntarily . . . often scientists-turned-administrators find their scientific skill obsolete if too many years have intervened since publication of their last scientific papers."

NEGOTIATING THE CANCELLATION

The toughest part of cancellation management is telling the concerned faculty member. Not telling the faculty member is unprofessional via either arrogance or cowardice. Keys to successful cancellations include:

– Having the facts straight before negotiating.
– Adjusting the level of explicit spoken argumentation to the level of resistance.
– Avoiding giving the impression of passing judgment on the faculty member's overall value to the school.
– Avoiding letting the matter become personal.

The factual information of which the librarian should be sure prior to a meeting with the candidate includes:

– The actual record of the faculty member's publications, including not only papers and book chapters but printed convention abstracts and invited talks.

—The costs and space consumption of the existing publications and the proposed savings that will result. (The identity of any proposed beneficiary of reassigned funds or space need not be revealed initially.)
—The assurance that there is little reasonable likelihood of disciplinary crossover damage through the proposed cancellations.
—A backup plan of providing some coverage in the subject field through awareness services like *Current Contents*, broad overviews services like the *Annual Reviews* services and legitimate document delivery systems like *The Genuine Article* or Copyright-Clearance-Center-paid interlibrary loans.
—A backup plan of alerting the faculty member to library holdings in fields for which he may now hold some new responsibility: higher education administration, issues in premedical education, faculty evaluation, etc.
—Fallback lines of compromise in terms of given journals that must go even if others stay.

In the best of circumstances there is little need for extensive explanation. The faculty member views himself as quietly having made a change in emphasis in his career. He tells himself that he is now simply consenting to a discreet change in library holdings. A gratuitously elaborate explanation of the librarian's reasoning might be counterproductive.

In the worst of circumstances the faculty member questions the "nerve" of the librarian in making such an assessment. The proper response is a calm offer to let the College Dean or Treasurer arbitrate, including in the librarian's submission to those officers an estimate of the annual cost of subscriptions multiplied by the number of years the faculty member has until retirement, with adjustments for inflation and building costs. As a practical matter, few inactive faculty wish to have the top administration reminded just how inactive they are, or just how expensive the soothing of their indignation might be.

It is in the intermediate situation of a faculty member requesting continuance for advanced instructional support that the librarian must be prepared to give and take with a mix of confidence in generalized student collateral reading behavior that might be tempered by local exceptions. Stankus[9] has demonstrated that the most widely adopted Biochemistry texts rarely suggest readings in specialty research journals, overwhelmingly stressing instead more readable overview articles in *Science, Nature, Scientific American* and in hardbound continuing series such as the *Annual Reviews* . . . the professor might still insist that his assignments (and his own level of preparation) go beyond the textbook. A reasonable compromise is a mutually agreed upon test of the actual amount of use of contested titles (via reserve room housing) for three cycles of having the pertinent courses taught. If in these days of student evaluation, the professor successfully risks forcing the use of these difficult materials on his students, he has made his point. If an argument remains, in spite of student disuse, that the material is necessary for his own professional updating, and the professor is not receptive to a combination of current awareness services and legitimate document delivery, suggest that he take tax-deductible personal subscriptions.

SUMMARY

Rising costs and shrinking shelf space can force librarians to purchase and house specialty subscriptions for active scientists at the expense of the subscriptions and space allotted for their inactive colleagues. A study of the research careers of 53 liberal arts college chemists who eventually stopped publishing suggests that after a four-year interval without a paper, the librarian can reasonably infer no further papers are ever again likely to appear from that author, and can negotiate at least some specialty journal cancellations. The arguments again this policy are anticipated and a negotiating strategy is suggested.

NOTES

1. Stankus, Tony. Negotiating journal demands with young scientists using lists derived from thesis advisor records. *Collection Management*, 5(3/4): 185-198, 1983 Fall/Winter.

2. Stankus, Tony. New specialized journals, mature scientists, and shifting loyalties. *Library Acquisitions Practice and Theory*, 9(2), 1985 Spring, in press.

3. Andreen, Brian, editor, *Research in chemistry at private undergraduate colleges*. Minneapolis, MN: Council on Undergraduate Research: 1979.

4. Spencer, James N.: Yoder, Claude H. A survey of undergraduate research over the past decade. *Journal of Chemical Education*, 58(10): 780-786, 1981 October.

5. Porter, Alan L. et al. The role of the dissertation in scientific careers. *American Scientist*, 70(5): 475-481, 1982 Sept./Oct.

6. Stankus, Negotiation . . . p. 189.

7. Bensman, Stephen J. Journal subscriptions and acquisitions: The view from the library. A paper presented to the Annual Meeting of the Association of American University Presses. Spring Lake, NJ, June 18, 1984 (to appear in revised form in *College & Research Libraries*, 1985).

8. Sinderman, Carl J. *Winning the games scientists play*. New York: Plenum; 1982: p. 138.

9. Stankus, Tony, Collection development: journals for biochemists. *Special Collections*, 1(2): 51-74; 1981 Winter.

THEME TWO

The Role of Language and Cultural Forces in Shaping Journals and Their Users

This section is based on the observation that scientists and science journals collections *en masse* resemble nothing so much as the situation at a major international airport. There are many nationalities of passengers and carriers. The loudspeakers are a babble of several languages, and the native tongues of the travelers are even more varied. But ultimately everyone is dependent upon the English, fluent or not, of the air traffic controller. The recognition of a need for a common language in English and the adoption of certain American-style practices has probably saved lives in the air and scientific careers on the ground. Of course this sense of American superiority must be regarded with bemusement. The American scientific journal writer is not unlike the "American" tourist at our archetypal airport: one wearing a Scottish tweed jacket, carrying Italian designer luggage, with a strap for a Japanese camera around his neck, headed for a Lufthansa flight on which he or she will drink Russian vodka and eat French cuisine.

English Language Trends in German Basic Science Journals: A Potential Collection Tool

Tony Stankus
Rashelle Schlessinger
Bernard S. Schlessinger

ABSTRACT. Americans traditionally avoid reading articles in science journals published in foreign languages. By way of response the publishers of some of these journals have progressively increased the proportion of articles in English. That trend is studied here for German basic science journals. Trends tables such as the one reported (for 18 years of 35 journals) can serve librarians in their future decisions about storage and purchase.

Some of the most difficult decisions facing today's librarians relate to the purchase and storage of journals. Methods of studying journals for storage or purchase decisions, such as user questionnaires,[1] tallies of bound volumes left unshelved after use,[2] photocopy requests,[3] circulation records,[4] user publication citation habits,[5] or more generalized citation behavior,[6] have all been reported. To complement these methods in the case of foreign-language journals, this study presents the changing percentage of English-language articles in German basic science journals over time in a table that may serve librarians in future collection development decisions.

INTRODUCTION

The background for this study lies in the historical fact that prior to the Second World War, American scientists generally viewed German

Reprinted from *Science & Technology Libraries*, volume 1, number 3, pages 55-66, 1981.

(and, to a lesser degree, French) research as very important. This was translated into a requirement in undergraduate programs for language training of one (or both) of these languages, and into a requirement in PhD programs for demonstration of reading proficiency in one (or both) of the languages.

After the Second World War, many American scientists gradually accepted the views that:

1. American research was the bellwether research in the scientific community.
2. Most, if not all, substantive research output would eventually be available in the English language.
3. English was moving toward acceptance as *the* international scientific language.
4. The language of computers was more important to the scientist than reading knowledge of German.

Although these historical perspectives are the interpretations of the authors, their direct manifestations, (1) the elimination of the reading proficiency requirements and substitution of computer language proficiency requirements and (2) the tendency of American library users to ignore foreign language references, can be well-documented.[7-10]

Notwithstanding the changed perceptions of English-language versus foreign-language research noted above, many American researchers still felt a need to use foreign-language materials.[11] This need resulted in two early solutions: (a) provision of accompanying abstracts of foreign-language research and (b) separately requested provision of full translations. Both of these have proved generally unsatisfactory.[12]

Foreign-language journals have recognized that, as the trends noted above developed, their sales to the lucrative American market have decreased. In response, German journals in particular have increasingly allowed or encouraged articles written in English and even "Americanized" or "Internationalized" their titles, formats, and editorial boards.[13] Thus, one can find in the "Instructions for Authors" in *Naturwissenschafften*

> English is now the *Lingua Franca* of the sciences and many scientists simply do not read papers published in other languages. Thus, in response to numerous suggestions, and in keeping with the journal's international standing, we herewithal appeal to authors intending to submit short communications to write in English.[14]

Similarly there is this note in *Liebig's Annalen der Chemie*[15]—"In an attempt to break down language barriers, the journal has internationalized itself by publishing either German or English papers with summaries in both languages."

Garfield has reported that the "internationalization" movement by German journals has resulted in those journals receiving increasing shares of the citations in their fields.[16] This has obvious implications for increased demand for current subscriptions and for those back years with the better cited English language articles.

The tables should be of aid in determining: (1) which back years contain sufficient percentages of English-language articles to warrant consideration of purchase, (2) which German journals have moved in the direction of "internationalization" and should be considered (or reconsidered) for inclusion in the collection, and (3) which German journals might be considered for storage only (or for weeding or microform use).

METHODOLOGY

German-language journals were chosen for this study, because of the general feeling, both in the literature[17-18] and of the authors that American scientists consider them the most important foreign-language medium in science.

The German journals with the heaviest citations or highest impact listed by Garfield[19] were used for research provided that:

1. They had a history of publication in Germany in the German language and currently published some papers in English.
2. They were basic-science-oriented. This excluded journals such as those in medicine, pharmacology, medical microbiology, and psychology, etc.

The list of journals used may be found in Table 1.

Each journal issue for the years 1960, 1965, 1970, 1975, 1978 was physically examined by one of the authors, who counted the number of articles in English and determined percentages. Included in the count were full-length articles, communications and letters of at least one page, and extended corrections or replies to criticism of at least one page. Excluded were book reviews, abstracts or oral reports at conferences, obituaries and commemorations, political commentary, and society business.

Table 1. List of Journals Used in the Research

1. Annalen der Physik
2. Anatomy and Embryology
3. Archive for Rational Mechanics and Analysis
4. Archives of Microbiology
5. Astronomy and Astrophysics[a]
6. Berichte der Bunsengesellschaft fuer Physikalische Chemie[b]
7. Cell and Tissue Research[c]
8. Chromosoma
9. Communications of Mathematical Physics[d]
10. Contributions to Mineralogy and Petrology[e]
11. Ctyolobiologie[f]
12. European Journal of Biochemistry[g]
13. Histochemistry[h]
14. Hoppe-Seylers Zeitschrift fuer Physiologische Chemie
15. Inventiones Mathematicae[i]
16. Journal of Comparative Physiology[j]
17. Journal fuer Praktische Chemie
18. Mathematische Annalen
19. Mathematische Zeitschrift
20. Molecular and General Genetics[k]
21. Naturwissenschaften
22. Pflugers Archiv-European Journal of Physiology[l]
23. Physica Status Solidi A+B
24. Planta
25. Synthesis[m]
26. Theoretica Chimica Acta[n]
27. Wilhelm Roux's Archives of Developmental Biology[o]
28. Zeitschrift fuer Anorganische und Allgemeine Chemie
29. Zeitschrift fuer Metallkunde
30. Zeitschrift fuer Naturforschung. Teil A. Physikalische Chemie

TABLE 1 (continued)

31. Zeitschrift fuer Naturforschung. Teil B. Anorganische und Organische Chemie
32. Zeitschrift fuer Naturforschung. Teil C. Biosciences
33. Zeitschrift fuer Pflanzenphysiologie
34. Zeitschrift fuer Physik A and B
35. Zeitschrift fuer Krystallographie

a. established by combination of five journals Annales des Astrophysik, Bulletin of the Astronomical Institute of the Netherlands, Bulletin Astronomie, Journal des Observatorie, and Zeitschrift fuer Astrophysik

b. formerly Zeitschrift fuer Elektochemie

c. formerly Zeitschrift fuer Zellforschung und Mikroskopische Anatomie

d. started in 1965

e. formerly Beitrage zur Mineralogie und Petrologie

f. started in 1969

g. formerly Biochemische Zeitschrift

h. formerly Histochemie

i. started in 1966

j. formerly Zeitschrift fuer Vergleichende Physiologie

k. formerly Zeitschrift fuer Verebungslehre

l. formerly Pfluger's Archiv fuer die Gesamte Physiologie des Menschen

m. started in 1969

n. started in 1962

o. formerly Wilhelm Roux Archiv fuer Entwicklungsmechanik

p. started in 1973

RESULTS AND DECISIONS

Table 2, which presents the percentage of English-language articles of each journal for the years 1960, 1965, 1970, 1975, and 1978, is interesting in that, of the 35 journals included, 33 show striking increases in percentage of English-language articles from the time they first appear in the table to 1978. Of the two which do not show such a

Table 2. Percentages of English-Language Articles 1960-78

	1960	1965	1970	1975	1978
1. Annalen der Physik	16.2	15.6	19.2	58.8	61.2
2. Anatomy and Embryology	10.0	34.2	36.9	95.6	98.9
3. Archive for Rational Mechanics and Analysis	26.6	88.2	76.1	96.3	94.7
4. Archives of Microbiology	22.0	29.7	72.3	92.3	96.8
5. Astronomy and Astrophysics	38.5	47.7	93.2	95.6	96.4
6. Berichte der Bunsengesellschaft fuer Physikalische Chemie	15.0	4.7	19.9	34.8	79.7
7. Cell and Tissue Research	31.3	54.7	75.4	100.0	100.0
8. Chromosoma	56.3	79.4	91.4	99.1	100.0
9. Communications of Mathematical Physics	----	100.0	98.3	100.0	100.0
10. Contributions to Mineralogy and Petrology	7.1	16.0	80.9	97.5	100.0
11. Cytobiologie	----	----	23.6	76.7	88.6
12. European Journal of Biochemistry	1.5	24.0	93.6	99.6	99.9
13. Histochemistry	43.2	50.5	81.7	93.9	92.6
14. Hoppe-Seylers Zeitschrift fuer Physiologische Chemie	0	0.8	31.8	68.5	91.3
15. Inventiones Mathematicae	----	44.4	71.1	89.6	90.4
16. Journal of Comparative Physiology	21.3	31.1	45.8	70.8	100.0
17. Journal fuer Praktische Chemie	5.6	15.2	16.2	10.9	32.8
18. Mathematische Annalen	39.1	51.8	66.5	66.9	68.9
19. Mathematische Zeitschrift	36.9	50.6	63.2	65.5	66.1
20. Molecular and General Genetics	39.6	39.3	90.1	100.0	99.5
21. Naturwissenschaften	13.3	19.8	37.0	55.2	63.7
22. Pflugers Archiv-European Journal of Physiology	1.6	15.2	71.0	97.1	100.0
23. Physica Status Solidi A+B	11.0	93.0	95.2	99.1	98.4
24. Planta	4.8	24.6	71.2	88.6	100.0
25. Synthesis	----	----	60.9	78.8	82.5
26. Theoretica Chimica Acta	22.2	52.3	82.5	92.5	94.2
27. Wilhelm Roux's Archives of Developmental Biology	20.4	20.8	52.4	71.7	80.4
28. Zeitschrift fuer Anorganische und Allgemeine Chemie	7.9	5.7	12.6	14.3	11.2
29. Zeitschrift fuer Metallkunde	0.8	1.5	20.6	35.9	39.2
30. Zeitschrift fuer Naturforschung Teil A. Physikalische Chemie	7.9	22.9	40.2	65.4	82.3

TABLE 2 (continued)

	1960	1965	1970	1975	1978
31. Zeitschrift fuer Naturforschung Teil B. Anorganische und Organische Chemie	4.8	8.6	23.6	28.2	22.7
32. Zeitschrift fuer Naturforschung Teil C. Biosciences	----	----	----	67.2	76.8
33. Zeitschrift fuer Pflanzenphysiologie	0	11.1	37.4	69.0	75.7
34. Zeitschrift fuer Physik A and B	11.2	19.5	69.3	88.2	99.2
35. Zeitschrift fuer Krystallographie	53.0	71.6	61.0	78.4	80.6

striking increase, one, *Communications of Mathematical Physics*, is already in the 90-100% range on first appearance, while one, *Zeitschrift fuer Anorganische und Allgemeine Chemie* starts out in 1960 at 7.9% and shows only a modest increase to 14.3% in 1975 and 11.2% in 1978. This evidence of internationalization is even more striking if one notes (see Table 3) that 28 of the journals were in the percentage range of 0-50 in 1960, while 27 were in the percentage range of 75-100 in 1978 (Table 4 lists the 27 journals in the percentage range 75-100). It is of further interest to note that the major shift in philosophy came between 1965 (when 24 journals fell in the 0-50 range) and 1970 (when 22 journals appeared in the 50-100 range). This would seem to have obvious implications for the question of whether to seek back issues before 1970.

Percentage figures show trends, but one must also look at the numbers of articles since that is a possibly more accurate predictor of the demand for a specific journal. Table 5 presents the data for numbers of English-language article sin the 35 journals, 1960-1978. As with the data for percentages in Table 2, these data for numbers show striking increases in English-language articles for each of the 35 journals, with an overall increase in totals from 606 published in English-language articles in 1960 to 7,172 in 1978, a 10.83-fold increase over the 18-year period.

No arguments can be made from these data that include the element of importance to the field of the journals involved. However, the data can be used to provide a picture of those journals that are major volume contributors to English-language publication. In Table 6, it can be seen that five journals contributed 46.4% of all English-language

Table 3. Percentage Ranges for English-Language Articles 1960-78

Percentage range	Number of Journals in Range in 1960	1965	1970	1975	1978
0-25	21	16	6	2	2
25-50	7	8	6	2	2
50-75	2	4	11	10	4
75-100	0	4	11	2	27

Table 4. The 27 Journals Publishing Better than 75% English-Language Articles in 1978

Anatomy and Embryology

Archive for Rational Mechanics and Analysis

Archives of Microbiology

Astronomy and Astrophysics

Berichte der Bunsengesellschaft fuer Physikalische Chemie

Cell and Tissue Research

Chromosoma

Communications of Mathematical Physics

Contributions to Mineralogy and Petrology

Cytobiologie

European Journal of Biochemistry

Histochemistry

Hoppe-Seylers Zeitschrift fuer Physiologische Chemie

Inventiones Mathematicae

Journal of Comparative Physiology

Molecular and General Genetics

Pflugers Archiv-European Journal of Physiology

Physica Status Solidi A+B

Planta

Synthesis

Theoretica Chimica Acta

Wilhelm Roux's Archives of Developmental Biology

TABLE 4 (continued)

Zeitschrift fuer Naturforschung. Teil A. Physikalische Chemie

Zeitschrift fuer Naturforschung. Teil C. Biosciences

Zeitschrift fuer Pflanzenphysiologie

Zeitschrift fuer Physik A and B

Zeitschrift fuer Krystallographie

Table 5. Numbers of English-Language Articles 1960-78

	1960	1965	1970	1975	1978	Totals
1. Annalen der Physik	6	12	15	30	19	82
2. Anatomy and Embryology	6	13	24	65	90	198
3. Archive for Rational Mechanics and Analysis	41	67	35	78	36	257
4. Archives of Microbiology	20	27	128	168	182	525
5. Astronomy and Astrophysics	82	113	277	499	396	1367
6. Berichte der Bunsengesellschaft fuer Physikalische Chemie	42	11	53	88	200	394
7. Cell and Tissue Research	42	117	307	409	410	1285
8. Chromosoma	18	54	118	110	235	535
9. Communications of Mathematical Physics	----	10	60	116	128	322
10. Contributions to Mineralogy and Petrology	1	4	93	115	92	305
11. Cytobiologie	----	----	13	33	78	124
12. European Journal of Biochemistry	2	49	73	720	726	1570
13. Histochemistry	19	50	125	184	125	503
14. Hoppe-Seylers Zeitschrift fuer Physiologische Chemie	0	1	69	150	136	356
15. Inventiones Mathematicae	----	8	32	43	85	168
16. Journal of Comparative Physiology	13	14	60	138	232	457
17. Journal fuer Praktische Chemie	3	22	24	14	44	107
18. Mathematische Annalen	25	71	145	107	124	472
19. Mathematische Zeitschrift	31	78	134	76	109	428

TABLE 5 (continued)

	1960	1965	1970	1975	1978	Totals
20. Molecular and General Genetics	19	24	128	231	405	807
21. Naturwissenschaften	87	164	125	132	135	643
22. Pflugers Archiv-European Journal of Physiology	4	25	137	134	235	535
23. Physica Status Solidi A+B	9	465	1040	1466	924	3904
24. Planta	6	29	148	171	277	631
25. Synthesis	----	----	53	227	250	530
26. Theoretica Chimica Acta	2	34	132	135	81	384
27. Wilhelm Roux's Archives of Developmental Biology	11	10	22	33	41	117
28. Zeitschrift fuer Anorganische und Allgemeine Chemie	20	20	39	33	35	147
29. Zeitschrift fuer Metallkunde	1	2	32	51	51	137
30. Zeitschrift fuer Naturforschung. Teil A. Physikalische Chemie	15	75	141	191	204	626
31. Zeitschrift fuer Naturforschung. Teil B. Anorganische und Organische Chemie	10	30	90	66	104	300
32. Zeitschrift fuer Naturforschung. Teil C. Biosciences	----	----	----	121	139	260
33. Zeitschrift fuer Pflanzenphysiologie	0	3	55	107	153	318
34. Zeitschrift fuer Physik A and B	36	60	278	351	637	1362
35. Zeitschrift fuer Krystallographie	35	63	47	69	54	266
TOTALS	606	1733	4252	6661	7172	20424

articles published over the 18-year period. Of the five, three are predominantly in Physics, one in biology, and one in Biochemistry. If more chemical-interest journals are desired, one can move to the second level in Table 6, which includes the nine additional journals that bring the total contribution to 72.5% of all English-language articles published 1960-78. The distribution of the 14 journals thus included by predominant subject area would be Biology - 6, Chemistry/Biochemistry - 4, Physics - 3, Science - 1. The analysis can be further

Table 6. Publication of English-Language Articles Rank-Ordered by the Numbers of Such Articles Published

Journal	Numbers of Articles (1960-78)	Total Number of Articles (1960-78)	Percentage of the Total
Physica Status Solidi A+B	3904		
European Journal of Biochemistry	1570		
Astronomy and Astrophysics	1367		
Zeitschrift fuer Physik A and B	1362		
Cell and Tissue Research	1285		
Subtotal for top 5 Journals	9488	20424	46.4
Molecular and General Genetics	807		
Naturwissenschaften	643		
Planta	631		
Zeitschrift fuer Naturforschung. Teil A. Physikalische Chemie	626		
Chromosoma	535		
Pflugers Archiv-European Journal of Physiology	535		
Synthesis	530		
Archives of Microbiology	525		
Histochemistry	503		
Total for top 14 Journals	14823	20424	72.5

applied to the other 21 journals that are responsible for the final 26.6% of English-language publication not reflected in Table 6.

CONCLUSION

This analysis of English-language article publication in German Basic Science journals with high citation or high impact provides a model for developing tools to assist in purchasing or storing foreign language journals.

NOTES

1. Schloman, Barbara Frick; Ahl, Ruth E. Retention periods for journals in a small academic library. *Special Libraries*, 70:377-383; 1979 September.

2. Tibbetts, Pamela. A method for estimating the in-house use of the periodical collection in the University of Minnesota Bio-Medical Library. *Bulletin of the Medical Library Association*, 62:37-48: 1974 January.

3. Basile, Victor A.; Smith, Reginald W. Evolving the 90% pharmaceutical library. *Special Libraries*, 61:88; 1970 February.

4. Kilgour, Frederick G. Use of medical and biological journals in the Yale Medical Library. *Bulletin of the Medical Library Association*. 50:429-443; 1962 July.

5. Chalmers, G. R.; Healey, J. S. Journal citations in masters theses; one measurement of a journal collection. *Journal of the American Society for Information Science*, 24:379-401; 1973 May.

6. Garfield, Eugene, *Journal citation reports; a bibliometric analysis of science journals in the ISI data base*. Philadelphia: ISI; 1979.

7. Schmidt, Jean Mace. Translation of periodical literature in plant pathology. *Special Libraries*, 70:12-17; 1979 January.

8. Gingerich, Owen. PhD. language requirement. *Physics Today*, 30:9-10; 1977 November.

9. Sherwood, Bruce A. Universal language requirement. *Physics Today*, 32:9; 1979 July.

10. Leck, Charles F. Foreign languages and biologists today. *Bioscience*, 28:367; 1978 June.

11. Wetzel, Robert G. On foreign languages. *Bioscience*, 28:620; 1978 October.

12. Schmidt, *op. cit.*, p. 13.

13. Schmidt, *op. cit.*, p. 13-14.

14. Instructions for Authors. *Naturwissenschaften*, Inside front cover, each issue.

15. Verlag Chemie International (Prospectus). *Scientific and Technical Journals* 1979, p. 28.

16. Garfield, Eugene. *Essays of an information scientist*. Philadelphia: ISI Press; 1977; p. 470, 473.

17. Schmidt, *op. cit.*, p. 13.

18. Wetzel, *op. cit.*, p. 20.

19. Garfield, *op. cit.*, pp. 471-472.

American Authors in Foreign Science Journals: Reviewing the Range of Initial Attitudes and Adjusting Library Investment to Client Experiences

Tony Stankus

ABSTRACT. Using the literature of three foreign countries in four disciplines, files were constructed of 457 authors with American affiliations who chose to publish abroad. Arguments for and against their choices are listed. Three tests of the citation performance of the American papers in the twelve foreign titles selected were conducted. While the results disallow some of the more extreme viewpoints—they do allow for continuing controversy concerning the papers' quality and the underlying motivation for their placement outside domestic channels. A final test shows that while a majority of Americans did not reappear as authors in these journals within three years, a sizable minority published there again and again. It is suggested that librarians quietly gauge the individually varying post-publication perspectives of their institution's authors before making collection management decisions.

RATIONALE

At least two factors suggest that another look at American library involvement with foreign science journals is worthwhile. American librarians are facing discriminatory pricing policies from some foreign publishers.[1] Moreover, American librarians are being called upon to evaluate faculty publications[2-4] and much less is known about foreign journals as vehicles for American reports or of the motivation of those Americans who publish within them.

METHODS

Publications from three foreign countries were analyzed. Four disciplines were studied through a matched set of twelve journals issued during 1981. Canadian, British, and West German titles were chosen because of their often habitual inclusion in many American collections. The assortment of fields included Mathematics, Chemistry, Physics and Microbiology. This was intended to provide some items of interest for librarians serving any of the clients in the pure or applied, and life or physical sciences.

Only those papers by scientists with a clearly designated American affiliation were included. Papers that Americans coauthored with foreign scientists which appeared in the latter's national journals were excluded. This disallowed the notion that the American partners published there solely as a matter of courtesy. See Figure 1 for a statistical summary.

THE CONFLICTING PERSPECTIVES

Arguments in favor of Americans publishing within foreign science journals – and having American libraries take them – include:

- Many of these journals have a very long and distinguished publication history. The roll call of their successive editors reads like chapter headings in the history of the discipline, with current editors preserving a rather strong personal involvement in manuscript consideration.
- Even in modern specialties, foreign scientific communities may have strong emphases that best match those of given American authors.
- Foreign journals have increasingly "Americanized" the language of publication of most of their papers, as well as the instructions for authors, citing style, and layout[5]
- Foreign journals rarely assess page charges which, particularly for American society-sponsored journals, can often run several hundred dollars per article.

Arguments against foreign science journals include:

- Some Americans feel that even if an American journal is not the first to be established in a field, sooner or later, the journal and

CHEMISTRY

Canadian Journal of Chemistry (21)
Journal of the Chemical Society
- Chemical Communications
(limited to first 69 authors)
Synthesis (37)

MICROBIOLOGY

Canadian Journal of Microbiology (59)
Journal of General Microbiology (38)
Archives of Microbiology (50)

NUMBER AMERICAN AUTHORS BY DISCIPLINE

Chemistry 127
Physics 81
Microbiology 147
Mathematics 102

PHYSICS

Canadian Journal of Physics (18)
Journal of Physics A (48)
Zeitschrift fuer Physik A (15)

MATHEMATICS

Canadian Journal of Mathematics (42)
Proceedings of the London Mathematical Society (21)
Mathematische Annalen (39)

NUMBER AMERICAN AUTHORS BY JOURNAL NATIONALITY

Canadian 140
British 176
West German 141

FIGURE 1. Foreign Journals Studied for this Paper. Numbers of American authors identified in 1981 issues, noted in parentheses.

its American contributors will rise to the top and become the most-cited.

- Foreign journal editors often do not provide carbons of anonymous referees' reports as is commonly done in major American journals. This suggests to some critics that experts outside the editorial boards are not called in often enough, possibly allowing inferior manuscripts to slip through, particularly those already rejected by American journals.
- Linguistically limited Americans note that many foreign journals still publish some papers in languages other than English, and that those papers that are in English are often very awkwardly written.
- Americans also complain about the lack of close correspondence between the cover date of an issue (e.g., January) and its arrival in the library (e.g., July), usually with allusions to foreign inefficiency in production and mail handling.
- Even apart from the current controversy on exchange rates, subscription costs for foreign journals are very high. Very few individual scientists take many of them. Even the number of libraries taking some of the more expensive ones is dropping. Critics suggest that all this reduces the chances of a given American contribution being noticed.

Without affirming the validity of any of the above comments from either side, we will designate these conflicting perspectives as the cosmopolitan and chauvinist viewpoints.

TEST ONE: DO AMERICAN PAPERS BOOST CITATIONS TO THE FOREIGN JOURNALS THAT PUBLISH THEM?

Both chauvinists and cosmopolitans might guess that American papers would improve foreign journal citation rates, albeit for very different reasons. Chauvinists might well base their judgments on the alleged superiority of even domestically rejected American papers. Cosmopolitans would point out the journal's intrinsic attraction for good papers, including good American papers. Using a procedure analogous to *Journal Citation Reports*,[6] we compared the average annual rate of citations earned by the American papers in the foreign journals to that reported for the journal overall.

Figure 2 provides both schools with an unpleasant surprise. In only four out of twelve cases did American papers earn as much as 90% of

CHEMISTRY

Canadian Journal of Chemistry 55%
Journal of the Chemical Society
- Chemical Communications 77%
Synthesis 75%

MICROBIOLOGY

Canadian Journal of Microbiology 75%
Journal of General Microbiology 112%
Archives of Microbiology 83%

AVERAGES BY DISCIPLINE

Chemistry 69%
Physics 95%
Microbiology 90%
Mathematics 71%

PHYSICS

Canadian Journal of Physics 97%
Journal of Physics A 89%
Zeitschrift fuer Physik A 100%

MATHEMATICS

Canadian Journal of Mathematics 100%
Proceedings of the London Mathematical Society 58%
Mathematische Annalen 56%

AVERAGES BY JOURNAL NATIONALITY

Canadian 82%
British 84%
West German 78%

FIGURE 2. Citation Performance of American Papers in Foreign Journals Compare to the Average for All Papers in the Journals. A score of 100% or more would suggest that American papers are cited as often or more than the resident foreign papers. This proved not to be generally true.

the foreign total. American physicists did the best as a disciplinary group; the average for microbiologists being unduly skewed by the *Journal of General Microbiology*. There is an equally surprising uniformity by nationality of publication. Americans did not perform better in any one of the nationalities than in another. Foreign journals do not seem to need American papers to bolster citations, at least during the early years when the ratings sweep is typically conducted.

TEST TWO: DO AMERICANS DELIBERATELY DUMP THEIR INFERIOR PAPERS ABROAD?

The only real test for the conscious disposal of inferior manuscripts in foreign journals could come from lie detector exams. Somewhat less drastically, a tendency in this direction might be detected by comparing citations to the American-issued vs. foreign-issued papers of the same authors on similar subjects in the same year. A search of our 457 authors disclosed that the files of 184 yielded matched pairs. When the American-issued paper exceeded its foreign peer, the dumping hypothesis of the chauvinists was credited. If not, the cosmopolitans were credited.

Figure 3 shows the surprising results: an almost perfect balance overall. Only about half the time in most pairs did the American-issued paper prevail. The worse case for the foreign-issued journal was 15 to 9 against the *Canadian Journal of Microbiology*. But this was almost perfectly balanced by 14 to 9 for the German journal *Synthesis*. This hardly suggests consistent abuse of foreign outlets. If the chauvinists are deliberately dumping, they're throwing away the wrong paper about half the time.

TEST THREE: WHAT ABOUT ESPECIALLY PROMISING PAPERS?

The previous test contains a bias in favor of the ordinary paper. There is no extra credit awarded to a journal for having published a truly significant paper. All a paper had to do was equal its peer or exceed it by a single citation. In this new test we search for papers which show signs, within approximately two years, of becoming heavily cited. This is done by achieving at least twice the citations suggested by the foreign journals' impact factors. Sixty-one papers from the 184 pairs in the previous test filled this additional criterion.

CHEMISTRY

Canadian Journal of Chemistry 50%
Journal of the Chemical Society
- Chemical Communications 54%
Synthesis 61%

MICROBIOLOGY

Canadian Journal of Microbiology 50%
Journal of General Microbiology 50%
Archives of Microbiology 48%

AVERAGES BY DISCIPLINE

Chemistry 55%
Physics 54%
Microbiology 49%
Mathematics 52%

PHYSICS

Canadian Journal of Physics 57%
Journal of Physics A 47%
Zeitschrift fuer Physik 57%

MATHEMATICS

Canadian Journal of Mathematics 45%
Proceedings of the London Mathematical Society 60%
Mathematische Annalen 50%

AVERAGES BY JOURNAL NATIONALITY

Canadian 50%
British 53%
West German 54%

FIGURE 3. How often is the foreign-issued paper by an American author cited as his domestically published one? A score substantially less than 50% would indicate that they were predictably inferior. This turns out not to be so.

This time the result was somewhat more conclusive. On average, seventy percent of the heavy hitting papers appeared in the American-issued journals. This result was reasonably consistent across nine of twelve journals, with an exceptional single showing by the *Zeitschrift fuer Physik*, and a 50-50 showing by two British journals. This test would seem to favor the chauvinist viewpoint. But the apparent contradiction between this and the previous tests may yield a generally satisfactory resolution across the three tests as follows.

Most scientists, including Americans, work up a great many "journeyman" manuscripts. The authors honestly assess them as worthwhile but of only ordinary citations prospects. It appears that those Americans willing to try foreign journals, divide up their journeyman manuscripts between domestic and foreign outlets without special favor or contempt. This behavior gives us the cosmopolitan result of test two. But many of the same scientists occasionally work up what they regard as a "master" manuscript, one that they feel will perhaps be highly cited. They generally prefer their domestic national outlet for these. While this gives us the chauvinist result of test three, it also gives us a cosmopolitan insight concerning test one. Perhaps the reason that the American papers did so poorly as a group relative to the foreign papers as a group lies in the largely journeyman representation of papers in the American contingent. By and large these could not compete with the resident foreign contingent which included not only journeyman papers but more master papers as well. In short, these foreign journals do in fact publish some of the more cited papers in the field, and have their own intrinsic advantage in their ability to recruit them at least regionally. See Figure 4.

This last interpretation is open to controversy. Garfield[7] has shown that many of the better-cited papers from some foreign nationals appear in American journals. Our study does not contradict that possibility, it merely suggests that the majority of heavy hitter papers appear in the resident national journals, at least for authors from major scientific powers.

REPEAT SUBMISSIONS AS AN INDICATOR OF AUTHOR SATISFACTION

Sustained involvement with a foreign journal is suggested by a pattern of repeated publications. An isolated paper is probably neutral in terms of the chauvinist-cosmopolitan dichotomy, but there are implications for collection managers when the American author appears

CHEMISTRY

Canadian Journal of Chemistry 0%

Journal of the Chemical Society - Chemical Communications 37%

MICROBIOLOGY

Canadian Journal of Microbiology 31%

Journal of General Microbiology 50%

Archives of Microbiology 25%

AVERAGES BY DISCIPLINE

Chemistry 31%

Physics 56%

Microbiology 35%

Mathematics 44%

PHYSICS

Canadian Journal of Physics 33%

Journal of Physics A 37%

Zeitschrift fuer Physik A 100%

MATHEMATICS

Canadian Journal of Mathematics 33%

Proceedings of the London Mathematical Society 100%

Mathematische Annalen 0%

AVERAGES BY JOURNAL NATIONALITY

Canadian 24%

British 56%

West German 46%

FIGURE 4. In any given matched pair of papers by American authors, which journals domestically-issued or foreign, captured the larger shares of especially well-cited papers? A score representing substantially less than 50% for foreign titles suggests that domestic journals do better, as turned out to be the case most often.

there on a recurring basis. In this portion of the study, we followed the output of our original author group through 1984, using the Source Index of *Science Citation Index*.

Once again, two seemingly contradictory findings emerged. See Figure 5. On average in no disciplinary group or foreign nationality is there a majority of repeat publishers in the approximately three year waiting span. (Physical and German journals seem to have retained their authors at a somewhat higher rate, however.) But, among those who do repeat there is an average of between two and three papers, suggesting a rather strong author loyalty. In this observation of individual differences lies the key to the decision in a given library situation.

IT WORKS FOR ME

The perceptive librarian realizes that a blunt immediate approach to a faculty member, questioning his involvement with a foreign journal might well provoke a defensive reaction. It may even set off a temporary flurry of resentful use of the title. There is much that can be learned inobtrusively prior to any interview on the subject. The central question must be: Has this journal "worked" for the author to such a degree that his library use justifies its library costs? Consider the following preliminary steps instead:

- Tabulate the citations to the author's foreign-issued papers? Are they equal to, or more numerous than, his domestically published papers on the same subjects?
- Check the subsequent domestic publications of the author. From among the many publications in his past with which he can document his assertions, how often does he mention his work in the foreign-issued journals?
- See if the author's foreign-issued papers are among those posted in his section of the departmental reprints bulletin board. Alternatively, see if the author includes them in graduate program recruiting posters or in the Peterson's Guide to Graduate Studies entries submitted by his department. (Authors are disinclined to advertise failures.)
- Monitor use of the foreign journal by students. Has the faculty member assigned readings there? Recall that faculty mentors have a strong influence on the young scientist's journal world view.[8]

CHEMISTRY

Canadian Journal of Chemistry 19% (2.5 papers)
Journal of the Chemical Society
- Chemical Communications 46% (2.3 papers)
Synthesis 32% (3.5 papers)

PHYSICS

Canadian Journal of Physics 33% (1.5 papers)
Journal of Physics A 42% (4.1 papers)
Zeitschrift fuer Physik 60% (1.9 papers)

MICROBIOLOGY

Canadian Journal of Microbiology 30% (1.9 papers)
Journal of General Microbiology 26% (2.4 papers)
Archives of Microbiology 44% (1.5 papers)

MATHEMATICS

Canadian Journal of Mathematics 5% (1 paper)
Proceedings of the London Mathematical Society 19% (1 paper)
Mathematische Annalen 15% (2.2 papers)

AVERAGES BY DISCIPLINE

Chemistry	32%	(2.8 papers)
Physics	45%	(2.5 papers)
Microbiology	33%	(1.9 papers)
Mathematics	13%	(1.4 papers)

AVERAGES BY JOURNAL NATIONALITY

Canadian	22%	(1.7 papers)
British	33%	(2.4 papers)
West German	38%	(2.3 papers)

FIGURE 5. What proportion of foreign-published American authors will return to their journal? How many more papers over a three year period? (Averages in parenthesis.)

– Are laboratory assistants or departmental secretaries making photocopies to fill reprint requests sent to the faculty member?

If these initial checks suggest positive experiences, the librarian can more frankly discuss with the faculty member how his papers were treated editorially and typographically. Moreover, did they attract the amount of attention he expected? Does he see himself turning to the journal as an outlet again?

The tougher circumstance occurs when all the preliminary checks look negative. Approaching the faculty member now will still elicit a defensive reaction, but the librarian will at least be able to see through any short-lived masking behavior.

THE NEED FOR MORE RESEARCH

These findings are probably strong enough to support the limited practical approaches in collection management recommended. Especially in tenure cases, more disciplines and more nationalities need investigation. Perhaps longer study periods are needed as well, particularly in slow-rate-of-publication fields like pure mathematics. There are undoubtedly gray areas in the definition of nationality as well. While it is clear that the *Canadian Journal of Chemistry*, is Canadian, it is not so clear, for example, that *Biochimica et Biophysica Acta*, a product of the Amsterdam-based multinational Elsevier-North Holland, is Dutch. Nonetheless, it is hoped that collection managers, and even the more perspicacious tenure evaluators, have gained some insights into expatriate papers and their authors.

NOTES

1. Siegfried Ruschin, "Why are Foreign Subscription Rates Higher for American Libraries Than They are for Subscribers Elsewhere?", *The Serials Librarian* 9, No. 3 (Spring 1985): 7-17.

2. Barbara A. Rice & Tony Stankus, "Publication Quality Indicators for Tenure and Promotion Decisions: What Can the Librarian Ethically Report?", *College & Research Libraries* 44, no. (March 1983): 173-178.

3. Eugene F. Garfield, "How to Use Citation Analysis for Faculty Evaluations, and When Is it Relevant?" *Current Contents* 26 (Part One), No. 44: 5-13 (Part Two), No. 45: 5-14 (both 1983).

4. A. Carolyn Miller & Sharon Serzan, "Criteria for Identifying a Refereed Journal," *Journal of Higher Education* 55, No. 6 (Nov.-Dec., 1984): 673-699.

5. Tony Stankus, Rashelle Schlessinger, & Bernard S. Schlessinger, "English Language Trends in German Basic Science Journals: A Potential Collection Tool," *Science & Technology Libraries* 1, No. 3 (Spring 1981): 55-66.

6. The actual method used in *Journal Citation Reports* takes the consecutive years of a journal's papers, than counts the citations they earned in the third year and divides the total citations by the number of papers. Our method is based on one year's papers, and the following two years of citations, divided by two. We balance the "inflationary" bias of dealing with two years of citations by the division. Our variation allowed us to keep the 1981 American papers in step with the rest of the journal's 1981 papers whose ratings were not fully reported until the 1983 *JCR* (published late in 1984).

7. See, for example, Eugene Garfield, "The 1981 Most-Cited Chemistry Papers. Part One. Pure and Synthetic Chemistry. Or, Should I Say, Most-Cited Papers Published in 1981 in the *Journal of the American Chemical Society*?" *Current Contents* 25, No. 12 (March 25, 1985): 3-16.

8. Tony Stankus, "Negotiating Journal Demands With Young Scientists Using Lists Derived From Thesis Advisor Records," *Collection Management* 5, No. 3/4 (Fall/Winter 1983): 185-198.

The Americanization of Journal Loyalties of Foreign-Born, Foreign-Trained Scientists and Physicians Who Emigrate to the United States

Tony Stankus
Kevin Rosseel

ABSTRACT. An analysis of the publication patterns of fifty-two immigrant scientists and physicians at three points in their career is reported. The data suggests that there are substantial differences in the depth and duration of loyalty on the part of emigrating Britons, Continental Europeans and Asian Indians to the journals of their homeland, although virtually all the immigrants share an eventual "Naturalization" of the bulk of their journal outlets in the long run. A subtle interplay of any residual advantage in maintaining the use of their original language of publication, and the relative prestige in America of their old country outlets, seems to govern the degree and frequency with which these authors will return to them after arrival. The fluctuating but persistent role of commercially issued "international" journals in the careers of all three migrant groups is also charted.

The arrival of foreign-born, foreign-trained scientists or clinicians as permanent library customers should prompt a review of the collection that must now serve them. Will they demand the journals of their native lands? Will they use the American journals that are already likely to be there? To what degree will they request "third party journals," those international titles not emanating from either their native countries or the United States? Do immigrant scientists of differing nationalities have differing demands? While there is a substantial literature on handling the library orientation needs of foreign students, there is little on collection adaptation, or on foreign born clients who

---

Kevin Rosseel was Daytime Supervisor, at the Science Library, Swords Hall 100, College of the Holy Cross, 1 College Street, Worcester, MA 01610.
He is currently a candidate for a Master's Degree in Library and Information Science at Indiana University.

not only have their initial professional degree or research doctorate, but papers in technical journals as well.

MODELS OF THE IMMIGRANTS AND THEIR JOURNALS

There have been three waves of scientific and clinical immigrants. While they all share some common characteristics, they can be distinguished by:

- the onset of their movement to America;
- their ethnic composition;
- the mix of their motives;
- the relative advantage or disadvantage of continued involvement with the journals of their homeland.

The first wave continues even today. It started in colonial times and is essentially a more educated version of the mainstream immigration from Western and Northern Europe. Its early make-up generally favored English speakers from the British Isles, but Continental Europeans made considerable gains after the Civil War. Both groups tended to share, with differing emphasis, four motives for immigration. Since the other two waves tend to enjoy some of the benefits mentioned, we'll treat them expansively.

> *Economic Gain*. Competition for a laboratory position or for a clinical practice that pays well represents an immediate concern of many of these skilled immigrants. While the educations and initial training of most immigrants are subsidized at their native universities, their governments do not always thereafter guarantee them a substantial income for life. Opportunities in America have been, and continue to appear, more lucrative. Even a relatively affluent group, British physicians who come to America, list money as their primary motive.[1]
>
> *Career Advancement*. A major attraction of America is the more rapid advancement possible in research institutes, universities, and clinical services. European institutions typically have many more layers of rank to work up through before one is given serious supervisory authority over funding and facilities. Moreover, there tend to be many more junior candidates for senior positions in Europe than positions. Many senior positions are still vacated only by the death of their tenants. In America there tend to be

many more opportunities for advancement created through the national propensity for job-changing and the ongoing establishment of new labs and hospitals. Fleming Kolby, Danish born director for Scandinavia of the world's largest bank has aptly said: "In Europe, by contrast, development goes step by step, . . . the European executive or scientist moves too slowly for his own good or for the good of the country . . . this turns personal drive sour."[2]

Comparative Political Stability and Tolerance. Apart from the upset of wars and revolutions in Europe, there has tended to be governmental intervention in the affairs of politically active scientists and clinicians. As will be seen in the next wave this could include dismissal or exile, but more typically it involves a subtle slowing down of an already slow career climb. While the United States certainly has had episodes of repressing Reds, it has a longer history of bemusement at professorial posturing. Steinmetz, the leading electrical engineer of the first quarter of this century had to flee Europe owing to his radical Socialist beliefs. Perhaps only in America would he ultimately be hired by the very much capitalist General Electric Company. Even then, he ran for political office repeatedly on the Socialist ticket with no serious detriment to his corporate standing.[3]

The Welcome Mat. Many Europeans have been actively recruited for positions in America. Since the 1800s both official commissions and streams of individuals have come back from Germany in particular, favorably impressed. The first catalog of the University of Michigan announced: "The State of Michigan has copied from Prussia what is acknowledged to be the most perfect educational system in the world.[4] At the turn of the century professorships with tenure were commonly offered as lures. In 1876, J.J. Sylvester, later the founder of the *American Journal of Mathematics*, demanded a fully paid passage from Britain, and the then titanic annual salary of $5,000 in gold, and received it from Johns Hopkins University.[5] Of course, there were trade-offs. The average American, who holds no special awe of the professorate, liked to know what he was getting for his money. In 1915 Jacques Loeb, a renowned Franco-German biologist, reports that Berkeley had offered him "a pure research position as an inducement . . . but very soon the community and newspapers resented the idea that I should receive full pay and do little teaching."[6]

Whatever the British and continental Europeans had in common in terms of motivation, there was a substantial difference in later years in the relative advantage their journal traditions conferred on their emigrants. Both groups tended to come from countries that had very well established and highly respected journals. (As late as 1935 Germans garnered 36 percent of all citations in the five leading journals of physics.)[7] And until the 1960s American scientists and clinicians could reasonably be expected to be conversant with the foreign language literature. It was at least theoretically possible for foreign-born scientists to continue demonstrating their research progress to their new American colleagues in their own customary European language outlets. But American foreign language proficiencies, rarely voluntarily pursued or part of a generally accommodating attitude to non-English speakers, essentially collapsed as formal university requirements for them faded in many disciplines. It became highly unlikely that publishing in anything other than English would impress American scientific or clinical audiences.

The second type of immigrant wave is episodic rather than continual. It often brings in a new ethnic assortment. The motivation is survival. A kind of journal disorientation is characteristic. The archetypal episode has been the Nazi repression of the Jews during the period between the world wars. While the Jews of all occupied countries were affected, some of the more numerous victims of this forced migration were hitherto less represented Central Europeans: Austrians, Hungarians, Czechs and Poles. Sixty-six percent (3,357) of all physicians arriving in the United States between 1933-1940 were Jewish refugees.[8] The racist Civil Service Laws of 1933 emptied out so many universities that they could barely continue to function in some cases. Hilbert, one of Germany's most distinguished gentile mathematicians, was asked by the Nazi minister of education how his world famous but newly purged institute was faring. Hilbert replied: "Mathematics at Goettingen? There is really none anymore." In all, twenty contemporary or future Nobel laureates left their posts. The advantage of having appeared in prestigious German-language journals, as many Central Europeans had eagerly done, was scarcely likely to be sustained under these circumstances. To a great degree, these victims became not only people without a country but scientists without a journal.

The refugee type of wave can recur with its abrupt onset, its ethnic concentration, its survival motivation, and the dispossession of any journal background. There were Hungarians in the '50s, Cubans in the '60s, Indochinese in the '70s, and Soviet Jews and Polish Catholics in the 1980s. How many of these can expect to return to the pages of their native journals as authors again?

In contrast the third wave is continuous and not of acute refugee character. Its distinguishing characteristics are its late onset (after World War II), its Third World basis, and a certain disregard for native journals by the natives themselves. Some would include the continuing migration of Europeans in this "Brain Drain," but the Western European countries are themselves recipients of 30 percent of these scientific and medical guest workers.[10] Moreover in terms of this study, there is no comparison of journal traditions or loyalties.

The "Brain Drain" motivation involves several interlocking circumstances. First a great many third world countries have at least one technologically advanced university where the very finest local students matriculate. The best of imported American, Japanese and Western European equipment and literature is provided for them. Then, on graduation day, the young scientists and physicians face the possibility of returning to whatever social and economic circumstances they came from, and doing whatever science or medicine is possible with the typically very limited means available. Many have no wish to leave their university city, but there is already an oversupply based on previous graduating classes. Ironically, those with the most financial resources and best grades quite simply follow the frank advice of their own professors and emigrate. Their journal orientation is likewise skewed. A given scientist or clinician may publish locally for a local audience, but many third world authors already know that they have no local future.

AN INFORMAL TEST OF THESE MODELS

These characterizations of immigrant scientists and clinicians and their journal loyalties can be subjected to a test that may have implications for collection adaptation. Using standard directories[11] a group of fifty-two life scientists and clinicians who met certain criteria were identified:

- They must have been born in a foreign country (typically theU.K., India, or German-speaking Europe).
- They must have earned their initial professional degree or doctorate in a foreign country (typically in the U.K., India, or German-speaking Europe).
- They must have published before and after coming to America.[12]
- And while some have had experiences in other countries prior to arrival in the United States, all of them appeared to have become permanent residents of the United States for at least the duration of the study. (In fact most become citizens.)

- –There was an attempt to provide some balance between British and Continental authors (20 authors each). The Indian immigration, being of more recent onset, was represented by twelve authors.
- –The Continental authors were further divided into pre- and post-World War II era immigrants. Half of the pre-World War II authors, were according to our admittedly imperfect but earnest judgement, refugee Jews, although this sort of information is rarely frankly reported in our sources.

The underlying rationale for the selection of these groups is as follows:

- –The British represent a first wave group whose journals had the dual advantage of both prestige and readability in American eyes.
- –The Continentals, a largely German-speaking contingent, represents a mixed first and second wave group whose journals had the advantage of prestige if not readability in American eyes.
- –The Indians represent a third wave, "brain drain" group whose journals had the advantage of readability, if not always prestige, in American eyes.

JOURNAL PATTERNS BEFORE COMING TO AMERICA

Figure 1 represents the output of our groups before their arrival in America.

The British picture is clearest. Every British author had at least some papers in British journals before coming to America (100% participation). About three of every five of their papers appeared in their native journals (62% share of output). About half of the Britons contributed to either (or sometimes both) "third party" international journals or American titles, each type accounting for one in five of their papers. The third party journals were typically the products of the major German, Dutch, or Swiss commercial houses: Springer, Elsevier, Karger, etc.

The Continental Europeans also showed a strong initial loyalty to their native national journals. Sixteen of twenty authors contributed to them (80% participation) with a 70 percent share of output. Of the four authors who did not follow this pattern, two were from "minor" science journal powers (Italy and Denmark) and had primarily published in third party journals. Two Nazi era Jews understandably contributed exclusively to British journals. The remaining Jews contributed to

FIGURE 1

PUBLICATION PATTERNS

BEFORE COMING TO AMERICA

% Group Participating	Share of Their Output
Publishing in Their Native National Journals	
British 100%	Continentals 70%
Continentals 80%	British 62%
Indians 50%	Indians 26%
Publishing in Non-Native, Non-US "Third-Party" Journals	
Indians 83%	Indians 58%
Continentals 75%	Continentals 24%
British 60%	British 19%
Publishing in American Journals	
British 50%	British 19%
Indians 33%	Indians 16%
Continentals 15%	Continentals 6%

some German titles, but also to Austrian titles (which remained open to them a little longer) and to Scandinavian and American titles. Interestingly virtually all Continental authors contributed a greater share of their output to third party international journals as opposed to American titles (75% contributing a 24% share vs. 15% contributing a 6% share). This bias persists even excluding those affected by wartime circumstances, and suggests that the language factor is operating: third-party international journals accept some papers in German, American journals, by and large, do not.

Indian authors present a striking contrast to their British and Continental counterparts. Only half of them contributed to native journals, and only a quarter of their papers were involved. Three-quarters of the Indians in fact sent nearly 60 percent of their papers to third party journals: British, Canadian and European titles. The British and Canadian titles are a part of an intellectually enduring commonwealth link, a network that still operates in terms of medical licensing and university transfers. The commercial European titles may well have been chosen because of several advantages. They are truly international in the sense that they are not owned by Americans and they are widely subscribed to around the world despite their considerable cost to libraries. The flip side to this approach to journal revenue is that Indian authors do not have to pay several hundred dollars for page charges as can be the case with less expensive American professional society journals. These journals are nonetheless published primarily in English, invariably the language of the Indian contributors in our study, and American papers appear alongside theirs. Perhaps most importantly, many of these third-party international journals have sympathetic third world editors.

It is important to note that Indians do contribute to American titles (33% participation). Their share of output is about equal to that of the British (16% vs. 19%) and almost three times that of the Continental group (6%). This may again reflect the Indian advantage in academic English or perhaps their earlier anticipation of emigrating to America.

In summary, the British and Continentals generally showed strong initial loyalty to their native journals, while the Indians did not. And while the Indians and Continentals contributed somewhat more frequently and heavily to third-party international titles than the British, the British and Indians, perhaps using their language advantage, appeared more often in American titles.

THE EARLY YEARS IN AMERICA

The publishing patterns of the newly arrived immigrants were followed using approximately five years' coverage of indexing/abstracting services. See Figure 2.

The change in the pattern of the Continentals is the most striking. They went from an 80 percent participation in native journals with a 70 percent share of output to a 95 percent participation in American journals with an 82 percent share. Moreover, this shift is clearly at the expense of their native journals (down to a 10% participation and 2%

FIGURE 2

PUBLICATION PATTERNS

DURING EARLY YEARS IN AMERICA

% Group Participating	Share of Their Output
Publishing in Their Native National Journals	
British 75%	British 17%
Continentals 10%	Continentals 2%
Indians 8%	Indians 1%
Publishing in Non-Native, Non-US "Third-Party" Journals	
British 60%	Indians 32%
Indians 58%	British 22%
Continentals 55%	Continentals 16%
Publishing in American Journals	
Continentals 95%	Continentals 82%
Indians 83%	Indians 81%
British 80%	British 61%

share). Their participation in third party journals is down somewhat (75% vs. 55%) as is their share of papers (24% vs. 16%) but not enough to account for most of the increase in American journal activity. Of interest is the fact that virtually all the papers now submitted by this group to third party journals are also in English. Strikingly both refugee wave Jewish Continentals and non-Jewish first wave Continentals share about the same degree of "Americanization." The only clear difference is the total absence of refugees from their native journals, but even nonrefugees made infrequent appearances. Perhaps the expulsion momentum operating with refugees merely accelerates for them the inevitable separation of virtually all non-English immigrant authors from non-English-language journals.

The Indian experience would be just as dramatic if it weren't so well foreshadowed. Their never high participation rate in native titles (50%) plummets to 8% and the share of output goes from 26 percent to 1 percent. As with the Continentals, most authors switch over to an even heavier participation in American titles (33% vs. 83%) with output shares increasing from 16 percent to 81 percent. Again, as with the Continentals, there is a drop in both participation (75% vs. 60%) and share of papers (58% vs. 32%) devoted to third party titles. The drop in share of output (-26%) was more serious than that of the Continentals (only -8%) and some of the increase in American titles must be explained as a partial disengagement from them. Perhaps knowing that their careers must now be made in America, makes the few uncommitted Indian scientists less tentative about putting more of their eggs into the explicitly American basket. More likely is the fact that their comparatively wealthy American institutions or granting agencies will now pay the page charges for them.

The British experience is similar to their Continental and Indian colleagues. Their participation in American journal publishing goes from 50 percent to 80 percent, and the share of output has grown from 19 percent to 61 percent. Their participation (60%) in third party outlets remains the same, while their share of output actually rises a little (19% vs. 22%). What sets the British apart is that while the share of output devoted to their native journals is substantially diminished (62% vs. 17%), their level of participation remains very high (100% vs. 75%). The British, it appears, do not give up their old ship.

In summary both the Continentals and the Indians rather wholeheartedly go over to American journals in their early years, very substantially reducing both their participation and their share of output in their native journals. The Indians also reduce their participation in third party journals. The British increase both their participation and share of output in American journals, maintain their third-party levels, and yet keep up a relatively frequent participation in their native journals as well.

THE PATTERNS OF THOSE STILL ACTIVE TODAY

While the numbers of authors still active today has understandably decreased (some of them are now in their eighties) a majority (90%

Britons, 80% Continentals, 92% Indians) continue to be active. All the authors have now been here at least ten years with a majority closer to twenty or thirty. See Figure 3 for the results of their last three years of output. There are three stories here. One is the essential convergence of all three national groups in terms of participation (93%-100%) and share of output (72%-76%) devoted to American titles. In short, the given nationalities are now much more alike one another than than they were at any other stage of of their careers. The second story is that the non-Jewish Continentals make a modest comeback in terms of participation in their native titles. Those titles are much

FIGURE 3

PUBLICATION PATTERNS

OF THOSE STILL ACTIVE

% Group Participating	Share of Their Output
Publishing in Their Native National Journals	
British 67%	British 11%
Continentals 19%	Continentals 3%
Indians 0%	Indians 0%
Publishing in Non-Native, Non-US "Third-Party" Journals	
British 78%	Continentals 24%
Indians 58%	Indians 24%
Continentals 50%	British 17%
Publishing in American Journals	
British 100%	Indians 76%
Indians 100%	Continentals 73%
Continentals 93%	British 72%

changed now, however. They are published now virtually entirely in English.[13] Essentially these titles have become much more similar to "third party" international journals. The third story is the enduring loyalty of British-born authors to British titles. Once again it is not so much the absolute share of output (11%) as the level of participation (still a remarkable 67%).

IMPLICATIONS FOR COLLECTION ADAPTATION

The first finding is that, giving some credence to this small historical study, the collection need not be drastically altered to suit most immigrant scientists. It is eminently clear that in dealing with third wave, "brain drain" scientists, we have a group who have long ago left behind whatever native journal loyalties they had, and are quite unlikely to resume participation in them as authors. In working terms, take only those third world titles that either are expressly requested (and then only those that are inexpensive if the client is unlikely to publish within them), or are among the few that have international citability (an example might be Current Science).

The situation with the gradual first wave and refugee second wave seems to be dependent more on linguistic considerations than motive for immigration. In particular virtually all non-English speaking authors tend to abandon publication in non-English language journals, and librarians should be leery of adding these in any great number or at great expense. Select only those titles published substantially in English with high citability. It appears that most non-English origin authors recognize that their future must be an English language one, in much the same way as the publishers of many formerly German language titles have. By sharp contrast the arrival of a British client presents a clear message: the librarian must be careful to have at least the major British titles in his field. British-trained clients seem likely to sustain a pattern of authorship, and will want to maintain contact with their native titles.

MORE RESEARCH IS NEEDED

While the facts of this study seem strongly suggestive in terms of working librarianship, much more work needs to be done before its conclusions are definitive. The size of the groups might well be expanded. Interviews with surviving immigrant scientists could be conducted. Other immigrant groups should be examined: do immigrating English-speaking Canadians have an advantage over French-speaking Canadians? What about Japanese scientists or Filipino clinicians? What about the experiences of scientists who emigrate to other Western countries? Do Indians who go to work in Germany write their papers in German or in English? Scientists are always migrating somewhere and their librarians need to know what they'll use.

NOTES

1. Rosemary Steven et al., *The Alien Doctors: Foreign Medical Graduates in American Hospitals* (New York: Wiley, 1978), p. 55.
2. D.N. Chorafas, *The Knowledge Revolution: An Analysis of the International Brain Market* (New York: McGraw-Hill, 1968), p. 24.
3. Robert A. Chipman (in the) *Dictionary of Scientific Biography* (New York: Scribners, 1976), v. 13, p. 24.
4. John Albrecht Walz, *German Influence in American Education and Culture* (Freeport, NY: Books for Libraries, 1969), p. 52.
5. J.D. North (in the) *Dictionary of Scientific Biography* (New York: Scribners, 1976), v. 13, p. 218.
6. Nathan and Ida H. Reingold, *Science in America, A Documentary History (1900-1939)* (Chicago: University of Chicago Press, 1981), p. 144.
7. Alan D. Beyerchen, *Scientists Under Hitler: Politics and the Physics Community in the Third Reich* (New Haven: Yale University Press, 1977), p. 184.
8. David L. Edsall and Tracy J. Putnam, "The Emigre Physician in America, 1941," *Journal of the American Medical Association* 117 (November 29, 1941): 1881-1888.
9. Beyerchen, *Scientists Under Hitler . . .* , pp. 33-34.
10. J.N. Bhagwati, ed., *The Brain Drain and Taxation: Theory and Empirical Analysis* (New York: North Holland, 1976), pp. 6-7.
11. These were typically *American Men and Women of Science*, 15th ed. (New York: Bowker, 1982), 7 v. for more recent immigrants and *Modern Scientists and Engineers* (New York: McGraw-Hill, 1980), 3 v. for older immigrants.
12. *Biological Abstracts, Chemical Abstracts, Index Medicus*, and the "Source Index" of *Science Citation Index* were used as appropriate. While attempts at completeness and accuracy were extensive, confusion over persons with similar names and the incompleteness of even this bibliographic armamentarium remains a possibility, a certain consistency of pattern within the members of the given groups seems reassuring. Good luck to researchers working with Korean Kim's or Chinese Wu's.
13. Tony Stankus et al., "English Language Trends in German Basic Science Journals: A Potential Collection Tool," *Science & Technology Libraries* 1, no. 3 (Spring 1981): 55-66.

THEME THREE

What Journals Tell Us About the Fields They Cover

As a practical matter I know very little biochemistry, anatomy or mathematics, yet I am able to put together without too much difficulty some comments on the journals of these disciplines. I have learned to ask questions of both faculty scientists and the journals themselves, and surprisingly enough, answers are forthcoming. The technique comes from Garfield. He asked questions and got answers in the form of citation data. I get a few more from abstracts, indexing codes and author's affiliations, most of which can be interpreted with a little help from others and from histories of the disciplines.

Collection Development: Journals for Biochemists

Tony Stankus

ABSTRACT. The types of serials of interest to biochemists are reviewed, as are the schools of science journal collection development. Results of pilot studies are presented: where American biochemists publish; authorship of articles in selected journals; publication patterns of authors in for-profit firms and in small liberal art colleges; journals most frequently cited in widely used biochemistry texts. A list of journals discussed is included.

INTRODUCTION

In addition to the intellectual curiosity involved, the study of serial collection development for biochemists worthwhile because of the cost and complexity of the materials involved. The decision to add or cancel a single subscription may involve several hundred dollars and comparison of numerous titles. To compound the problem, publication in biochemistry is growing at a rapid rate. Garfield (1979) reports three journals which published more than a thousand papers in 1977 (one of them exceeded two thousand papers) and estimates the total production of papers in that year as 20-25,000. Virtually every library with a substantive collection in the life sciences will have biochemistry serials and should have a policy for their selection.

HISTORICAL BACKGROUND

The development of the serial literature in biochemistry has been discussed by Sengupta (1973). Between the late 1800s and the First World War, the French, Germans, Americans, and British established

Reprinted from *Special Collections*, volume 1, number 2, pages 51-74, 1981. Copyright, The Haworth Press.

scientific societies devoted to better understanding the relationship between chemistry and living organisms. these national societies sponsored journals to publish in their native languages the results of specifically biochemical work. These include, respectively, *Biochimie, Hoppe-Seylers Zeitschrift fuer Physiologische Chemie*, the *Journal of Biological Chemistry*, and the *Biochemical Journal*. These journals gave increased visibility and respectability to the field and, gradually at first, drew biochemically oriented manuscripts away from the neighboring disciplines of general and organic chemistry, microbiology, and physiology. After the Second World War, the science publishing world exploded with many new biochemistry journals, some no longer directly sponsored by a scientific society and most dominated by English-language articles. Some of the more alert journals of neighboring disciplines sought to hold on to their biochemically concerned readers and have increasingly featured papers using biochemical methods. This time of rising status for biochemistry also saw increased acceptance of biochemistry papers in the prestigious multiscience journals. As a consequence of these trends, Sengupta too sees more and more biochemistry papers in more and more kinds of journals, although he sees the more specifically biochemical journals as most important.

Types of Serials for Biochemists

Serials for biochemists may be classified in at least two ways: (1) by the function and/or length of the papers ordinarily published and (2) by the subject orientation of the papers ordinarily published.

In the function/length category, several subclasses of journals are found.

1. A journal that publishes primarily the result of original research in longer articles with structural elements such as abstracts, introductions, experimental details, results, and discussions may be referred to as a FULL-LENGTH ORIGINAL REPORTS JOURNAL. Examples include the *Journal of Biological Chemistry* and *Biochemistry*. Publishing in one of these journals is prestigious, in part because of the very rigorous examination of a given paper's worth by a somewhat lengthier refereeing process.
2. The delay between submission and appearance of articles in Full-Length Original Reports Journals (due to the lengthier refereeing procedures and the large numbers of papers, chronically backlogged) and the fact that not all studies lend themselves to this for-

mat have led to the development of the RAPID, PRELIMINARY COMMUNICATIONS (or "LETTERS") JOURNAL. The studies reported in these journals are in the form of shorter papers, often reporting preliminary results. Newsworthiness is stressed; the format is not as structured. Referees are instructed to quickly assess submitted papers and to make reasonable allowance for very new or speculative interpretation in the interests of rapid dissemination. *Biochemical and Biophysical Research Communications* is an example of all of these characteristics, while *FEBS Letters* stresses a more conclusive finding equally with brevity and speed of processing.

3. The desire for speed and priority of announcement, especially of reports presented at meetings, has resulted in appearance of the MEETING ABSTRACTS JOURNAL or the MEETING ABSTRACTS SPECIAL ISSUES (of either a full-length or rapid preliminary communications journal). In these journals, presenters scheduled for meetings publish paragraph-sized summaries of their presentations. The journals usually appear in print well before the conference. Examples of these journals are found in the special issues of the *Biophysical Journal* and the *Journal of Supramolecular Structure*.
4. Biochemists have felt a necessity to grasp the central themes and generalizing theories of their profession. They have recognized that one is in danger of seeing only the thousands of trees (full-length articles; rapid, preliminary communications; meetings abstracts) and failing to comprehend the totality of the forest. For this reason, the REVIEW SERIAL was born. In Review Serials, authors present long essays which summarize and classify the main channels of work in a given specialty by discussing a great many papers written over a given time span. The physical appearance of the type of review serial defined here is usually hardbound, and issuance is often irregular A well-known hardbound series is the *Annual Review of Biochemistry*; a familiar softbound is the *CRC Critical Reviews in Biochemistry*.

In the subject-orientation category, six subclasses are also present, divided into two classes of specialty journals in biochemistry and four classes of more general journals or journals in other disciplines of importance to biochemists.

The first class of specialty journals is devoted to classes of biochemical substances. SUBSTANCE SPECIALTY JOURNALS vary in format from the full-length *Journal of Lipid Research* to the rapid communication-like *Nucleic Acids Research* to the evaluative essays in *Advances in Protein Chemistry*.

The second class of SPECIALTY JOURNALS deals with a central theme or phenomena, a class of organism, a methods approach, or with an applied biochemistry field. Examples include, respectively, the *Journal of Immunology*, *Insect Biochemistry*, *Analytical Biochemistry*, and *Clinical Chemistry*.

In the more general or other-discipline journals can be found:

1. The MISSION-ORIENTED JOURNALS. The contents focus on a societal or medical problem. Examples are *Cancer Research* and the *Biology of Reproduction*.
2. The MULTISCIENCE JOURNALS. Both original and review papers in biochemistry and many other sciences are published here. A mix of short, newsworthy rapid communications and extended, authoritative reviews dominate in journals such as *Science* and *Nature*, while a medium-length paper dominates journals such as the *Proceedings of the National Academy of Sciences*.
3. The HYBRIDIZED JOURNALS. These attract the biochemically oriented researchers in other disciplines to publish with biochemists in one common journal at the mutual border of the two disciplines. Examples include *Biochemical Genetics, Biochemical Medicine,* and *Biochemical Pharmacology*.
4. The NEIGHBORING DISCIPLINE JOURNALS. The journals in biochemistry, as noted earlier, took their content from journals in fields such as microbiology, medicine and chemistry. Biochemists still publish within and cite these journals. Prominent examples include the *Journal of Bacteriology,* the *Journal of Clinical Investigation* and the *Journal of the American Chemical Society*.

CURRENT SCHOOLS OF SCIENCE JOURNAL COLLECTION DEVELOPMENT

There are two current schools of thought on how librarians select from among the wide variety of journals described above for their scientific journals collection. Each of these schools may be said to have its own principal tool.

The first school of thought focuses on the sponsorship of the journal and its publication in English. The importance of selecting English-language journals published by well-known societies is reflected in the lists of periodicals in the common science literature texts (Chen, 1975; Malinowsky, 1976; Mount, 1975). The frankest statement of this school of thought can be found in what is probably the most widely consulted library journals selection tool, *Magazines for Libraries* (Katz & Richards, 1978): "Titles have been selected to include the main English-language research journals sponsored by distinguished societies in the United States, Canada, and Great Britain (and) some high quality commercial publications commonly found in academic/ special libraries."

What is not clear is to what degree the "Society Sponsorship & English-Language Publication" rule is to be applied when selecting journals from non-English-speaking countries. For example, Stankus, Schlessinger, and Schlessinger (1981) have shown that a large number of basic science journals, both society sponsored and commercial, based in Germany and formerly publishing in German, are now publishing the vast majority of their material in English. Katz and Richards endorse many of them and thereby seem to be extending their rule, at least in the cases of the society-sponsored titles. But this still leaves us with the problems of many commercial titles and with those foreign-language journals with a society sponsorship. The librarian cannot expect a resolution in Katz and Richards, for they note that they cannot list every good journal and that *Magazines for Libraries* serves many libraries for whom the price of the commercial journals and the difficulties of comprehension of foreign-language material by patrons would argue against selection.

One help for selection of foreign-language journals is afforded by the second school of thought about scientific journal selection, the citation analysis approach (Garfield, 1972, 1976). This approach is based on the cumulative citation behavior of tens of thousands of scientists as they publish their papers and cite their own work and that of others. A basic assumption of citation analysis is that the scientific community within a given discipline will, over the long run, cite the better works in the better journals more often, and that the citation count can serve as an indicator of the importance of a journal. That librarians should select journals with articles heavily cited, in the disciplines they work with seems reasonable, since citation frequency should correlate with user demand (Stankus & Rice, 1981).

In actual operation, the use of citation data in scientific journal selection would require that the librarian screen a list of journals in citation frequency order and select those pertinent journals at the top of the list. Such lists exist in *JCR (Journal Citation Reports)* (Garfield,

1975). The lists of "most cited," "highest impact," "immediacy indexes," etc. and the individual analyses of specific journals gain in validity with comparisons made using several years' data.

The *JCR* and its parent *Science Citation Index* data base have been the source for much literature evaluating journals in given fields, including some dealing with biochemistry. In one recent study, Garfield (1979) closely analyzes the citation behavior of 40 biochemical journals, those "core" journals which publish exclusively papers in biochemistry. Two tables in the article list journals of all types ranked by the frequency with which they cite, or are cited by, these "core" biochemistry journals. Many of these "core" journals are on both lists, an expected tight interaction. The lists also contain surprisingly many multiscience, mission-oriented, hybridized, and neighboring discipline journals. (All journals from either of the lists, and any others mentioned in this paper, are listed in Appendix 1.) This citation analysis approach also poses some questions, for example:

1. Should the librarians select the more narrowly defined biochemistry "core" journals as a general rule?
2. Or, should the librarians select, within funding limits, any journals that cite or are cited by biochemists?
3. Is a special collection for biochemists better served with its own subscriptions to American journals like *Cell*, the *Journal of Bacteriology*, and the *Journal of Clinical Investigation* rather than to foreign journals like the *Journal of Biochemistry (Tokyo)*, *Hoppe-Seyler's Zeitschrift fuer Physiologische Chemie*, or *Biochimie*?

Many other questions can be posed. They lead to the conclusion that the works of Garfield warrant analysis and sophistication on the part of working librarians before casual attempts at application.

One final point should be made on the use of citation analysis. The Garfield data is all-inclusive in its audience. It speaks to scientists and librarians, to foreign as well as to American audiences. When, for example, the data show that the *Journal of Biochemistry (Tokyo)* is the 16th most-cited journal of any kind among the core journals of biochemistry, that statement is made on the basis of inclusion of all citations made by the Japanese within that journal (and any others within which they publish) as well as the more occasional American references to it. (The same statement may be made for journals published by the Germans, French, etc.) Garfield has explored the citation behavior of certain foreign groups of journals (Garfield, 1977), but largely with the view of persuading them to increase their use of English by demonstrating the "under-citedness" of articles and journals written in languages other than English. What American librarians need is some indication of specific American involvement, possibly through study of citation made by Americans. This has not yet been done but may one day be available.

OTHER TOOLS FOR SELECTION

The two schools noted above can be helpful in decisions of collection development. One either possible tool rests upon an analysis of where specifically American biochemists publish. This type of study has been approached in the following pilot investigation by the author. A sample of American institutions or departments likely to publish regularly in biochemistry journals was identified in four different categories: Medical Schools, Universities, Federal Establishments, and independent Research Foundations. Using recent issues of the "Corporate Index" of *Science Citation Index* for a period of time long enough to avoid peaks and valleys in publication, the output of the various units was tabulated, with the intent of identifying for each group over a three-year span 25-30 journals in which some group members published each year. Table 1 presents the results for 40 institutions and departments (the specific locations are included in Appendix 2). It can be seen that society-sponsored journals published in English do well, as for example, *Journal of Biological Chemistry, Biochemistry*, and *Biochemical Journal*. It may also be observed that every journal on the list in Table 1 is very highly cited, and, in fact, all 12 of the "core" biochemistry journals on the Garfield list of the top 100 journals of any disciplines also appear on this list. Other observations are worth making:

1. Only a handful of foreign-editorially-based journals appear on any of the lists. These include *Nature*; the *Journal of Molecular Biology*; *Biochemical Journal*; *Biochemical et Biophysica Acta*; and the *European Journal of Biochemistry*.
2. Despite the fact that they accept English-language papers, neither *Biochimie*; *Hoppe-Seylers Zeitschrift . . .* ; the *Journal of Biochemistry (Tokyo)*, nor any Eastern Bloc journals appear on the list. American librarians must consider whether they can afford to spend hundreds of dollars annually on these and other "bridesmaid journals" (i.e., journals that the librarians's research cus-

Table 1. Journals Published in by American Biochemists Working in Specific Areas, 1977-1979

Part 1. Medical Schools and Universities

	Medical Schools		Universities	
1.	J. Biol. Chem.	238	Biochemistry	196
2.	Proc. Nat. Acad. Sci.	96	J. Biol. Chem.	179
3.	Biochemistry	86	Proc. Nat. Acad. Sci.	155
4.	Biochim. Biophys. Acta	46	Cell	83
5.	Fed. Proc.	42	J. Bacteriol.	72
6.	Cell	32	J. Mol. Biol.	56
7.	Anal. Biochem.	29	Biochem. Biophys. Res. Commun.	54
8.	Biochem. Biophys. Res. Commun.	28	Biochim. Biophys. Acta	44
9.	J. Bacteriol.	23	Nature	44
10.	Arch. Biochem. Biophys.	22	Nucleic Acid Res.	44
11.	J. Cell Biol.	21	J. Cell Biol.	36
12.	Nature	17	Arch. Biochem. Biophys.	33
13.	Nucleic Acid Res.	16	Virol.	33
14.	FEBS Letters	16	J. Virol.	30
15.	J. Mol. Biol.	15	Science	28
16.	J. Immunol.	15	Anal. Biochem.	27
17.	Endocrinology	14	J. Am. Chem. Soc.	26
18.	J. Clin. Invest.	13	Biopolymers	21
19.	Science	13	Mol. Gen. Genet.	17
20.	Carbohydrate Res.	12	Cold Spring Harbor Symp. Quant. Biol.	13
21.	Biochem. J.	11	J. Immunol.	12
22.	Mol. Pharmacol.	11	FEBS Letters	12
23.	Pediatric Res.	10	J. Cell Physiol.	12
24.	Biochem. Pharmacol.	9	Cancer Res.	8
25.	Exp. Cell Res.	9	Exp. Cell Res.	7
26.	J. Supramol. Struct.	9	Phytochem.	6
27.	Eur. J. Biochem.	7	J. Neurochem.	5
28.	Annu. Rev. Biochem.	7	Biochem. Genet.	4

Part 2. Independent, Non-Profit Research Foundations and Federal, Veterans and Military

	Independent, Non-Profit Research Foundations		Federal, Veterans and Military	
1.	Proc. Nat. Acad. Sci.	67	J. Biol. Chem.	57
2.	Biochem. Biophys. Res. Commun.	44	Proc. Nat. Acad. Sci.	40
3.	Fed. Proc.	40	Biochemistry	28
4.	J. Biol. Chem.	38	Clin. Chem.	27
5.	Nature	37	J. Cell Biol.	17
6.	J. Virol.	36	Biochem. Biophys. Res. Commun.	16
7.	Endocrinology	35	Cell	16
8.	Biochim. Biophys. Acta	33	J. Immunol.	13
9.	Biochemistry	27	J. Virol.	12

Table 1. (cont.)

10.	Cell	27	Fed. Proc.	11
11.	J. Nat. Cancer Inst.	24	J. Mol. Biol.	11
12.	Cancer Res.	24	Science	11
13.	J. Cell Physiol.	22	Nature	11
14.	Proc. Amer. Assoc. Cancer Res.	19	J. Gen. Virol.	10
15.	Biol. Reprod.	19	Anal. Biochem.	10
16.	Science	18	Biochim. Biophys. Acta	10
17.	Virology	16	J. Chromatography	9
18.	Life Sci.	16	Arch. Biochem. Biophys.	9
19.	Biochem. Pharmacol.	14	Cancer Res.	7
20.	Exp. Cell Res.	13	Clin. Res.	7
21.	J. Immunol.	12	J. Cell Physiol.	7
22.	J. Mol. Evol.	11	J. Supramol. Struct.	6
23.	J. Exp. Med.	11	Mol. Pharmacol.	6
24.	Biophys. J.	8	FEBS Letters	4
25.	J. Mol. Biol.	8		
26.	J. Gen. Virol.	6		
27.	Cytogenet. Cell Genet.	6		
28.	Mol. Pharm.	4		
	28 journals produced 635 articles of 177 journals producing 908 articles		24 journals produced 363 articles of 106 journals producing 599 articles	

Note: Three meetings abstracts equal one paper.

tomers might only cite from time to time) in contrast to "bride journals" (i.e., journals that these customers not only cite but publish in).

3. There is a strong presence of the multiscience, hybridized, and neighboring-discipline journals. It appears that for Americans these related journals have equal status to most "core" biochemistry titles with the exceptions of the most highly regarded *Journal of Biological Chemistry* and *Biochemistry*. It should be further noted, however that Americans do appear to choose only the more-cited of these related journals in which to publish, e.g., *Cell* or the *Journal of Cell Biology*, rather than *Cytobios*.

As a further investigation, the author analyzed the authorship (U.S. vs. others) in articles in some of the journals in question. The most recent year available at the time of this study, 1978, was chosen for analysis and samples used, of no less than 50% (excepting for 25% for the titanic *Biochimica et Biophysica Acta*) of the total publication in that year. The results are shown in Table 2. Analysis of the results indicates that:

Table 2. Geographic Affiliation of Authors in Journals of Biochemical Interest

Journal	Editorial Control U.S.	Editorial Control Foreign	Number and (%) of Papers U.S.	Number and (%) of Papers Foreign	Number of Papers and (%) of Annual Output in Sample
J. Biol. Chem.*	X		686(83)	142(17)	828(57)
Biochem. Biophys. Res. Comm.*	X		547(53)	479(47)	1026(100)
Science*(B)	X		100(92)	14(8)	114(100)
Biochemistry*	X		415(83)	89(17)	504(57)
Proc. Nat. Acad. Sci.*(B)	X		252(77)	75(23)	327(70)
Arch. Biochem. Biophys.*	X		271(75)	99(25)	370(100)
Anal. Biochem.*	X		284(60)	172(40)	456(100)
J. Mol. Biol.*		X	172(54)	151(46)	323(100)
Nature*(B)		X	171(52)	156(48)	327(50)
Biochim. Biophys. Acta*		X	301(38)	509(62)	810(25)
Biochem. J.*		X	101(16)	492(84)	593(65)
FEBS Letters*		X	104(13)	681(87)	785(80)
Eur.J.Biochem.*		X	70(9)	700(91)	770(100)
Experientia(B)		X	56(25)	171(75)	227(100)
Int.J.Biochem.		X	39(28)	101(72)	140(100)
Mol.Cell Biochem.		X	27(40)	40(60)	67(100)
Biochimie		X	13(8)	150(92)	163(100)
Can. J. Biochem.		X	9(6)	153(94)	162(100)
Naturwissensch.(B)		X	8(29)	20(71)	28(100)
J.Biochem.(Tokyo)		X	6(3)	245(97)	351(100)
Hoppe-Seyler's Z.		X	2(1)	177(99)	179(100)
Biochemistry(USSR)		X	0(0)	239(100)	239(100)
			3624	5155	8779

*Journals Containing a "Critical Mass" of American Papers

(B) Only Biochemistry papers counted in this multiscience journal

U.S. papers in journals with "Critical Mass" = 3474
U.S. papers in journals without "Critical Mass" = 150

1. Generally, Americans publish in journals controlled by U.S. editors, foreign authors in journals controlled by editors of similar persuasion.
2. A "critical mass" for publication by Americans in foreign journals seems to be about 100 American papers per year. It would seem that publication by American authors in foreign journals is effectively a socialization phenomenon and is based on knowing that a reputable American colleague or research group has published there.

The author also analyzed publication practices of authors in for-profit firms and in small liberal arts colleges.

In the case of for-profit firms, the director *Industrial Research Laboratories of the U.S.* (Cattell Press, 1970) was used to develop a list of for-profit institutions that were biochemistry oriented. Analysis of three years of the Corporate Index of *Science Citation Index* produced some indications of industry-by-industry patterns. It would appear that:

1. Authors in pharmaceutical firms regularly publish in the hybridized *Biochemical Pharmacology*, *Molecular Pharmacology*, and the rapid preliminary communications journal *Life Sciences*.
2. Authors in biochemical and clinical laboratory supply firms publish heavily in *Clinical Chemistry* and less frequently in *Clinica Chimica Acta*, *Clinical Biochemistry*, and the *Journal of Laboratory and Clinical Medicine*.
3. Authors in firms dealing with food and agricultural products publish in the *Journal of Food Science*: the *Journal of Agricultural and Food Chemistry*: the class of biochemical substance specialty journals (the *Journal of the American Oil Chemists Society* and *Cereal Chemistry*, and three kinds of neighboring discipline jounals (the *Journal of Nutrition*, *Plant Physiology*, and the *Journal of the Association of Official Analytical Chemists*).
4. Authors in laboratories involved with cancer screening and product safety favor *Food and Cosmetic Toxicology* and *Toxicology and Applied Pharmacology* and in particular announce their findings in a Meeting Abstracts special issue (*Proceedings of the American Association for Cancer Research*) of *Cancer Research*.
5. Authors working in the new area of genetic engineering have appeared in *Nature* and *Science*, as well as in the *Proceedings of the National Academy of Sciences*, *Journal of Biological Chemistry*, *Journal of Molecular Biology*, *Journal of Bacteriology*, and the virological journals. *Molecular and General Genetics* and *Gene* appear to be oriented toward these authors.

For investigating the publication habits of the liberal-arts-college biochemists, a group of eighty schools was identified (Cass, 1978) and publication patterns developed, using the Corporate Index of the *Science Citation Index* for the periods 1965-71 and 1972-78. the results are shown in Table 3. Analysis of the results are shown in Table 3. Analysis of the results show that:

1. While the preferential order of the biochemistry journals is altered, many of the same journals are on this list as well as on those lists developed earlier.
2. The *Journal of Biological Chemistry* and *Biochemistry* do not

Table 3. Publication Habits of Biochemists in Liberal Arts Colleges

	1972-78 (39 schools)	1965-71 (23 schools)
	Articles (Number) in Indicated Journals	
1.	Comparative Biochemistry Physiology (19)	Biochem. Biophys. Res. Commun. (15)
2.	Biochem. Biophys. Res. Commun. (18)	J. Am. Chem. Soc. (15)
3.	Nature (10)	Biochim. Biophys. Acta (11)
4.	Biochemistry (7)	Comp. Biochem. Physiol. (11)
5.	Science (7)	Biochemistry (11)
6.	Arch. Biochem. Biophys. (6)	Nature (11)
7.	Biochim. Biophys. Acta (6)	Proc. Nat. Acad. Sci. (6)
8.	J. Am. Chem. Soc. (5)	Arch. Biochem. Biophys. (5)
9.	Analyt. Biochem. (4)	J. Biol. Chem. (4)
10.	Biopolymers (4)	Science (4)
11.	J. Biol. Chem. (4)	Analyt. Biochem. (3)
12.	Bioorganic Chem. (3)	Canad. J. Biochem. (3)
13.	FEBS Letters (3)	J. Mol. Biol. (3)
14.	J. Histochem. Cytochem. (3)	Biochem. J. (2)
15.	J. Nat. Cancer Inst. (3)	J. Chromat. (2)
16.	Mutation Res. (3)	All Others (17)
17.	Proc. Nat. Acad. Sci. (3)	
18.	Steroids (3)	
19.	Canad. J. Biochem. (2)	
20.	Immunol. (2)	
21.	J. Lipid Res. (2)	
22.	J. Membrane Biochem. (2)	
23.	J. Mol. Biol. (2)	
24.	Thrombosis Haemostasis (2)	
	All Others (22)	
	Abstracts (Number) in Indicated Journals	
1.	Fed. Proc. (12)	Fed. Proc. (8)
2.	Biophys. J. (6)	Biophys. J. (3)
3.	Proc. Soc. Exp. Med. Biol. (1)	J. Dent. Res. (1)

dominate as they do on other lists. This is probably due to the comprehensive, full-length, and conclusive nature of papers accepted by these journals. Most research in liberal-arts colleges is limited. This also probably explains the favored position of *Biochemical Biophysical Research Communications* (which specialized in more preliminary and shorter works for these authors). The popularity of *Comparative Biochemistry and Physiology* may be explained in that instructors at some of these smaller institutions are hired for double duty, combining their interests in biochemistry and animal physiology.

One additional pilot investigation carried out for this paper was an analysis of the journals most frequently referred to in six widely used biochemistry texts. As a historical comparison to test the ability of the current list, a matching set of six texts from the period 1968-1971 was constructed and similarly analyzed (see Appendix 3 for the list of tests). Table 4 presents, for those serials scoring at least one percent of the total in any text, the rankings arranged by number of tests in which the one percent measure was exceeded. In the table, those serials primarily devoted to review articles or regularly publishing review articles are indicated.

The following observations may be noted:

1. Many of the journals favored for authorship by American biochemists appear.
2. There is a strong dominance of review serials and other journals that regularly carry review articles.

It is apparent that a library that serves organized instructional needs should seriously consider including some of these latter titles, particularly in light of their strength over time (as noted in the historical group). The Garfield study particularly mentions the importance of review serials.

THE FINAL SELECTION DECISION

Although journal lists based on any school of selection are helpful, the librarian is the final decision-maker, often faced with a selection decision on a journal recommended by an important patron. Some helpful suggestions follow for the ultimate decision on an unknown journal.

1. Has the patron seen or used the journal? If not, *Current Contents* entry pages from past issues should be given to him to examine for appropriateness of language of publication and subject.
2. Use the Author and Address Index of *Current Contents* for as many issues as possible to determine authorship orientation. Is your type and level of institution regularly represented? Does this journal show promise for authors of your type of institution?
3. Consult as many Citing Journal Packages as possible from *Science Citation Index Annuals*. What journal does this candidate journal habitually cite year after year? Does the subject orientation derived from this agree with the patron's conceptions of what the journal is about?

Table 4. Journals Cited in Six Widely Used Biochemistry Texts with Average Citation Share in Those Texts.

	1980 Texts		1968-71 Texts	
	Journals Cited in Six Texts with Percentage of Citations			
1.	Annu. Rev. Biochem.*	14.3	Annu. Rev. Biochem.*	16.8
2.	Science*	9.2	Science*	8.4
3.	Sci. Am.	8.2	Nature*	5.6
4.	Nature*	7.5	Advan. Enzymol.*	3.4
5.	Advan. Enzymol.*	3.7	Fed. Proc.*	1.3
6.	Curr. Top. Cell Regul.*	1.8		
	Journals Cited in Five Texts with Percentage of Citations			
1.	Proc. Nat. Acad. Sci.	7.6	J. Biol. Chem.	15.0
2.	J. Biol. Chem.	6.8	J. Mol. Biol.	4.5
3.	New Eng. J. Med.	4.3	Biochem. J.	2.6
4.	J. Mol. Biol.	4.0		
	Journals Cited in Four Texts with Percentage of Citations			
1.	Fed. Proc.*	2.5	Proc. Nat. Acad. Sci.	11.7
2.	Cold Spring Harb. Symp. Quant. Biol.	2.3	Biochemistry	4.7
3.	Biochemistry	2.3		
4.	Biochim.Biophys.Acta	2.3		
5.	Adv. Protein Chem.*	2.3		
	Journals Cited in Three Texts with Percentage of Citations			
1.	Essays in Biochem.*	3.7	Angew.Chem.Int.Ed.Eng.*	4.5
2.	Arch. Biochem. Biophys.	1.7	Sci. Am.*	4.0
3.	Biochem. J.	1.7	J. Am. Chem. Soc.	3.4
			Biochem. Biophys. Res.Comm.	2.7
			Harvey Lect.*	1.8
			Prog.Nucl.Acid.Res.Molec. Biol.*	1.7
			Adv. Protein Chem.*	1.5
	Journals Cited in Two Texts with Percentage of Citations			
1.	Annu. Rev. Physiol.*	3.0	Annu. Rev. Plant Physiol.*	5.2
2.	Physiol. Revs.*	3.0	Biochim.Biophys. Acta	3.5
3.	FEBS Letters	2.0	Proc.Roy.Soc.Lond.B	2.2
4.	Meth. Enzymol.*	2.0	Arch. Biochem. Biophys.	2.0
5.	Vitamins and Hormones*	2.0	Vitamins and Hormones*	1.7
6.	Eur. J. Biochem.	1.5	Eur. J. Biochem.	1.6
7.	Ann. NY Acad. Sci.*	1.0	J. Clin. Invest.	1.6
8.	Bacteriol. Rev.*	1.0	Advan. Carb. Chem.*	1.5
9.	Horizons in Biochem. and Biophys.*	1.0	Advan. Enzyme Regul.*	1.2
10.	Prog. Biophys. Mol. Biol.*	1.0		

*Journals that regularly feature review-type articles.

4. Consult as many Cited Journal Packages as possible from the *Science Citation Index Annuals*. What use is made of the articles from this journal? Have better known journals in this field cited this candidate journal often?
5. How does this journal compare in gross citations or citations per article published with comparable journals?
6. Calculate the cost of subscribing to the journal versus legitimate Interlibrary Loan fees when the Copyright Clearance Charge is also regularly paid. (A sample issue will contain, at the bottom of the first page of each article, the fee for copying.) Consider the use of legitimate commercial article suppliers such as the Institute of Scientific Information's *OATS* service. It may well be worth suggesting to your patron that you might provide him with either of these forms of services rather than subscribing to the journal.

The point in making these suggestions is not to avoid purchase, but merely to note that librarians have much more information at their command than they suppose and that they should use all that information before committing several hundred dollars per year for years to come for a journal of unknown value.

THE OLDER STOCK

The final issues to be addressed here are the interlocking questions of back-year purchases and older-volume retirement. Research by both indirect (Smith, 1970; Tibbetts, 1974) and direct (Schlomann & Ahl, 1979) methods yields a 15-20 year active-life estimate for most journals. This may also be accepted as the outside limit for retrospective holdings. For journals involving foreign languages, particularly German, recent work indicates that the trend towards anglicization is at most 15 years old and closer to 10 in some cases (Stankus, Schlessinger, & Schlessinger, 1981). Finally, a new citation ranking table in *JCR*, the "Half-Life" table, shows that the bulk of references to biochemical journals are to papers at most 10 years old.

REFERENCES

Cass, James, & Birnaum, Max. *Comparative Guide to American Colleges*. New York: Harper and Row, 1978.

Cattell Press. *Industrial Research Laboratories of the U.S.* New York: R.R. Bowker, 1970.

Chen, Ching-Chih. *Scientific and Technical Information Services*, Cambridge, MA: MIT Press, 1975.

Garfield, Eugene. Citation Analysis as a Tool in *Journal Evaluation, Science*, 1972, 1978, 471-9.
Garfield, Eugene. *Essays of an Information Scientist*. Philadelphia: ISI Press, 1977.
Garfield, Eugene. *SCI Journal Citation Reports*. Philadelphia: ISI Press, 1975.
Garfield, Eugene. Trends in Biochemical Literature. *Trends in Biochemical Sciences*, 1979, 4, 290-5.
Katz, Bill, and Richard Berry. *Magazines for Libraries*. New York: R.R. Bowker, 1978.
Malinowski, H. Robert, Gray, Richard, & Gary, Dorothy, *Science and Engineering Literature*. Littleton CO: Libraries Unlimited, 1976.
Mount, Ellis. *University Science and Engineering Libraries*. Westport, CT: Greenwood Press, 1975.
Scholoman, Barbara, and Ahl, Ruth. Retention Periods for Journals in a Small Academic Library. *Special Libraries*, 1979, *70*, 377-83.
Sengupta, I. N. Recent Growth of the Literature of Biochemistry and Changes in Ranking of Periodicals. *Journal of Documentation*, 1973, *29*, 192-211.
Smith, Joan. A Periodical Use Study at Children's Hospital of Michigan. *Bulletin of the Medical Library Association*, 1970, *58*, 65-7.
Stankus, Tony, Schlessinger, Rashelle, & Schlessinger, Bernard S. English-Language Article Publication in German Basic Science Journals. *Science & Technology Libraries*, 1981.
Stankus, Tony, and Rice, Barbara. Handle with Care: Use and Citation Data for Science Journal Management. *Collection Development*, 1981.
Strauss, Lucille, Sheve, Irene, & Brown, Alberta. *Scientific and Technical Libraries*. New York: Becker and Hayes, 1972.
Tibbets, Pamela. A Method for Estimating the In-House Use of the Periodical Collection in the University of Minnesota Biomedical Library. *Bulletin of the Medical Library Association*, 1974, *64*, 37-48.

Appendix 1. Journals Noted Within the Paper
Collection Development: Journals for Biochemists

1. Acta Biochimica et Biophysica (G)
2. Acta Biochimica Polonica (G)
3. Advances in Enzymology and Related Areas of Molecular Biology (G)
4. Advances in Protein Chemistry
5. Agricultural and Biological Chemistry - Tokyo (G)
6. American Journal of Physiology (G)
7. Analytical Biochemistry (G)
8. Analytical Chemistry (G)
9. Annals of the New York Academy of Sciences (G)
10. Annual Review of Biochemistry (G)
11. Annual Review of Physiology
12. Archives of Biochemistry and Biophysics (G)
13. Bacteriological Reviews (G)
14. Biochemical and Biophysical Research Communications (G)
15. Biochemical Genetics
16. Biochemical Journal (G)
17. Biochemical Pharmacology (G)
18. Biochemical Society Transactions (G)
19. Biochemistry - U.S. (G)
20. Biochimica et Biophysica Acta (G)
21. Biochimie (G)
22. Bioinorganic Chemistry (G)
23. Biokhimiya (Biochemistry - USSR)
24. Biology of Reproduction
25. Bioorganic Chemistry (G)
26. Bioorganicheskaya Khimiya (G)
27. Biophysical Journal

Appendix 1 (Cont.)

28. Biopolymers (G)
29. Canadian Journal of Biochemistry (G)
30. Cancer Research (G)
31. Carbohydrate Research
32. Cell (G)
33. Cereal Chemistry
34. Chemistry and Physics of Lipids (G)
35. Clinica Chimica Acta
36. Clinical Biochemistry
37. Clinical Chemistry
38. Clinical Research
39. Cold Spring Harbor Symposia (G)
40. Comparative Biochemistry
41. CRC Critical REviews in Biochemistry (G)
42. Current Topics in Cellular Regulation
43. Cytogenetics Cell Genetics
44. Endocrinology (G)
45. Enzymes (G)
46. Essays in Biochemistry
47. European Journal of Biochemistry (G)
48. Experientia
49. Experimental Cell Research (G)
50. FEBS Letters (G)
51. Federation Proceedings (G)
52. Food and Cosmetic Toxicology
53. Gene
54. Hoppe-Seyler's Zeitschrift Fuer Physiologische Chemie (G)
55. Horizons in Biochemistry and Biophysics
56. Immunology
57. Indian Journal of Biochemistry and Biophysics (G)
58. International Journal of Biochemistry (G)
59. International Journal of Peptide and Protein Research (G)
60. Italian Journal of Biochemistry (G)
61. Journal of Agricultural and Food Chemistry
62. Journal of Bacteriology (G)
63. Journal of Biochemistry-Tokyo (G)
64. Journal of Biological Chemistry (G)
65. Journal of Cell Biology (G)
66. Journal of Cellular Physiology
67. Journal of Chromatography (G)
68. Journal of Clinical Investigation (G)
69. Journal of Cyclic Nucleotide Research (G)
70. Journal of Dental Research
71. Journal of Experimental Medicine (G)
72. Journal of Food Science
73. Journal of General Microbiology (G)
74. Journal of General Physiology (G)
75. Journal of General Virology
76. Journal of Histochemistry and Cytochemistry
77. Journal of Immunology
78. Journal of Laboratory and Clinical Medicine
79. Journal of Lipid Research (G)
80. Journal of Membrane Biochemistry
81. Journal of Molecular Biology (G)
82. Journal of Molecular Evolution
83. Journal of Neurochemistry (G)
84. Journal of Nutrition (G)
85. Journal of Physiology - London (G)
86. Journal of Supramolecular Structure
87. Journal of the American Chemical Society (G)

Appendix 1 (Cont.)

88. Journal of the American Oil Chemists Society
89. Journal of the Association of Official Analytical Chemists (G)
90. Journal of the National Cancer Institute
91. Journal of Virology (G)
92. Life Sciences (G)
93. Lipids (G)
94. Methods of Enzymology (G)
95. Molecular and Cellular Biochemistry (G)
96. Molecular and General Genetics (G)
97. Molecular Pharmacology (G)
98. Mutation Research
99. Nature (G)
100. Naturwissenschaften
101. New England Journal of Medicine
102. Nucleic Acids Research (G)
103. Pediatric Research
104. Physiological Chemistry and Physics (G)
105. Physiological Reviews
106. Physiologist
107. Phytochemistry (G)
108. Plant Physiology (G)
109. Postepy Biochemii (G)
110. Preparative Biochemistry (G)
111. Proceedings of the American Association For Cancer Research (a special issue of Cancer Research)
112. Proceedings of the National Academy of Sciences - USA (G)
113. Proceedings of the Societies for Experimental Biology and Medicine (G)
114. Progress in Biophysics and Molecular Biology
115. Revue Romaine de Biochimie (G)
116. Science (G)
117. Seikagaku (G)
118. Steroids
119. Thrombosis Haemostasis
120. Toxicology and Applied Pharmacology
121. Ukrainskii Biokhimicheskii Zhurnal (G)
122. Virology (G)
123. Vitamins and Hormones

(G) - included on Garfield's lists.

Appendix 2. Selected Units Studied in Table 1.

Selection of the units in this appendix was made from the indicated sources with attention paid to geographical diversity, type of institution, and specific biochemical orientation.

Medical Schools

Selection Source: Garfield, Eugene. "Most-Cited Articles of the 1960's 3. Preclinical Basic Research."
Current Contents, 1980, 23, 5-13.

East: Harvard University
School of Medicine, Boston, MA
(Dept. Biol. Chem.)

Cornell University
College of Medicine, New York City, NY
(Dept. Biochem.)

New York University
Medical Center, New York City, NY
(Dept. Biochem.)

Midwest: Case-Western Reserve University
School of Medicine, Cleveland, OH
(Dept. Biochem.)

University of Chicago
Pritzker School of Medicine, Chicago, IL
(Dept. Biochem.)

Washington University of St. Louis
School of Medicine, St. Louis, MO
(Dept. Biochem.)

South: Vanderbilt University
School of Medicine, Nashville, TN
(Dept. Biochem.)

Duke University
Medical Center, Durham, NC
(Dept. Biochem.)

West: University of Washington at Seattle
School of Medicine, Seattle, WA
(Dept. Biochem.)

University of California at San Francisco
Medical School, San Francisco, CA
(Dept. Biochem.)

APPENDIX 2 (continued)

Universities

Selection Source: Roose, Kenneth, and Anderson, Charles. A Rating of Graduate School Programs. Washington, DC American Council on Education, 1970.

East: Princeton University
Princeton, NJ
(Dept. Biochem.)

Brandeis University
Waltham, MA
(Dept. and Graduate Dept. Biochem.)

M.I.T.
Cambridge, MA
(Depts. Biol. and Chem.)

Midwest: University of Illinois
Urbana-Champaign, IL
(Dept. Biochem.)

Purdue University
West Lafayette, IN
(Dept. Biochem.)

Indiana University
Bloomington, IN
(Dept. Biol. Sciences and Chem.)

South: Oklahoma State University
Stillwater, OK
(Dept. Biochem.)

Florida State University
Tallahassee, FL
(Depts. Biol.; Chem.; Inst. Mol. Biophys.)

West: Caltech
Pasadena, CA
(Depts. Biol.; Chem.)

University of Oregon
Eugene, OR
(Inst. Molec. Biol.)

Independent, Non-Profit Research Foundations

Selection Source: Association of Independent Research Institutes. Constitution and Bylaws. 1977.

East: The Wistar Institute
Philadelphia, PA
(All article output examined.)

APPENDIX 2 (continued)

The Worcester Foundation For Experimental Biology
Shrewsbury, MA
(All article output examined.)

Midwest: Cancer Research Center
Columbia, MO
(All article output examined.)

Michigan Cancer Foundation
Detroit, MI
(All article output examined.)

Mayo Clinic and Research Foundation
Rochester, MN
(Depts. Biochem. and Molec. Medicine)
Note: Mayo Clinic is not a member of this Association and does have medical school ties, but national reputation and need for geographic representation helped its inclusion.

South: Oklahoma Medical Research Foundation and Inst.
Oklahoma City, OK
(All article output checked.)

Papanicolau Cancer Research Inst.
Miami, FL
(All article output checked.)

West: Salk Inst. Biological Studies
San Diego, CA
(All article output checked.)

Pasadena Found. for Medical Research
Pasadena, CA
(All article output checked.)

Scripps Clinic and Research Foundation
La Jolla, CA
(Dept. Biochem.)

Federal, Veterans and Military

Selection Source: Author's study of available institutes in Washington, DC and other areas.

East: Veterans Administration Hospital
Buffalo, NY
(All article output checked.)

U.S. Food and Drug Administration
Bethesda, MD
(Bureau of Biologics examined.)

National Cancer Institute
Bethesda, MD
(Biochem. Lab.)

APPENDIX 2 (continued)

National Inst. of Arthritis, Metabolic Diseases and Diabetes
Bethesda, MD
(Molec. Biol. Lab.)

National Inst. Dental Research
Bethesda, MD
(Biochem. Lab.)

Walter Reed Army Inst.
Washington, DC
(Dept. Biochem.)

Midwest: Veterans Administration Hospital
Ann Arbor, MI
(All article output checked.)

South: Veterans Administration Hospital
New Orleans, LA
(All article output examined.)

Center for Disease Control
Atlanta, GA
(All article output examined.)

West: Veterans Administration Hospital
Palo Alto, CA
(All article output checked.)

Appendix 3. Texts Used for Data in Table 4.

Current Group

Bohinski, Robert C., Modern Concepts in Biochemistry. 3rd edition, Boston: Allyn and Bacon, 1979.

Lehninger, Albert L. Biochemistry: The Molecular Basis of All Structure and Function. New York: Worth, 1975.

McGilvery, Robert W. Biochemistry: A Functional Approach. Philadelphia: Saunders, 1979.

Metzler, David E. Biochemistry: The Chemical Reactions of Living Cells. New York: Academic Press, 1977.

Stryer, Lubert. Biochemistry. San Francisco: W. H. Freeman, 1975.

White, Abraham, et al. Principles of Biochemistry. 6th edition, New York: McGraw-Hill, 1978.

APPENDIX 3 (continued)

Historical Comparison Group

Harrow, Benjamin and Mazur, Abraham. Textbook of Bio-Chemistry. 10th edition. Philadelphia: Saunders, 1971.

Lehninger, Albert L. Biochemistry. New York: Worth, 1970

Mahler, Henry R. and Cordes, Eugene H. Biological Chemistry. New York: Harper and Row, 1968.

Mallette, M. Frank, et al. Introductory Biochemistry. Baltimore: Williams and Wilkins, 1971.

McGilvery, Robert W. Biochemistry: A Functional Approach. Philadelphia: Saunders, 1970.

White, Abraham, et al. Principles of Biochemistry. New York: McGraw-Hill, 1968.

Journals for Anatomists in Medical versus Nonmedical Biological Research Institutions

Tony Stankus

ABSTRACT. A sharp distinction of journal needs between anatomists in medical vs. nonmedical biological research institutions is documented by diverging publication patterns between 1965-79. This is traced to an historical drifting apart beginning in the nineteenth century. Medically affiliated researchers, who dominate most anatomy journals, are general microscopists who also require journals of embryology, cell biology, pathology, and neurology. Anatomists affiliated with university departments of the zoological sciences and physical anthropology, or with natural history museums, have maintained a small share of papers in some anatomy journals and often continue to stress the classical dissection or reconstruction of remains. They need journals of zoology, marine biology, evolution, paleontology, and physical anthropology. Museum bulletins are shown to be uniquely important to the nonmedical group, while multiscience and academic clinical investigation journals are frequent outlets for only the medically affiliated group. The tables from this study, *Journal Citation Reports*, and *Current Contents*, are suggested as interacting selection tools.

INTRODUCTION

Human and comparative anatomy share a colorful past that sheds light on the differing journal needs of their current researchers. Surprisingly, it is not so much a division based on human vs. animal material that best characterizes the biases of medical vs. nonmedical researchers but differences in scale of biological structure studied, tools used, and systems of professional specialty designation.

Until the mid-1800s the compartmentalization of medical vs. nonmedical faculties, curricula, and research interests was quite flexible.

Reprinted from *Science & Technology Libraries*, volume 2, number 2, pages 61-85, 1981.

Comparative anatomy was taught in medical schools while students of the liberal arts and sciences learned some human anatomy as a part of "natural philosophy." Researchers of either nominal affiliation cut away, measured, weighed, and described their specimen's anatomy. They concerned themselves with its most accurate portrayal and attempted a functional analysis. As this approach was being exhausted on man and many common animals at the readily visible and low magnification dissection ranges (gross anatomy), medically affiliated workers slowly started to leave the field. While the tradition of some common interests remained, leaders in the evolving and increasingly distinct academic programs made personal career choices and opened new fields that were more consistently followed by one or the other of the groups.[1]

Medically affiliated workers were particularly lured by the promise of a deeper understanding of nature afforded by increasingly sophisticated microscopes whose greater magnifying power was being made useful by new lenses and chemical stains that enhanced the visualization of details on slides (the beginnings of modern histology and stain technology). This trends was clearly reflected in the career of Johannes Muller (Medical Faculty, Univ. Berlin), perhaps the most influential medical researcher and teacher of the first half of the nineteenth century. He literally lent his microscopes to several of the founders of embryology as a real science. Happy borrowers include Remak (Medical Faculty, Univ. Berlin) and Reichert (Muller's immediate successor). Another of Muller's pupils, Schwann (Medical Faculties, Univs. Berlin, Louvain, and Liege), combined his human and animal microscopical studies with the plant microscopical studies of Schleiden (Botanical Faculty, Univ. Jena) to establish that the cell was the fundamental unit of all life, furthering the study of its normal anatomy, cytology. The study of diseased cellular anatomy, modern anatomic pathology, is most closely identified with Virchow (Medical Faculty, Univ. Berlin). He was another of Muller's pupils and was himself perhaps the most influential medical researcher and teacher of the second half of the nineteenth century. Two other microscopists who were eventually to win the Nobel Prize for Medicine in 1906 began their careers both apart from each other and in relative isolation from most of the major scientific centers of the time. The work of an Italian, Golgi (Medical Faculty, Univ. Padua), and a Spaniard, Ramon y Cajal (Medical Faculty, Univ. Zaragoza), centering on findings based on new metallic stains for slides of nervous system tissue, was made better known through invitations to international congresses and subsequent publication of their papers in journals of greater international circulation than their own local journals. Their professional association sponsors were two presidents of the Anatomische Gesellschaft, an international group associated with the leading journal of the time, the *Anatomischer Anzeiger.*[2-3] Not surprisingly the first of these, von Koelliker (Medical Faculty, Univ. Wurzburg) was yet another of Muller's pupils, while the second, Waldeyer-Hartz (Medical Faculties, Strasbourg and Berlin) was one of Reichert's, Muller's successor.

Yet work involving gross anatomy received its own reinforcements: the founding or expansion of the great natural history museums; the international surge of colonization and its accompanying land and sea scientific expeditions; the intensification of debate over the classification and origins of species. The scientific generation before the split of anatomy had a mania for the collection and classification of plants, animals, and even minerals (all "nature" or all "natural history"). It was probably most avidly pursued by Buffon (who abandoned medical studies to become a botanist at Versailles) and Linneaus (who exchanged his Chair of Practical Medicine for that of Botany at the University of Uppsala). Blumenbach, a somewhat younger contemporary was unique both for remaining in Medicine (Univ. Gottingen) and for stressing the systematicization of the races of man, effectively promoting physical anthropology as a science founded upon gross anatomy.

The legacy of this earlier generation then was essentially of two parts: an urge for a valid organizing principle for all life forms; many very large collections in need of housing, arrangement and interpretation. Small, older museums of curiosities had to be expanded, redefined and more formally administered. New museums were constructed in Europe and the United States with a kind of competitive zeal among wealthy patrons, scientific societies, universities and municipalities that one associates today with some of the same groups and sports complexes or shopping malls. This had immediate consequences for gross anatomy as a livelihood by providing employment apart from Medicine and publishing outlets apart from those used by medically affiliated microanatomists.

Owen, for example, left surgery to become director of the Hunter and subsequently the British Museums. There he was to develop many of the conceptual ground rules and systems of argumentation used even today in comparative anatomy. Hyrtl left his position as Professor of Anatomy in the Faculty of Medicine at the University of Vienna for two pursuits of importance to gross anatomy: the standardization of terms for anatomical structures and the improvement of anatomical exhibits for museums.[4] By the time of his death the university's zoology department museum had become the fourth largest in the world. Cuvier (Director, French National Natural History Museum), a disciple of Buffon, and a strong influence in his later years on the young Owen, pioneered a new direction in gross anatomical studies involving not so much the dissection (for which he was also famous but the reconstruction of animals from their fossil remains, thereby laying the foundation of vertebrate paleontology.

One of Cuvier's pupils, Louis Agassiz, published a four volume treatise on fossil fishes, laying the foundation of the anatomical portion of modern ichthyology. Agassiz then emigrated to the United States. Here he founded Harvard University's Museum of Comparative Zoology, and, in the spirit of the age, urged his new countrymen in spellbinding and immensely popular lectures to mount expeditions for specimens with which to fill it from both land and sea. Understandably the British Navy and Royal Society were the leaders in deep ocean research.[5] The cruises of their converted warship *Challenger* under the leadership of C.W. Thomson (Dept. Natural History, Univs. Belfast and Edinburgh) and John Murray (an independently wealthy member of the Royal Society) provided many specimens of not only fish but also the larger marine invertebrates for Morrison Watson (Prof. Anatomy, Univ. Edinburgh) and museum workers in the British Museum to dissect. The North Sea and Baltic powers heavily financed research related to commercially important fish. C.G.J. Petersen (Director, Danish Mobile Marine Station) worked on the growth and migration patterns of fish. Heincke (Prof. Zoology, Univ. Kiel) worked on anatomic methods of their age determination and recorded variations in structure over geographic ranges. Sars and Hjort (Prof. Zoology, Univ. Oslo) worked on fish larval structures and life histories.

Yet the most important expedition of the century was largely unheralded at the time. Charles Darwin spent five years on a British warship collecting specimens with a special attention to the variations in animal anatomy with respect to geography, diet and lifestyle. He incubated his conclusions for 22 years before ultimately collaborating with Wallace (who himself spent several years on expeditions) on a paper published, appropriately enough, in the *Journal of the Proceedings of the Linnean Society*, setting forth the outline of what is now known as the theory of evolution. Evolution provided an overriding explanation of the abundance and variety of species, as well as new yardstick with which to measure the validity of the various systems of classification. Virtually all the gross anatomical sciences (and even embryology for a time) have been since under its influence.

Two developments in this century have affected anatomy research.

The electron microscope, developed for other uses in the 1930s, eventually saw applications in anatomy after the Second World War. It opened up a whole new range of magnification called ultrastructure that included the smallest portions of cells and even aggregations of the larger molecules. While a few journals exclusively devoted to ultrastructure have appeared, papers involving it have been readily accepted in both general and histological anatomy journals as well. The x-ray and functionally related tools such as the CAT scan and ultrasonic imaging have added new instruments at the opposite, gross, size range of anatomy. However, most of the journals devoted to their use stress clinical diagnosis rather than studies of fundamental anatomy.

METHODS

The journal needs of anatomists in both medical and nonmedical institutions were analyzed from the viewpoint of their publication patterns. Gross anatomy was approached through entries in *Biological Abstracts*.[6] In accordance with the *Abstracts'* own subject searching recommendations, not only were entries under "Chrodate Anatomy" examined but also "Vertebrate Zoology," "Invertebrate Zoology," "Evolution," "Physical Anthropology," all the organ systems, as well as many other entries suggested in the "CROSS" indexes under "COMPARATIVE" and "GROSS ANATOMY." Authors, institutional types, topic, and journal title were noted for three, six-month spans in 1965, 1972, and 1979. A total of over 30,000 entries were examined yielding 1,298 appropriate abstracts.

Since, as will shortly be demonstrated, the *Abstracts* study confirmed the continuing abandonment by medically affiliated anatomists of work involving gross anatomy for that involving histology and ultrastructure, the latter two fields were more readily approached through a tabulation and analysis of the journals in which 196 medical schools' departments of anatomy published for the years 1965-1979 as reported in the "Corporate Index" of *Science Citation Index*.[7] Twenty schools (all sixteen of Canada's) for each national, linguistic, or political bloc were selected with the aid of a standard directory.[8] Attention was directed to diversity within each bloc of cities, sponsorship, and institutional age. A total of 14,536 papers were recorded and categorized by type of subject journal involved. Percentages by category were calculated for each bloc. Then, giving each bloc equal weight, these percentages were averaged (normalized) for the results to be discussed in the second portion of this paper.

RESULTS AND DISCUSSION – GROSS ANATOMY

Table 1 is a clear demonstration of the declining relative contribution of medically affiliated anatomists to gross anatomy. Their share went from 50% to 23% during the study. The contribution of nonmedical anatomists increased proportionally. The combined output more than doubled.

Table 2 shows that only a portion of work involving gross anatomy appears in anatomy journals. This is not surprising in light of the editorial board domination of most anatomy journals by medically affiliated, microscopically oriented workers. The fact that many of these journals still rank as major outlets for gross work is a reflection of the relatively large number of papers they publish annually, typically 100-200. Even though these journals stress microscopical work, the number of appears remaining for gross work is large enough to be significant in the less prolific world of gross anatomy.

An important consideration was the relative international involvement of authorship of the journals. Americans publish primarily in the journals based in their own country with the relative frequency indicated in the first column of Table 3, and while foreign authors also publish primarily in their own journals, up to a quarter of their papers are published in journals "foreign" to them, including American journals. In return, Americans contributed in this study to *Acta Anatomica*, *Antomischer Anzeiger*, and *Zoomorphologie*. But certain journals, indicated in the second column of this table, rarely feature work from authors outside their own bloc. Many of these latter journals are also among the rarer to be found in American library collections. It is likely that their contribution to current publication in gross anatomy is thereby unrecognized. Combining the results of the study thus far provides an explanation of the popular misconception, perhaps based on a scan of the better known, medically affiliated journals, e.g., *Anatomical Record*, that work involving gross anatomy is declining, a notion

Table 1. The changing relative contribution to publication in gross anatomy by number of papers from medical vs. nonmedical institutions 1965-1979.

	1965	1972	1979
Medical	139 (50%)	181 (40%)	132 (23%)
Nonmedical	141 (50%)	271 (60%)	434 (77%)
Totals	280 (100%)	452 (100%)	566 (100%)
Net Change	---	(+62%)	(+201%)

Table 2. Primary subject classification of journals publishing A: Gross Anatomy and B: Works from Medical School Departments of Anatomy, by percentage of papers, 1965-1979.

A. GROSS ANATOMY (1,298 papers, predominantly from nonmedical institutions worldwide.)		B. HISTOLOGY & ULTRASTRUCTURE (14,536 papers from the medical schools of ten multinational blocs, average share per bloc.)	
Anatomy	22%	Anatomy	32%
Zoology	17%	Cytology	5%
Marine Biology	5%	Embryology	3%
Evolution	4%	Pathology	3%
Paleontology	5%	Neurology	14%
Physical Anthropology	6%	Multiscience & General Clinical Investigation	19%
Museum Bulletins	9%	*Others	23%
*Others	32%		
	100%		100%

*Others included papers individually verified as dealing with gross anatomy, but appearing only rarely in a wide assortment of outlets including experimental, physiological and comparative psychology; wildlife management; biomechanics; orthopedics; veterinary science, science education, etc.

*Others included papers verified as coming from a medical school department of anatomy, but which often did not deal with anatomy. Included many papers in biochemistry, physiology, endocrinology, genetics, microbiology, etc.

contradicted by Table 1. Rather, it is scattered in some less obvious outlets. As mentioned in the introduction, half the work originating in medical centers appear in clinical journals of diagnostic radiology and related fields. As seen in Table 2 A, much of the remainder from any source appears in zoology journals, museum bulletins, etc. As shown in Table 3, column two, of those papers which do appear in journals devoted exclusively to anatomy, half are in those of limited interaction and availability owing to linguistic or political isolation. The results suggest that nonmedically dominated western journals such as the *Journal of Morphology* or *Zoomorphologie*, or the more broadly minded medically-affiliated journals such as the *Journal of Anatomy*

Table 3. Journals of general anatomy publishing gross anatomy by number of papers in study sample.

INTERNATIONAL	APPARENTLY LIMITED TO THEIR OWN NATIONALS
Acta Anatomica 46 (Switz.)	Archiv Anatomii Gistologii i Embriologii 62 (U.S.S.R.)
Anatomischer Anzeiger 23 (E. Ger.)	Folia Morphologica, Warsaw 15 (Poland)
Journal of Morphology 19 (U.S.)	Archives d'Anatomie Pathologique 9 (France)
Journal of Anatomy 18 (U.K.)	Journal of the Anatomical Society of India 9
Anatomical Records 14 (U.S.)	Indian Journal of Zootomy 7 (India)
Anatomy and Embryology 9 (W. Ger.)	Folia Morphologica, Prague 6 (Czechoslovakia)
American Journal of Anatomy 8	Acta Anatomica Nipponica 5 (Japan)
Zoomorphologie 8 (W. Ger.)	Archives d'Anatomie, d'Histologie et d'Embryologie 4 (France)
Acta Morphologica Neerlando-Scandinavica 7 (Neth.)	Okajimas Folia Anatomica Japonica 4
Anatomia, Histologia, et Embryologia 2 (W. Ger.)	Quaderni di Anatomia Pratica 4 (Italy)
	9 other Journals / 12 Papers
10 Journals / 144 Papers	19 Journals / 137 Papers

or *Anatomischer Anzeiger* would provide a better indicator of the persistence, if not also the growth, of a minority of gross level work.

Zoology journals are the next most frequent outlet for work involving gross anatomy. (See Table 4.) As is the case with many Europeans, Americans contribute most of their papers to their own national journals with a small but regular portion appearing in foreign international journals. A distinction between the American and European situation is that most Europeans have both general and specialized (phyletic) zoology journals to which to contribute freely, while Americans do not. The *American Zoologist* is a journal of invited symposia papers, and while a rather large number of these have involved gross anatomy, American anatomists must generally submit their work aborad if they prefer a general zoology outlet.

Journals of marine and freshwater biology (see Table 5 A) are

Table 4. Journals of general and specialized zoology publishing gross anatomy by number of papers in study sample.

GENERAL ZOOLOGY

Journal of Zoology 32
(U.K.)

Zoologicheskii Zhurnal 26
(U.S.S.R.)

Canadian Journal of Zoology 15

Zoologische Anzeiger 11
(E. Ger.)

Vestnik Zoologii 9
(U.S.S.R.)

Acta Biologica Cracoviensis, Series Zoologia 6
(Poland)

Revue Suisse de Zoologie 6
(Switz.)

Symposia of the Zoological Society of London 6
(U.K.)

Acta Zoologica Sinica 5
(P.R. China)

Acta Zoologica, Stockholm 5
(Sweden)

American Zoologist 5
(U.S.)

Zoologische Abhandlungen 5
(E. Ger.)

Netherlands Journal of Zoology 4

Studii Cercetari de Biologie, Seria Zoologie 4

18 others / 28

ORNITHOLOGY

Auk 6
(U.S.)

Condor 3
(U.S.)

Ibis 3
(U.K.)

Journal fuer Ornithologie
(W. Ger.)

Pavo 3
(India)

Ornis Scandinavica 2
(Denmark)

Aves 1
(Venezuela)

Wilson Bulletin 1
(U.S.)

HERPETOLOGY

Copeia 11
(U.S.)

Herpetologica 4
(U.S.)

MAMMALOGY

Mammalia 9
(France)

Journal of Mammalogy 8
(U.S.)

Saeugertierkundliche Mitteilungen 6
(W. Ger.)

Acta Theriologica 3
(Poland)

Zeitschrift fuer Saeugertierkunde 2
(W. Ger.)

among the heirs of the all encompassing natural history tradition. These journals include not only papers dealing with aquatic animals, but their interactions with plants, currents, seabed, etc., as well. These journals are particularly important as one of the few categories of outlets for papers dealing with the anatomy of invertebrates large enough to be studied by dissection (usually with some magnification if little histochemical staining), such as many crustaceans (crabs, lob-

Table 5. Journals of A: Marine and Freshwater Biology and B: Evolution, Systematics, Natural History, and Biogeography publishing gross anatomy by number of papers in study sample.

A.

Voprosy Ikhtiologii 12
(U.S.S.R.)

Scientific Reports of the Whale Research Institute 7

Japanese Journal of Ichthyology 4

Journal of Fish Biology 4
(U.S.)

Crustaceana 3
(Netherlands)

Journal of the Fisheries Research Board of Canada 3

Journal of Experimental Marine Biology and Ecology
(Netherlands)

Veliger 3
(U.S.)

Arquivos de Ciencas do Mar 2
(Brazil)

Biologiya Morya 2
(U.S.S.R.)

Cybium 2
(France)

Helgolaender Wissenschaftliche Untersuchungen 2
(W. Ger.)

Journal of the Marine Biological Association of the United Kingdom 2

Marine Biology, Berlin 2
(W. Ger.)

16 other Journals / 20 Papers

B.

Evolution 12
(U.S.)

Zoological Journal of the Linnean Society 11
(U.K.)

Zeitschrift fuer Zoologische Systematik und Evolutionsforschung 6
(W. Ger.)

Journal of Natural History 5
(U.K.)

Biological Journal of the Linnean Society 4
(U.S.)

Systematic Zoology 3
(U.S.)

Great Basin Naturalist 3
(U.S.)

American Midland Naturalist 2
(U.S.)

Bulletin Mensuelle de la Societe Linneene 2
(France)

American Naturalist 1
(U.S.)

Evolutionary Theory 1
(U.S.)

Irish Naturalists Journal 1
(N. Ireland, U.K.)

Southwest Naturalist 1
(U.S.)

Terre et la Vie 1
(France)

Zoologische Jahrbuecher, Abteilung fuer Systematik, Oekologie, und Geographie der Tiere 1
(E. Ger.)

sters, shrimp, etc.), and molluscs (squid, octopi, and the sedentary shellfish, clams, mussels, etc.). With the exception of the *Journal of Morphology* and *Zoomorphologie* most general anatomy journals will not regularly publish invertebrate work, another reflection of their medical domination. Journals of this aquatic sciences class also share the publication of marine mammal papers two ways with journals of mammalogy and general anatomy, and fish anatomy papers two ways with journals of ichthyology and general anatomy. *Copeia*, a journal listed under the interrestial zoology tables, deserves special mention here since contributions to fish anatomy appear there along with those concerning reptiles and amphibians. Publications in the aquatic group understandably reflect a preponderance of maritime nations. Americans contribute not only to their own journals but those of North Atlantic and North Sea countries. The Japanese and most Europeans reciprocate with papers in American journals.

Journals that feature evolution, systematics, and related fields such as biogeography (see Table 5 B) represent a major forum for work involving gross anatomy. As was indicated in the introduction, controversies in these areas are the driving force for many papers in all the journals involved in this study thus far, but most especially so in the frankly evolutionary (e.g., *Evolution*), frankly systematics (e.g., *Systematic Zoology*), and more general natural history journals. The American natural history journals in this table can be divided into those of an essentially regional character (*Great Basin* . . . , and, *Southwest* . . .) and national outlets (*American Midland* . . . and *American Naturalist*). All of these titles involve ecology as well, with the last journal particulary noted for this and general evolutionary theory. Publication patterns closely follow national lines. Americans publish abroad somewhat rarely, and only a small amount of foreign work appears in American publications.

Since paleontology (see Table 6 A) is essentially the reconstruction of the gross anatomy of extinct animals on the basis of their fossilized skeletal remains, findings in this small field can be important in the larger fields of zoology and evolution. A third interaction is with journals of geology, a byproduct of the use of fossils to date geologic formations. Publications patterns in this field are narrowly nationalistic, with some interplay between British and American authors and journals.

Physical anthropology (see Table 6 B) is one of the few anatomical sciences involving many gross level workers from medical institutions. This is partly due to the historical reasons mentioned in the introduction, and partly due to the continuing use of clinical facilities and procedures for study in living humans. The study also discovered authors from university departments of anthropology and zoology. The zoologist shares an interest in this field both for reasons of its evolutionary implications and its inclusion of the anatomy of apes, who share with humans the zoological classification of "primate."

Table 6. Journals of A: Paleontology and B: Physical Anthropology publishing gross anatomy by numbers of papers in study sample.

A.	B.
Journal of Paleontology 15 (U.S.)	American Journal of Physical Anthropology 39 (U.S.)
Paleontology 13 (U.K.)	Folia Primatologica 11 (Switz.)
Annales de Paleontologie Vertebres 10 (France)	Journal of the Anthropoligical Society of Nippon 6
Lethaia 4 (Norway)	Bulletins et Memoires de la Societe d'Anthropologie de Paris 4
Paleobiology 4 (U.S.)	Anthropologie 3 (France)
Paleontologischeskii Zhurnal 3 (U.S.S.R.)	Human Biology 3 (U.S.)
Acta Paleontologica Polonica 3	Mitteilungen der Anthropologischen Gesellschaft im Wien 3 (Austria)
Geobios 3 (France)	Zeitschrift fuer Morphologie und Anthropologie 3 (W. Ger.)
Canadian Journal of the Earth Sciences 1	Archives Suisses d'Anthrologie Generale 2 (Switz.)
Eclogae Geologicae Helvetiae 1 (Switz.)	Journal of Medical Primatology 2 (Switz.)
Geological Magazine 1 (U.S.)	Primates 2 (Japan)
Geologica Romana 1 (Italy)	7 other Journals / 7 Papers
Studia Geologica Polonica 1	

(See, for example in this table, *Folia Primatologica*, *Journal of Medical Primatology*.) An initial surprise to this author was the involvement of many dental school researchers, until it was realized that teeth and jawbones, the stuff of dentists, are among the hardest, most enduring and ultimately most available of primate remains for study. Publication patterns in this field are narrowly national for Americans, with somewhat greater interplay for Europeans, who also contribute with frequency to American outlets.

Museum bulletins and related publications such as the proceedings of city, district, and the smaller national academies of science, as well as the "Occasional papers" of university departments are a frequent and historically very important outlet for work involving gross anatomy. The museums publishing these bulletins are sponsored by these societies and departments as well as by private foundations and governments at all levels as indicated by the representative sample in Table 7. Museum bulletins give priority to publishing the works of their permanent professional staff, visiting scholars in residence, and faculty from nearby universities. A few papers of exceptional pertinence owing to their being based on extensive examination of loaned museum specimens or resulting from an expedition funded by the museum may also be included. Consequently few foreign papers are pub-

Table 7. A selection of museums and their bulletins publishing gross anatomy by number of papers in the study sample.

U.S.	INTERNATIONAL
American Museum of Natural History (New York, NY) American Museum Novitates; Bulletin 8	Senckenbergische Naturforschende Gesellschaft (Senckenberg Museum, Frankfurt, W. Ger.) Senckenbergiana, 9
Carnegie Museum of Natural History (Pittsburgh, PA) Annals; Bulletin 7	Termeszettudomanyi Museum (Budapest, Hungary) Annales Historico-Naturales Musei Nationalis Hungarici 3
Museum of Comparative Zoology (Harvard U., Cambridge, MA) Breviora; Bulletin 6	Zoologisches Museum in Berlin (E. Ger.) Mitteilungen 1
Field Museum of Natural History (Chicago, IL) Fieldiana 5	Staatlichen Museum fuer Naturkunde (Stuttgart, W. Ger.) Stuttgarter Beitraege zur Naturkunde 1
Illinois State Academy of Sciences (Illinois State Museum, Springfield, IL) Transactions 4	Hamburgisches Zoologisches Museum (U. Hamburg, W. Ger.) Mitteilungen 1
Natural History Museum of Los Angeles County, CA Science Bulletin; Science Series 2	Naturhistorisches Museum in Wien (Vienna, Austria) Annalen 1
California Academy of Sciences (San Francisco, CA) Bulletin: Proceedings 2	South African Museum (Capetown, R.S.F.) Annals 1
San Diego Society of Natural History (San Diego, CA) Transactions 2	Queensland Museum (Brisbane, Australia) Memoirs 1
Smithsonian Institution (Washington, D.C.) Smithsonian Contributions 2	Yokosuka City Museum (Japan) Scientific Reports 1
Peabody Museum of Natural History (Yale U., New Haven, CT) Postilla 2	Museo de la Plata (National U., Argentina) Revista 1
Museum of Natural History (U. Kansas, Lawrence, KS) Bulletin 2	46 other Museums / 46 Papers
7 other Museums / 7 Papers	

lished. Some museums issue an assortment of bulletins with subject specialty titles, e.g., *Smithsonian Contributions to . . . Anthropology, . . . the Marine Sciences, . . . Paleobiology, . . . Zoology*. Other museums have published differing bulletins for comparatively shorter and longer papers, e.g., Harvard University's *Breviora* and *Contributions*, respectively. Most bulletins consist of one, two, or a few papers and appear very irregularly. On the other hand, most of the papers are very extensive by the standards of conventional journals, with articles running from fifty to literally hundreds of pages. This provides enormous scope for full-size, heavily illustrated work and exhaustive treatments of topics. Moreover bulletin issues generally remain in print for ten years and longer.

APPLICATION OF RESULTS – GROSS ANATOMY

The tables in the study thus far are not meant to be taken as literal, decreasing-preference, buying guides. While the sample analyzed is clearly large enough to argue the need for a variety of categories of journal to serve most gross anatomists, it is not large enough to indicate every title of value, and certainly not in preferential order. Nor is it suggested that every librarian should buy some journals in each category for every library situation. Rather the tables and previous discussion, added by a careful use of *Journal Citation Reports*[9] and *Current Contents*[10] as outlined below and talks with clientele, can together make for tailor-made collections.

The use of *Journal Citation Reports* in science collection management is receiving increasing attention and at least tentative validation through experience.[11] It works well in subject fields with a high volume of journal publication and many library journal users, but may not correlate well with actual circulation records in fields with less journal publication and typically fewer library journal users,[12] a possibility repeatedly acknowledged by its publishers.[13] A few examples of its use in this field, bolstered by a novel use of *Current Contents*, illustrate the need for caution, yet show how helpful guidance can be found.

For example, careful librarians may wish to test the method by checking several *JCR*s for the list of journals which, year after year, cite or are cited by, an obvious choice, e.g., the *Journal of Morphology*. They should not be discouraged at repeatedly seeing *Cell and Tissue Research* or the *Journal of Cell Biology* at the top of these lists. Rather, they should recall from our previous discussion that microscopical anatomy, which these latter two journals stress, is preponderant in most general journals of anatomy, even nonmedical ones. They may assign those citations then to the microscopical majority. Continuing down the lists they will find the fewer, but reassuringly persistent references annually made to, and by, many zoology journals. To confirm their working hypothesis, careful librarians should check several issues of *Current Contents* that include the *Journal of Morphology*. Having done so, they will likely agree with two standard buying guides that it represents a good buy in this category.[14-15]

As another example, librarians might wish to expand a collection serving bird anatomists. This study's tables and the librarians' clientele might well suggest *Auk* as a leader. Checking a few years' *JCR*s for other journals which cite or are cited by *Auk*, they will find, among several, the *Wilson Bulletin* and *Bird Banding*. A check with several issues of *Current Contents* that included both of these titles will likely confirm the first titles and disqualify the second. The *Wilson Bulletin*, like *Auk*, will show itself to be a general bird studies journal that will include work involving gross anatomy, while *Bird Banding* can be seen as generally limiting itself to field work.

Both librarians and their clientele can be given unexpected insights from the interplay of *JCR*s and long runs of *Current Contents*. both tools, for example, indicate that the general zoology title, the *Canadian Journal of Zoology*, might be a good candidate for a collection in the more specialized field of bird work. In short, the tables and discussion from the study thus far, a history of citation interactions in several years' *JCR*s, and suggestions from clientele, can all give leads for collection building in gross anatomy that can often be confirmed by checking a substantial run of *Current Contents*.

RESULTS AND DISCUSSION – MEDICAL SCHOOL HISTOLOGY AND ULTRASTRUCTURE

Table 2 B indicates that, as is the case with gross anatomy, only a portion of histological and ultrastructural anatomy is published in journals exclusively devoted to anatomy. Yet, as is also the case with gross anatomy, these anatomy journals constitute the largest category of journal outlet. An important difference, and one which *should* have greater effect, is that histologists and ultrastructuralists dominate these journals, many of which are the official organs of their professional associations. One explanation for the majority of papers appearing in a variety of other journals is the historical pattern of specialization mentioned in the introduction. Another is a general trend in medical funding towards "mission research," such as: cancer, birth defects, artificial organs, and so on. A final explanation is an identity and status crisis in some countries of their medical schools' departments of anatomy.[16-18] While this is now most sharply focused on the widespread reduction of curriculum time allowed for anatomy, it also concerns a general impression that even medical school anatomy is an unfashionable, declining, and archaic activity. This notion is rejected by the authors reporting the crisis, if not also by the volume of papers in this study. Their fears have some justification, however, given the proportion of papers going to disciplines with only a marginal connection to anatomy, e.g., the 23% "other" in this table.

Table 8 indicates the expected outlets for medical school anatomists, journals exclusively devoted to anatomy at all of its structural size ranges. The journals are ranked by a simple cumulative preference system that will be used throughout the remainder of this paper. According to this system, the most frequent outlet for each of the blocs mentioned in the Methods section was given ten points, the next most frequent, nine, and so on. The points from all the blocs for each individual title in the category of subject journal under discussion were then summed. This system has the unique property of indicating both significant international outlets (since they must score in more than one bloc to go over ten points) without denying some rating to those journals which are very, if not exclusively, important to a single bloc, or which have only a modest following in a few blocs (scores of ten or less).

It should be noted that since their coverage in *Science Citation Index* was absent or not continuous, two journals, *Archiv Anatomii Gistologii i Embriologii,* and *Anatomischer Anzeiger*, could not be included in the general anatomy journal category of this table. While this study repeatedly showed that few Soviet journals ever attracted authors outside the Soviet Union, giving the first journal at most ten points, and suggesting that the issue was moot, the case with *Anatomischer Anzeiger* merits one discussion. Recalling the historical introduction, *Anatomischer Anzeiger* has had an important role among general anatomy journals, and was in fact included in the early years of *SCI*. It was dropped from coverage more recently, presumably for low citation ratings. These reasons may have contributed to this apparent decline. First, the journal may have lost some of its appeal to Western authors when it fell into East German hands at the end of the Second World War. Second, while the journal was one of the first to allow the publication of English-language articles among German-based anatomy journals, the proportion of English, particularly

Table 8. Anatomy journals covering research on a variety of levels of biological structure ranked as publication outlets for ten international blocs representing 196 medical school departments of anatomy by a cumulative preference scheme described in the text.

GENERAL

(Publishing a Mix of Gross, Histological, & Ultrastructural)

Acta Anatomica 88 (Switz.)

Journal of Anatomy 66 (U.K.)

Anatomical Record 64 (U.S.)

Anatomy and Embryology 60 (W. Ger.)

Acta Morphologica Neerlando-Scandinavica 36 (Neth.)

American Journal of Anatomy 36 (U.S.)

Journal of Morphology 25 (U.S.)

Anatomia, Histologia, Embryologia 13 (W. Ger.)

Anatomia Clinica 8 (France)

Annales d'Anatomie Pathologique 8 (France)

Zoomorphologie 8 (W. Ger.)

Annales de Anatomia 6 (Spain)

ULTRASTRUCTURAL

(Usually Exclusively Ultrastructural)

Journal of Ultrastructure Research 69 (U.S. - Sweden)

Ultramicroscopy 26 (Neth.)

Journal of Electron Microscopy 19 (Japan)

HISTOLOGICAL

(Publishing Histology & Ultrastructure)

Cell and Tissue Research (W. Ger.)

Histochemistry 68 (W. Ger.)

Acta Histochemica 44 (E. Ger.)

Journal of Histochemistry and Cytochemistry 39 (U.S.)

Stain Technology 34 (U.S.)

Journal of Microscopy 26 (U.K.)

Acta Histochemica et Cytochemica 24 (Japan)

Journal de Microscopie 23 (Now Biologie Cellulaire) (France)

Zeitschrift fuer Mikroskopisch-Anatomische . . . 19 (E. Ger.)

Mikroskopie 17 (Austria)

Folia Histochemica et Cytochemica 15 (Poland)

Tissue and Cell 12 (U.K.)

Annales d'Histochemie 11 (Now Cellular and Molecular Biology) (France)

Archivum Histologicum Japonicum 9 (Japan)

Microscopica Acta 6 (W. Ger.)

smooth American English, and the frequently accompanying Americanization of layout, have been slower to follow than in some of this journal's Western competition. Third, the journal accepts one of the largest proportions of gross level work. Gross level work, as mentioned earlier, generally comes from a smaller, less prolific community, less able, and less inclined, to contribute the high volume of citations associated with the microscopically oriented, medical anatomists. Returning to those journals which are included in the table, the reader will find few surprises, save, should he have forgotten the historical introduction, the remarkable dominance of German-based journals as outlets for microscopic anatomy as indicated in the histology column.

Cell Biology (see Table 9 A) is a unique field which anatomists share with biochemists.[19] This diversity of devotees leads to some surprising rankings. *Cell* and the *Journal of Cell Physiology*, which share leading roles with the *Journal of Cell Biology* and *Experimental Cell Research* from the biochemist's point of view, share a modest ranking

Table 9. Journals of A: Cell Biology and B: Embryology ranked as publication outlets for ten international blocs representing 196 medical school departments of anatomy by a cumulative preference scheme described in the text.

A.	B.
Experimental Cell Research 78 (Sweden)	Teratology 83 (U.S.)
Journal of Cell Biology 65 (U.S.)	Journal of Embryology and Experimental Morphology 81 (U.K.)
Journal of Cell Science 42 (U.K.)	Developmental Biology 41 (U.S.)
Cell and Tissue Kinetics 26 (U.K.)	Wilhelm Rouxs Archives of Developmental Biology 25 (W. Ger.)
Cytobiologie 22 (W. Ger.)	Biology of the Neonate 22 (Switz.)
Biologie Cellulaire 20 (France)	Cell Differentiation 17 (Neth.)
Cytologia 16 (Japan)	Development, Growth, Differentiation 16 (Japan
Cell 15 (U.S.)	Growth 14 (U.S.)
Cytobios 15 (U.K.)	Archives d'Anatomie Microscopique et de Morphologie Experimentale 12 (France)
Cellular Immunology 11 (U.S.)	Differentiation 8 (W. Ger.)
Journal of Cell Physiology 11 (U.S.)	
Tsitologiya 10 (U.S.S.R.)	
5 Others	

with the biochemically unheralded *Cytologia* and *Cytobios* in this anatomist's preference study. This table also provides the reader with an example in which the scoring system indicates a journal (*Tsitologiya*) of great importance to a single bloc or country (the Soviet Union) whose medically affiliated anatomists stress cell biology to a high degree (10% of their total papers compared to the ten bloc average of 5%) but which (through its score of ten) is shown to have little international authorship. Other blocs with an above average proportion of their papers in this field (the Americans, 9%; Canadians and German-speaking, 7% each) published much more broadly and internationally among titles in the top half of this table.

Embryology (see Table 9 B) has become, even for its anatomy department adherents, a science that is as experimental as observation. Changing the environment of a developing fertilized egg or cultured tissue specimen prior to microscopical study has become as much a part of this discipline as is the systematic examination of its unadulterated developmental anatomy. This is clearly indicated by the titles of two of its journals: the *Journal of Embryology and Experimental Morphology* and *Archives d'Anatomie Microsopique et de Morphologie Experimentale*. The fact that many of these experimental alterations are intended to simulate or stimulate embryonic abnormalities, called teratogenies, is indicated by the title of another journal, *Teratology*. The Japanese (9% total papers) and German-speaking (8%) particularly stress embryology which otherwise takes up about 3% of the world's anatomy papers.

In its broadest sense modern pathology (see Table 10 A) includes infections, parasites, poisoning, injuries, the determination of cause of death, and laboratory procedures for the analysis of these conditions. Most anatomists working in pathology today, however, adhere to the microscopic study of diseased cells and tissues, very often as seen in biopsies performed in conjunction with cancer diagnosis or basic research. In light of the "Introduction" it is not surprising to find *Virchows Archiv* the international leader. Most of the remaining journals are national association publications for pathologists, or diagnostic, or basic research oncologists. (Cancer treatment reporting is shared by general clinical journals, which will be discussed soon, or in the journals of those specialists who currently dominate its treatment: hematologists, nuclear medicine therapists and surgeons, by a few journals exclusively devoted to treatment and by those including basic research.) Medical school anatomists in Canada (6% total papers) and German-speaking bloc (5%) stress pathology-oncology outlets greater than the ten bloc average (3%).

Table 10. Journals of A: Pathology and Oncology, and B: Neurosciences ranked as publication outlets for ten international blocs representing 196 medical school departments of anatomy by a cumulative preference scheme described in the text.

A.	B.
Virchows Archiv A & B 68 (W. Ger.)	Brain Research 88 (Neth.)
Laboratory Investigation 36 (U.S.)	Journal of Comparative Neurology 43 (U.S.)
Experimentelle Pathologie 27 (E. Ger.)	Experimental Brain Research 41 (W. Ger.)
Cancer Research 23 (U.S.)	Acta Neuropathologica 25 (W. Ger.)
Journal of the National Cancer Institute 21 (U.S.)	Journal of Neurocytology 23 (U.K.)
Journal of Pathology 20 (U.K.)	Neuroscience Letters 23 (Neth.)
Cancer 14 (U.S.)	Neuroendocrinology 21 (Switz.)
International Journal of Cancer 13 (Switz.)	Neuroscience 19 (U.K.)
Neoplasma 13 (Czech.)	Journal of Neurochemistry 18 (U.S.)
Experimental and Molecular Pathology 12 (U.S.)	Zhurnal Nevropatologii i Pskiatrii imeni S. S. Korsakova 10 (U.S.S.R.)
Journal of Cancer Research and Clinical Oncology 12 (W. Ger.)	Zhurnal Vysshei Nervnoi Deyaltel'nosti imeni I. P. Pavlova 9 (U.S.S.R)
Pathologia Europaea 11 (Belgium)	Journal of the Neurological Sciences 8 (Neth.)
Acta Pathologica et Microbiologica Scandinavica 10 (Denmark)	Journal of Neural Transmission 8 (W. Ger.)
Beitraege zur Pathologie 10 (W. Ger.)	Physiology and Behavior 7 (U.S.)
15 Others	Brain Research Bulletin 6 (U.S.)
	17 Others

Neuroscience journals (see Table 10 B) are the final subspecialty outlets for medically affiliated anatomists found in this study. It should be noted that most anatomists stress the microanatomy of the brain and nervous system as evidenced in journals such as the *Journal of Comparative Neurology* or the *Journal of Neurology* as opposed to journals of psychotherapy, psychiatry, learning and behavior, or even neurosurgery. The Japanese (19% total papers) and Americans (16%) publish the largest shares of their anatomy papers in this field although the involvement of the entire ten blocs tends to be high as indicated by the 14% group average.

Medically affiliated anatomists publish very regularly in multi-science and general clinical investigation journals. This is in marked contrast to their gross level counterparts. It is safe to say that among anatomists the medically affiliated have at least as strong and exclusive a hold on this category of journals as their gross level counterparts have on museum bulletins. As is also the case with museum bulletins, contributions made by anatomists to these journals tend to follow resident national lines save in all but the top six or seven titles in Table 11. The special considerations involved in museum bulletins were extended format and prolonged availability, with these it is a wider audience and higher visibility. (It is not clear, however, that the many papers that the 19% ten bloc average represents deal with anatomy, a real concern of those who warn of a crisis in anatomy.) Within each bloc then, there were typically one or two truly international titles and then a string of domestic ones.

The Indian experience is typical: the *Indian Journal of Medical Research* (ten points), *Experientia* (the sole frequent truly international outlet, nine), *Current Science* (eight), the *Indian Journal of Experimental Biology* (seven), the *Indian Journal of Experimental Medicine* (six), and so on. Even among these many characteristically narrow patterns, those of the Soviet Union and France stand out for extreme concentration on a few national, official publications, all of which could be listed in this table. The publication patterns of the Americans in journals of the category provide the reader with paradoxes similar to those found of this cell biology category. American anatomists published rarely in some otherwise distinguished journals. Examples, striking in their absence from the top of this frequency-as-outlets-for-anatomists-list included: the *New England Journal of Medicine*, the *Journal of the American Medical Association*, and the *Journal of Clinical Investigation*. Whether this is owing to some exlusionary editorial policy, historical circumstances or is in fact symptomatic of the low status of the work or workers in medical school departments of anatomy is not clear.

APPLICATION OF RESULTS – MEDICAL SCHOOL HISTOLOGY AND ULTRASTRUCTURE

The tables in this portion of the study are based on a much larger data base than the earlier, gross anatomy portion, and in many cases can be taken as literal, decreasing-preference buying guides. Since

Table 11. Multiscience and general clinical investigation journals ranked as publication outlets for ten international blocs representing 196 medical school departments of anatomy by a cumulative preference scheme described in the text.

Experientia 83
(Switz.)

Nature 67
(U.K.)

Science 25
(U.S.)

Lancet 21
(U.K.)

Proceedings of the National Academy of Science 17
(U.S.)

Naturwissenschaften 12
(W. Ger.)

Schweizerische Medizinische Wochenschrift 11
(Switz.)

Byulleten Eksperimental'noi Biologii i Meditsiny 10
(U.S.S.R.)

Comptes Tendus des Seances de la Societe de Biologie et ses Filiales 10
(France)

Indian Journal of Medical Research 10

Proceedings of the Society for Experimental Medicine and Biology 10
(U.S.)

Bulletin de l'Academie Polonaise des Sciences, Serie des Sciences Biologiques 9
(Poland)

Comptes Rendus Hebdomadaires des Seances de l'Academie des Sciences, Serie D 9
(France)

Doklady Akademii Nauk S.S.S.R. 9
(U.S.S.R.)

Scandinavian Journal of Clinical and Laboratory Investigation 9
(Sweden & U.K.)

Acta Biologica Academiae Scientarium Hungaricae 8
(Hungary)

Annals of the New York Academy of Sciences 8
(U.S.)

Current Science 8
(India)

Deutsche Medizinische Wochenschrift 8
(W. Ger.)

Medical Biology 8
(Finland)

Nouvelle Presse Medicale 8
(France)

Sovetskaya Meditsina 8
(U.S.S.R.)

Union Medicale Canadienne 8
(Canada)

Canadian Medical Association Journal 7
(Canada)

Federation Proceedings 7
(U.S.)

Indian Journal of Experimental Biology 7

Acta Biologica et Medica Germanica 6
(E. Ger.)

Indian Journal of Experimental Medicine 6

Journal of Experimental Medicine 6
(U.S.)

Zhurnal Obshaschei Biologii 6
(U.S.S.R.)

27 Others

most medical schools have several researching anatomists, automatically buying some journals within each of the categories discussed in this portion of the study is reasonable. *Journal Citation Reports* and *Current Contents* can be used with fewer special warnings and greater ease since the citation data at the top of the lists generally represent the influence of medical school based microanatomy. Ironically, this ease of identification of likely journal subscription candidates puts the focus in collection development as much on exclusion as inclusion. Two factors mentioned in a few specific cases earlier can serve as general sorting guides. The first is the aversion of many Western-alliance authors for non-Western-alliance journals. The second is related and partly explanatory of the first. When the literature of a scientific discipline is large enough to force a limitation on systematic reading and offers authors a wide variety of possible outlets, Americans will consistently avoid reading and contributing to journals published in a foreign language. Only when the journal "Internationalizes" (publishes in smooth American English, with a slick format, on a predictable schedule) will they regularly read or publish within it.[20] This seems to be the case for American microanatomists. By contrast, gross level anatomists are members of a smaller scientific literature community to both readership and publication outlets and are often reliant on older literature. They are generally quite cosmopolitan and tolerant of a variety of formats, publication schedules and at least the major Western European languages.

SUMMARY

The majority of gross anatomists are based in university departments of zoology, physical anthropology, marine biology, and paleontology, or in natural history museums. Apart from showing some interest in few mutually important anatomy journals, their subscription needs reflect their institutions' specialties and are consequently radically different from those of their microscopically-oriented medical school counterparts. Medical school anatomists have been focusing their attention on even smaller structures in embryos, cells, diseased tissues, and the nervous system. When not publishing their results in the many anatomy journals that they dominate, they publish in journals devoted to the subspecialties defined by their specimens. Typically among anatomists, only the gross level worker publishes in museum bulletins, while only the microscopically oriented worker publishes in multiscience and general clinical investigation journals. The librarian can look to history for an explanation of the origins of this overall situation and to the tables of this study, *Journal Citation Reports*, and *Current Contents* for collection development advice.

NOTES

1. The most convenient and authoritative source of biographical information, the one used throughout this introduction, is: *Dictionary of scientific biography*. New York: Scribner's; 1970. 16 vols.

2. Schierhorn, H. Die Multinationalitat der Anatomischen Gesellschaft und die Mehrsprachigkeit ihr Versammlungen. *Anatomischer Anzieger*, 148(7): 168-206; 1980.

3. Brooks, Chandler McC; Seller, Horst. Early and late contributions to our knowledge of the autonomic nervous system and its control made by German scientists. *Journal of the Autonomic Nervous System*, 3(2-4): 105-119; 1980.

4. Steyer, Gerhard Ernest. Joseph Hyrtl als komparativer Anatom. *Anatomischer Anzeiger*, 148(10): 462-473; 1980.

5. Schlee, Susan. *The edge of an unfamiliar world; a history of oceanography*. New York: Dutton; 1973; Chap. I, II, III and VI.

6. *Biological Abstracts*. (Volumes 46(1965), 53(1972) and 68(1979) were used for this study.)

7. *Science Citation Index*. (Volumes for 1965-1979 were used for this study.)

8. *World directory of medical schools*. 4th ed. Geneva: World Health Organization; 1970. (The blocs were: Canada; Eastern Europe (The Warsaw Pact minus the Soviet Union and East Germany, but with Yugoslavia); French-speaking Europe (France, French-speaking Belgium and Switzerland); German-speaking Europe (East and West Germany, Austria, and German-Speaking Switzerland); India; Japan; Scandinavia and the Netherlands (who share a leading anatomy journal); the United Kingdom and Eire; the United Sates; and the U.S.S.R.)

9. Garfield, Eugene, ed. and comp. *SCI Journal Citation Reports: a Bibliometric Analysis of Science Journals in the ISI Data Base*. Philadelphia: Institute for Scientific Information: 1977-(Annual).

10. *Current Contents. Agriculture, Biology and Environmental Sciences* (preferable for most gross level anatomists) and *Current Contents: Life Sciences* (preferable for most histologist and ultrastructuralist). Philadelphia: Institute for Scientific Information (Weekly).

11. Broadus, Robert N. Citation analysis and library collection building. *Advances in Librarianship*, 7: 299-333; 1970.

12. Stankus, Tony; Rice, Barbara. Handle with care; use and citation data for science journal management. *Collection Development*.

13. Garfield, *ibid*, 1979 ed., p. 9A.

14. Katz, Bill; Richards, Berry G. *Magazines for libraries*. 3d ed. New York: Bowker; 1978: p. 170.

15. Farber, Ira Evan. *Classified list of periodicals for the college library*. Westwood, MA: Faxon; 1972; p. 61.

16. Romanes, G.J. An anatomist looks at medical education. *Physical East*, 3(2): 20-23; 1981 Feb.

17. Sinclair, David. The two anatomies. *Lancet*, 1(7912): 875-878; 1975 Apr. 19.

18. Lehr, Robert P. A clarion for dissection. *New England Journal of Medicine*, 303(22): 1370; 1981 May 20.

19. Stankus, Tony. Collection development: journals for biochemists. *Special Collections*, 1(2).

20. Stankus, Tony; Schlessinger, Rashelle; Schlessinger, Bernard S. English language trends in German basic science journals: a potential collection tool. *Science & Technology Libraries*, 1(3): 55-66; 1981 Spring.

Selecting Multispecialty Mathematics Research Journals via Their Underlying Subject Emphases

Tony Stankus
Virgil Diodato

Mathematicians are like Frenchmen: whatever you say to them they translate into their own language and forthwith it is something completely different.

Goethe, *Maximen und Reflexionen*[1]

ABSTRACT. The problems of selecting mathematics research journals are reviewed, with particular emphasis on the best matching of multispecialty mathematics journals with given mathematical specialties. A simple method involving *Mathematical Reviews* classification numbers identified the specialties of 21,332 papers published between 1972 and 1979 in 30 multispecialty mathematics journals. The journals' underlying subject strengths are reported and compared. This reveals strong subject biases in several journals as well as a general pattern of subject polarization. The results are discussed in light of the current academic politics of Pure Mathematics versus Applied Mathematics.

INTRODUCTION

A librarian building a journal collection for pure and applied mathematicians often sees publishing patterns not usually encountered in other sci-tech literatures. Few sci-tech selection guidelines seem to apply to mathematics. The typical sci-tech literature in any given country and field is characterized by one or two general journals (such as the *Journal of the American Chemical Society*) and a large family of clearly designated subspecialty journals (such as *Biochemistry*, *Inor-*

Reprinted with permission from *Science & Technology Libraries*, volume 4, number 1, pages 61-78, 1983. Copyright, The Haworth Press.

ganic Chemistry, and *Macromolecules*). In mathematics the United States alone has over a dozen essentially general journals, while families of mathematics journals seem easier to characterize by article length than by subspecialty. The publishing of most other sci-tech journal literature has become monopolized by the major national professional societies and well-known commercial houses. However, in mathematics these sources share roughly equal status with individual university presses (Illinois, Duke, Oxford); regional associations Rocky Mountain Mathematics Consortium, London Mathematical Society, and sixteen institutions that together support the *Pacific Journal of Mathematics*); and less familiar commercial houses (Sithoff, Birkhauser, DeGruyter). While most other types of American scientists consistently read and publish within only American journals or those foreign titles characterized by English-language articles and American formats and schedules, American mathematicians are exceptionally cosmopolitan in their reading and choice of publishing outlets.[2-4] American mathematics journals feature French-language and German-language papers, with Italian occasionally seen. Even Latin is found in at least one prominent journal, the *Archive for Rational Mechanics and Analysis*.

While the journals of many of the other (generally larger) sci-tech disciplines annually have been ranked convincingly by *Journal Citation Reports*[5] in gross citations or impact factors – a process that promotes a consensus on journal selection between librarian and clientele – the results involving mathematics journals are usually not as clear. Factors in mathematics such as the higher frequency of citations to monographs, the lower rate of citations per paper, and the relatively small volume of papers in the field may be responsible.[6-7] There is uncertainty in the interpretation of the more complicated citing and cited relationships as well. In many other sci-tech disciplines, specialty journals that significantly cite more general journals in the same discipline are reassuringly cited in return, confirming a link in the mind of the collection developer. In mathematics this "love" often seems unrequited. For example, compare the citations made by the *Journal of Differential Equations* with those made by the *Transactions of the American Mathematical Society*, or those of the *Journal of Combinatorial Theory* with those of the *Proceedings* of the same society.

One strategy in the selection of mathematics journals would be to reverse the usual sci-tech selection procedure and first select the specialty journals that match the clientele before selecting any general journals. But this only delays the inevitable quandary about which of the more general journals to select. Guides such as Fedunok,[8] while being noteworthy for denoting the fields stressed in some journals, still tend to emphasize whether or not given titles are too technical for some collections. Contemporary guides to the general field or sci-tech literature (Malinowsky, Chen, Subramanyam)[9,10,11] and those specifically devoted to Mathematics (Pemberton, Dorling, Dick)[12,13,14] stress reference works and monographs. Attempts to sort journals by direct inspection of their content is likely to be frustrating for the librarian in light of mathematics' incredible terminology. Our study demonstrates a method, accessible to the librarian, of bypassing the terminology and of identifying the underlying subject strengths, where they exist, of mathematics research journals that each cover several specialties. We have labelled such journals as multispecialty journals.

METHODS

The journals involved in this study were chosen because they together covered various areas of mathematics, they were perceived as important by librarians and faculty at the author's institutions, and they represented both American and non-American titles. As a practical matter, their number was limited to 30, although many journals did meet our criteria. The first author of each paper appearing in these journals between 1972 and 1979 was searched in the 1972 through 1981 issues of *Mathematical Reviews (MR)*. Data gathered from *MR* were the first two digits of the primary subject classification code assigned to each paper. (A recent brief explanation of the classification system used by *MR* is in Kusma.[15] Major headings of the system are displayed on the front cover of most *MR* issues.) These codes were grouped into ten specialty categories modified from earlier work by Diodato.[16] And so, each paper was easily placed in one of the following specialty fields: mathematical foundations (including logic, set theory, combinatorics, universal algebra), algebra and group theory, algebraic geometry, complex and harmonic analysis, ordinary theory, algebraic geometry, complex and harmonic analysis, ordinary differential equations, partial differential equations, real and abstract analysis, differential geometry, topology, applied mathematics (including statistics, probability, numerical analysis). The process of categorization was straightforward and certainly required no special insight into mathematical terminology. The list of journals, the specialty field categories and corresponding *MR* classification codes, and the raw data for each journal are in the Appendices.

RESULTS

One result is clear from even a cursory glance at Tables 1-4. There is indeed substantial variation in subject emphasis among multispecialty mathematics research journals. In almost every specialty category there are some journals that devote much of their content to that field while others provide almost nothing. The selection of the appropriate multispecialty journal for matching with a clientele's specialties would not be a matter of random choice. Yet, if selection in these instances should not be random, should it be a matter for individual journal analysis every time a journal subscription is considered? While we later will argue for the ease and merit of making such individual determinations, the reader should be aware that there are some general characteristics of journals that ought to allow the librarian to make preliminary decisions for groups of journals.

A comparison of the results in Tables 1 and 2 suggests that there is an inverse relationship of specialty strengths for at least two sets of specialty fields. One set is algebra nd group theory, algebraic geometry, and topology. The other is ordinary differential equations, partial differential equations, and applied mathematics. Comparisons here are based on the ten or so journals – the top one-third of our 30 journals – the most frequently publish papers in each specialty.

We concentrate first on the algebra-algebraic geometry-topology set. The three specialties in this first set have many of the same journals in their respective top one-thirds. The *Illinois Journal of Mathematics*, *Quarterly Journal of Mathematics*, *American Journal of Mathematics*, *Compositio Mathematica*, *Annals of Mathematics*, and *Pacific Journal of Mathematics* are top third journals in two of the three fields. *Commentarii Mathematici Helvetici* and the *Proceedings of the American Mathematical Society* are top third journals for all three specialties in this set. In fact, the top two-third of the journals are almost the same – except for order – for any two of the three specialties. This implies a striking conclusion: the bottom third of journals for any one of the three specialties – algebra and group theory, algebraic geometry, topology – is likely to be the bottom third of "worst" group of journals for the other two as well.

The "worst" group provides evidence for the inverse relationship mentioned above. these journals from the top third of journals for the second set of specialties; ordinary differential equations, partial differential equations, and applied mathematics. The top third relationship is even stronger here than in the first set of specialties, for the following journals are in the top third of all three specialties of the second

TABLE 1. Journals ranked by shares devoted to Algebra & Group Theory, Algebraic Geometry, and Topology. The top twenty journals for any one of these specialties tends to be the same as for the other two, with only their order of rank changed. Note the consistent representation of the more Applied journals among the "Worst" group.

HIGHER ALGEBRA & GROUP THEORY	ALGEBRAIC GEOMETRY	TOPOLOGY
29% Math. Z.	40% Bull. Soc. Math. Fr.	29% Comment. Math. Helv.
26% Illinois J. Math.	39% Inventiones Math.	28% Illinois J. Math.
25% Quart J. Math. Oxf.	32% Am. J. Math.	27% Michigan Math. J.
23% Compositio Math.	29% Compositio Math.	26% Dissertationes Math.
20% Pacific J. Math.	25% Math. USSR Izvestija	25% Ann. Math.
20% Bull. Soc. Math. Fr.	23% Ann. Math.	24% Quart. J. Math. Oxf.
18% Proc. Am. Math. Soc.	18% Duke Math. J.	22% Trans. Am. Math. Soc.
18% Comment. Math. Helv.	14% Acta Math. Uppsala	21% Am. J. Math.
17% Commun. Pure Appl. Math.	12% Comment. Math. Helv.	20% Proc. Am. Math. Soc.
16% Math. USSR Izvestija	10% Proc. Am. Math. Soc.	20% Pacific J. Math.
16% Advan. Math.		
15% Inventiones Math.	9% Pacific J. Math.	19% Compositio Math.
15% Ann. Math.	9% Trans. Am. Math.	17% Duke Math. J.
14% Trans. Am. Math. Soc.	9% Advan. Math.	16% Inventiones Math.
13% Duke Math. J.	9% Mich. Math. J.	12% Rocky Mtn. J. Math.
13% Rocky Mtn. J. Math.	8% Math. Z.	11% Acta Math. Uppsala
12% Am. J. Math.	7% Rocky Mtn. J. Math.	10% Math. Z.
10% Mich. Math. J.	7% Illinois J. Math.	10% Bull. Soc. Math. Fr.
10% Acta Math. Uppsala	7% Quart. J. Math. Oxf.	9% Indiana J. Math.
10% Dissertationes Math.	7% Indiana J. Math.	7% Math. USSR Izvestija
	7% Arch. Math. Basel	6% Advan. Math.
8% Siam. J. Appl. Math.	2% Commun. Pure Appl. Math.	2% J. Math. Anal. Appl.
8% Arch. Math. Basel	1% Quart. Appl. Math.	1% Siam J. Math. Anal.
3% Siam Rev.	1% Dissertationes Math.	1% Commun. Pure Appl. Math.
2% J. Math. Anal. Appl.	1% Siam Rev.	1% Z. Ang. Math. Phys.
2% Z. Angen. Math. Phys.	0% J. Math. Anal. Appl.	1% Arch. Math. Basel
1% Siam J. Math. Anal.	0% Siam J. Appl. Math.	0% Siam J. Appl. Math.
1% J. Inst. Math. Appl.	0% Siam J. Math. Anal.	0% J. Inst. Math. Appl.
0% Arch. Rational Mech. Anal.	0% Arch. Rational Math. Mech.	0% Arch. Rational Mech. Anal.
0% Indiana J. Math.	0% J. Inst. Math. Appl.	0% Quart. Appl. Math.
0% Quart. Appl. Math.	0% Z. Ang. Math. Physik	0% Siam Rev.

TABLE 2. Journals ranked by shares devoted to Ordinary Differential Equations, Partial Differential Equations, and Applied Mathematics. Note that the best journals for any one of these specialties tend to be the same as for the other two. Recall that these journals are the worst contributors to the fields of Table 1.

ORDINARY DIFFERENTIAL EQUATIONS	PARTIAL DIFFERENTIAL EQUATIONS	APPLIED MATH. & OTHERS
20% Siam J. Math. Anal.	25% Commun. Pure Appl. Math.	84% J. Inst. Math. Appl.
15% J. Math. Anal. Appl.	22% Arch. Rational Mech. Anal.	72% Z. Ang. Math. Phys.
10% Siam. J. Appl. Math.	14% Indiana Math. J.	69% Quart. Appl. Math.
10% Siam Rev.	13% Siam J. Math. Anal.	64% Siam. J. Appl. Math.
8% Rocky Mtn. J. Math.	13% Z. Ang. Math. Phys.	61% Siam Rev.
8% Arch. Rational Mech. Anal.	13% Quart. Appl. Math.	51% Arch. Rational Mech. Anal.
8% Quart. Appl. Math.	11% Arch. Math. Basel	40% J. Math. Anal. Appl.
7% Quart. J. Math. Oxf.	8% J. Math. Anal. Appl.	26% Commun. Pure Appl. Math.
7% Commun. Pure Appl. Math.	8% Siam Rev.	23% Siam J. Math. Anal.
4% Proc. Am. Math. Soc.	7% Siam J. Appl. Math.	23% Rocky Mtn. J. Math.
4% Z. Ang. Math. Phys.		23% Advan. Math.
3% Pacific J. Math.	6% Math. Z.	14% Dissertationes Math.
3% Trans. Am. Math. Soc.	6% Acta Math. Uppsala	12% Indiana J. Math.
3% Math USSR Izvestija	5% Duke Math. J.	9% Math. Z.
3% J. Inst. Math. Appl.	5% Rocky Mtn. J. Math.	9% Acta Math. Uppsala
2% Math. Z.	4% Math. USSR Izvestija	9% Arch. Math. Basel
2% Indiana Math. J.	4% Advan. Math.	7% Trans. Am. Math. Soc.
2% Advan. Math.	3% Trans. Am. Math. Soc.	7% Bull. Soc. Math. Fr.
	2% Proc. Am. Math. Soc.	6% Pacific J. Math.
	2% Am. J. Math.	6% Math. USSR Izvestija
	2% Quart. J. Math. Oxf.	6% Comment. Math. Helv.
	2% J. Inst. Math. Appl.	
	2% Ann. Math.	
1% Am. J. Math.	1% Pacific J. Math.	5% Proc. Am. Math. Soc.
1% Duke Math. J.	1% Illinois J. Math.	5% Inventiones Math.
1% Illinois J. Math.	1% Inventiones Math.	5% Duke J. Math.
1% Inventiones Math.	1% Compositio Math.	5% Ann. Math.
1% Mich. Math. J.	1% Michigan Math. J.	4% Illinois J. Math.
1% Comment. Math. Helv.	1% Bull. Soc. Math. Fr.	4% Quart. J. Math. Oxf.
1% Acta Math. Uppsala	1% Comment. Math. Helv.	3% Am. J. Math.
1% Arch. Math. Basel	1% Dissertationes Math.	2% Compositio Math.
1% Dissertationes Math.		1% Michigan Math. J.
0% Ann. Math.		
0% Compositio Math.		
0% Bull. Soc. Math. Fr.		

TABLE 3. Journals ranked by shares devoted to Mathematical Foundations and Differential Geometry. While pure journals predominate in the upper groupings, some applied journals do well.

PURE FOUNDATIONS, COMBINATORICS, & OTHERS	DIFFERENTIAL GEOMETRY
20% Dissertationes Math.	16% Inventiones Math.
11% Advan. Math.	15% Comment. Math. Helv.
9% Quart. J. Math. Oxf.	14% Ann. Math.
6% Proc. Am. Math. Soc.	13% Acta Math. Uppsala
6% Pacific J. Math.	10% Am. J. Math.
6% Trans. Am. Math. Soc.	9% Commun. Pure Appl. Math.
6% Math. Z.	8% Advan. Math.
6% Siam J. Appl. Math.	7% Indiana J. Math.
5% Siam Rev.	7% Duke Math. J.
	7% Arch. Rational Mech. Anal.
	7% Dissertationes Math.
4% Duke Math. J.	6% Math. USSR Izvestija
4% Compositio Math.	6% Mich. Math. J.
3% Rocky Mtn. J. Math.	6% Compositio Math.
3% Ann. Math.	5% Trans. Am. Math. Soc.
3% Acta Math. Uppsala	5% Bull. Soc. Math. Fr.
2% Illinois J. Math.	4% Proc. Am. Math. Soc.
2% Comment. Math. Helv.	4% Math. Z.
2% Math. USSR Izvestija	4% Rocky Mtn. J. Math.
2% Michigan Math. J.	
1% J. Math. Anal. Appl.	3% Illinois J. Math.
1% Siam J. Math. Anal.	3% Siam Rev.
1% Inventiones Math.	3% Arch. Math. Basel
1% Arch. Rational Math. Mech.	2% Quart. J. Math. Oxf.
1% Z. Ang. Math. Mech.	1% J. Math. Anal. Appl.
1% Bull. Soc. Math. Fr.	1% Pacific J. Math.
1% J. Inst. Math. Appl.	1% Siam J. Appl. Math.
0% Am. J. Math.	1% Quart. Appl. Math.
0% Indiana J. Math.	1% Z. Ang. Math. Phys.
0% Commun. Pure Appl. Math.	0% Siam J. Math. Anal.
0% Arch. Math. Basel	0% J. Inst. Math. Appl.
0% Quart. Appl. Math.	

TABLE 4. Journals ranked by shares devoted to Complex and Harmonic Analysis, and Real and Abstract Analysis. Both pure and applied journals regularly feature Analysis, with pure journals leading in the first specialty and applied in the second.

COMPLEX AND HARMONIC ANALYSIS	REAL AND ABSTRACT ANALYSIS
21% Michigan Math. J.	42% Indiana J. Math.
21% Arch. Math. Basel	39% Arch. Math. Basel
19% Acta Math. Uppsala	37% Siam J. Math. Anal.
14% Comment. Math. Helv.	27% J. Math. Anal. Appl.
9% Pacific J. Math.	25% Proc. Am. Math. Soc.
9% Trans. Am. Math. Soc.	25% Pacific J. Math.
9% Duke Math. J.	24% Michigan Math. J.
	23% Math. USSR Izvestija
	22% Trans. Am. Math. Soc.
	22% Illinois J. Math.
7% Proc. Am. Math. Soc.	21% Duke Math. J.
7% Math. Z.	18% Math. Z.
7% Indiana J. Math.	18% Rocky Mtn. J. Math.
7% Math. USSR Izvestija	18% Dissertationes Math.
7% Rocky Mtn. J. Math.	17% Quart. J. Math. Oxf.
6% Illinois J. Math.	17% Advan. Math.
5% Commun. Pure Appl. Math.	15% Am. J. Math.
4% J. Math. Anal. Appl.	15% Bull. Soc. Math. Fr.
4% Arch. Rational Mech. Anal.	15% Acta Math. Uppsala
4% Am. J. Math.	13% Compositio Math.
4% Ann. Math.	
3% Siam J. Math. Anal.	9% Ann. Math.
3% Inventiones Math.	9% Siam Rev.
3% Advan. Math.	8% J. Inst. Math. Appl.
3% Z. Ang. Math. Phys.	7% Arch. Rational Mech. Anal.
3% Compositio Math.	7% Commun. Pure Appl. Math.
2% Quart. J. Math. Oxf.	6% Quart. Appl. Math.
2% Bull. Soc. Math. Fr.	4% Inventiones Math.
1% J. Inst. Math. Appl.	3% Siam J. Appl. Math.
1% Quart. Appl. Math.	3% Comment. Math. Helv.
1% Dissertationes Math.	3% Z. Ang. Math. Phys.
0% Siam J. Appl. Math.	
0% Siam Rev.	

set: *Zeitschrift fur Angewandte Mathematik und Physik*, *Quarterly Journal of Applied Mathematics, SIAM Journal of Applied Mathematics, SIAM Review*, *Archive for Rational Mechanics and Analysis*, *Journal of Mathematical Analysis and Applications* and *Communication on Pure and Applied Mathematics*. This collection of journals does not simply neglect algebra and group theory, algebraic geometry, and topology for the sake of a little more emphasis on the seven other specialty fields. Rather, as Table 2 suggests, this group concentrates on ordinary differential equations, partial differential equations, and applied mathematics.

These patterns of mutual emphasis and mutual devaluation are not accidental but rather reflect the current positions of pure mathematicians versus applied mathematicians on which mathematical specialties are worthwhile. Norwood states:

> Pure Mathematics asks, "What is? What different kinds of mathematical objects can exist? And how can we tell one when we have found one?
> It would be a mistake to conclude that mathematicians necessarily care whether a new discovery has some practical application. Mathematicians do what they do because it is beautiful, interesting, challenging.[17]

Norwood might put almost all geometry and topology into this description, as well as much of algebra save some areas like matrix algebra and parts of group theory.

The attitude of the applied mathematicians is represented most strongly by Kline, a former topologist whose feelings for pure mathematics are clear:

> Blinded by a century of ever purer mathematics, most mathematicians have lost the skill to read the book of nature. They have turned to fields such as Abstract Algebra and Topology, to abstractions and generalizations such as Functional Analysis, to existence proofs for differential quotations that are remote from applications, to axiomatizations of various bodies of thought, to arid brain games. Only a few still attempt to solve the most concrete problems, notably in Differential Equations and allied fields.[18]

While these two mathematicians cannot agree on which specialties are most valuable, they are likely to concur that pure workers dominate most general university mathematics departments and, thus, most general research journals. Norwood reports that much of statistics and computer science has broken away from mathematics (to become the responsibility of independent departments in larger academic institutions). Similarly, there have come to be many essentially independent journals devoted to those offshoots of mathematics. Kline reports that much of the best applied mathematics is done by other independent specialists as physicists and electrical engineers in their own departments and in some of their own journals. Still there are the minority applied mathematicians working in Pure Mathematics departments as well as closet purists at institutes of technology and schools of engineering. As fate and American library administration would have it, all these factions are often lumped together in the same science branch library with the same science librarian buying for them all.

Is there a way to determine quickly the pure or applied orientation of a journal, as a preliminary step in journal selection? The obvious marker is the word "applied" in the title or sponsoring agency's name. The Society for Industrial and Applied Mathematics (SIAM) and its journals were founded in strong reaction to the sense of isolation and perhaps even scorn founded in strong reaction to the sense of isolation and perhaps even scorn felt by applied workers from the American Mathematical Society and its journals. In addition to SIAM journals, the "applied" marker works well for journals such as *Communications on Pure and Applied Mathematics*, *Zeitschrift fur Angewandte Mathematik und Physik*, and the *Journal of Mathematical Analysis and Applications*. But the suggested marker is scarcely infallible. The *Journal fur die Reine und Angewandte Mathematik* is strongly oriented toward pure mathematics. And journals such as the *Rocky Mountain Journal of Mathematics* and the *Indiana University Mathematics Journal* contain much applied mathematics while lacking the "applied" marker altogether.

The distribution of journals over the other four specialty fields (mathematical foundations, differential geometry, complex and harmonic analysis, real and abstract analysis) does not display the same degree of polarity of pure vs. applied journals as the two sets of three specialties discussed above. (See Table 3.)

Mathematical foundations is a predominantly pure area that produces papers for journals such as the *Quarterly Journal of Mathematics*, Proceedings of the American Mathematical Society, *Pacific Journal of Mathematics*, and *Mathematische Zeitschrift*. Interestingly, the top one-third of journals for this specialty also includes two SIAM journals, while the *Rocky Mountain Journal of Mathematics* is in the middle one-third. A reason for this is the increasing applicability of combinatorics. A few journals otherwise regarded as pure show extremely low interest in mathematic foundations: *Inventiones Mathematicae*, *Bulletin de la Societe Mathematique de France*, and the *American Journal of Mathematics*. Thus, in this specialty the pure versus applied polarity is not complete.

Differential geometry is also a predominantly pure field. Its top third journals include *Inventiones Mathematicae*, *Commentarii Mathematici Helvetici* and *Annals of Mathematics*. Yet there are some surprising journals in the top third: *Communication on Pure and Applied Mathematics*, *Indiana University Journal of Mathematics*, and *Archive for Rational Mechanics and Analysis*. One reason for this intermingling between journals is that differential geometry can involve the use of differential equations. Also, there is a small vanguard of theoretical and mathematical physicists who hope to introduce this specialty to applications oriented audiences. The pure journals *(Illinois Journal of Mathematics*, *Arkiv for Mathematik*, *Quarterly Journal of Mathematics*, *Pacific Journal of Mathematics*) have surprisingly low representation in differential geometry. Again, polarization is not complete.

It is when we come to the enormous field of analysis that we see fairly cosmopolitan concerns form both pure and applied mathematicians. (See Table 4.) In the complex and harmonic analysis specialty it is still true that there is an academic flavor of predominantly pure journals in its top third, such as the *Michigan Mathematical Journal*, *Arkiv of Mathematik*, *Acta Mathematica*, and *Commentarii Mathematici Helvetici*. However, those journals noted for leaning to more applicable fields all make a good showing in the second third of complex and harmonic analysis: *Indiana University Journal of Mathematics*, *Rocky Mountain Journal of Mathematics*, *Communications on Pure and Applied Mathematics, Archive for Rationale Mechanics and Analysis*, the *Journal of Mathematical Analysis and Applications*. The other specialty of analysis is real and abstract analysis, and its top third is dominated by the journals in the second third of complex and harmonic analysis, plus the *SIAM Journal on Mathematical Analysis.* Also in the top third of real and abstract analysis are the purer *Proceedings and Transactions of the American Mathematical Society*, the *Pacific Journal of Mathematics*, *Michigan Mathematical Journal*, and *Duke Mathematical Journal*. This joint interest in real and abstract analysis is not accidental, for analysis is the last frequently used meeting ground of pure and applied mathematics, a fact acknowledged inside the cover of every issue of the *SIAM Journal on Mathematical Analysis*:

> [This journal] contains research articles on the part of Analysis which bridges pure mathematics and numerical, physical, and engineering applications. Topics include Asymptotic Analysis, Generalized Functions, Harmonic Analysis, Integral Transforms, and Special Functions.

This wide range of papers in analysis leaves the librarian in a good news/bad news situation. The good news is that almost any journal, except some extremely pure and some extremely applied journals, is likely to have some analysis content, and so the chance of making a radical selection mistake is rare in this specialty. The bad news is that the librarian must buy a lot of journals to get the same level of overage in analysis as might be gotten in less diffused fields requiring only a few strongly biased journals.

PRACTICALITY AND RELIABILITY

Reasonable questions can be asked about our approach. Are the time and expense worth the kind of selection data gathered? Must all eight years of a journals' content be studied? Are the underlying subject emphases of these journals likely to remain the same after an analysis is completed?

In the first instance, the task is so uncomplicated that the analysis of a journal can be assigned to a clerk and completed in several hours. It is not even necessary to have immediate access to a complete run of the journal. The clerk can work from tables of contents obtained via interlibrary loan. Alternatively, the procedure can be done online without using even the printed tables of contents. For our paper we analyzed eight years of *Zeitschrift fur Angewandte Mathematik und Physik* using MATHFILE, the online counterpart of *MR*. Compare our online investment of 27 minutes and $27.50 with the journal's current annual subscription rate of $262.

In the second instance, the time span of papers to be studied in a journal cannot be specified uniformly for all journals. Patterns of subject emphasis can be determined reliably only when enough articles are examined. As a rule of thumb, we suggest that two years of a journal, or 200 articles, whichever supplied fewer articles, should be sufficient.

In the third instance, the stability of subject analysis cannot be guaranteed, but there are three reassuring factors. First, consider that many of these journals have loyal clienteles who would be unlikely to support radical subject shifts. A good example would be the membership of SIAM, which worked so hard to establish journals emphasizing its particular interests. Second, the stability of editorial boards favor slow change. Many editors appear to serve quite long terms, and they tend to attract papers from authors who understand what subjects are likely to interest those editors. Even the selection of new editors is a gradual process. Candidates for an editorship are likely to include authors who have shown interest in the journal through their pattern of successful manuscript submissions appropriate to the journal's subject. Third, consider the rather tardy appearance of papers in many of these journals. For example, papers appearing in the January 1983 issue of *Annals of Mathematics* were submitted as long ago as January 1981. Many journals seem to have up to two years of backlogs of already accepted articles. Therefore, the evidence of an unlikely radical shift might take a couple of years to appear in print.

A FINAL WORD

While the authors feel that for the particular circumstances described our method offers advantages over the consulting of standard buying guides or the use of citation indexing data, we suggest that a combination of all these methods is likely to make for the most informative selection decisions.

NOTES

1. See: Hirsch, Morris W. *Differential geometry*. New York: Springer Verlag; 1976: p. 169.

2. Stankus, Tony; Schlessinger, Rashelle; Schlessinger, Bernard S. English language trends in German basic science journals: a potential collection tool. *Science & Technology Libraries*, 1(3): 55-66; 1981 Spring.

3. Stankus, Tony. Collection development: journals for biochemists. *Special Collections*, 1(2): 51-74; 1981 Winter. (See particularly the discussion on pages 57-60 and the summation at the bottom of Table 2.)

4. Stankus, Tony; Rice, Barbara. Handle with care: use and citation data for science journal management. *Collection Management*, 4(1/2): 95-110; 1982 Spring/Summer.

5. Garfield, Eugene. *Citation indexing – its theory and application in science, technology, and humanities*. New York: Wiley; 1979: Chapter 9.

6. Garfield, Eugene. Highly cited papers in mathematics. Part 1. Pure mathematics. Part 2. Applied mathematics. *Essays of an information scientist*. Philadelphia: Institute for Scientific Information: 1977; p. 504-13.

7. Garfield, Eugene, Journal citation studies, 36. Pure and applied mathematics journals: what they cite and vice-versa. *Current Contents*, 23(15): 5-13; 1982 April 12.
8. See: Katz, Bill; Katz, Linda Sternberg. *Magazines for libraries*. 4th ed. New York: Bowker; 1982: p. 633-41.
9. Malinowsky, H. Robert; Richardson, Jeanne M. *Science and engineering literature; a guide to reference sources*. 3d ed. Littleton, CO: Libraries Unlimited; 1980; Chapter 4.
10. Chen, Ching-Chi. *Scientific and technical information sources*. Cambridge, MA: MIT Press; 1977: p. 359-360.
11. Subramanyam, Krishna. *Scientific and technical information resources*. New York: Marcel Dekker; 1981: Chapter 18.
12. Pemberton, John E. *How to find out in mathematics*. Oxford Pergamon: 1970.
13. Dorling, A. R. *Use of mathematical literature*. London: Butterworths; 1977: Chapter 2.
14. Dick, Elie M. *Current information sources in mathematics: an annotated guide to books and periodicals, 1960-72*. Littleton, CO: Libraries Unlimited; 1973: p. 240-51.
15. Kusma, Taissa T. Computerization of *Mathematical Reviews* into MATHFILE. *Science & Technology Libraries*, 3(1): 49-62; 1982 Fall.
16. Diodato, Virgil P. Author indexing. *Special Libraries*, 72(4): 361-9; 1981 October.
17. Norwood, Rick. In abstract terrain. *The Sciences*, 22(9): 12-18; 1982 December.
18. Kline, Morris. *Mathematics: the loss of certainty*. New York: Oxford; 1980; Chapter XIII.

Appendix A.

Correspondence Between Specialty Categories and

Mathematical Reviews Classification Codes

Stankus/Diodato Specialty Categories	*MR* Classification Codes
1. Mathematical Foundations	00 through 08
2. Algebra and Group Theory	10,15,16,17,18,20
3. Algebraic Geometry	12,13,14,32
4. Complex and Harmonic Analysis	30,31,43
5. Ordinary Differential Equations	34
6. Partial Differential Equations	35
7. Real and Abstract Analysis	26,28,40,41,42
	44,45,46,47,56
8. Differential Geometry	53,58
9. Topology	22,54,55,57
10. Applied Mathematics	all others

Appendix B.

The Number of Articles per Specialty in Each Journal, 1972-1979

	Stankus/Diodato Category										
	1	2	3	4	5	6	7	8	9	10	Tot
Acta Mathematica (Uppsala)	4	14	20	27	1	9	21	19	16	13	144
Advances in Mathematics	38	57	30	11	8	15	61	28	21	82	351
American Journal of Mathematics	2	54	142	18	5	10	69	43	93	12	448
Annals of Mathematics	10	51	79	13	1	5	30	46	86	17	338
Archive for Rational Mechanics and Analysis	3	2	1	20	36	101	30	29	0	228	450
Arkiv for Mathematik (Basel)	0	11	10	31	1	16	57	5	1	13	145
Bulletin de la Societe Mathematique de France	1	34	69	4	0	2	25	8	17	12	172
Commentarii Mathematici Helvetici	7	55	38	42	2	2	10	47	89	18	310
Communications on Pure and Applied Mathematics	1	42	5	13	17	61	17	23	2	63	244
Compositio Mathematica	11	62	79	7	1	3	36	16	52	5	272
Dissertationes Mathematicae	15	7	1	1	1	1	13	5	19	10	73
Duke Mathematical Journal	22	71	95	47	4	29	112	35	92	26	533
Illinois Journal of Mathematics	9	114	31	27	4	5	94	13	122	16	435

Appendix B. (Continued)

The Number of Articles per Specialty in Each Journal, 1972-1979

	Stankus/Diodato Category										
	1	2	3	4	5	6	7	8	9	10	Tot
Indiana University Mathematics Journal	2	16	27	45	16	91	280	49	59	80	665
Inventiones Mathematicae	4	83	219	16	3	5	25	88	89	27	559
Journal of Mathematical Analysis and Applications	24	33	4	66	273	151	481	23	30	722	1807
Journal of the Institute of Mathematics and its Applications	1	4	1	4	14	8	34	0	1	355	422
Mathematics of the USSR - Izvestija	7	76	120	33	16	20	108	30	34	29	473
Mathematische Zeitschrift	77	351	94	89	25	78	226	55	124	111	1230
Michigan Mathematical Journal	6	33	30	72	3	3	80	19	91	3	340
Pacific Journal of Mathematics	150	481	205	221	68	28	610	20	478	138	2399
Proceedings of the American Mathematical Society	243	736	399	304	151	82	1042	173	842	213	4185
Quarterly of Applied Mathematics	1	0	3	2	19	30	14	3	0	156	228
Quarterly Journal of Mathematics (Oxford)	34	91	24	9	26	9	62	7	85	13	360

Appendix B. (Continued)

The Number of Articles per Specialty in Each Journal, 1972-1979

	Stankus/Diodato Category										
	1	2	3	4	5	6	7	8	9	10	Tot
Rocky Mountain Journal of Mathematics	11	58	32	33	37	24	80	16	53	101	445
SIAM Journal on Applied Mathematics	51	68	4	2	83	57	28	7	4	549	853
SIAM Journal on Mathematical Analysis	7	6	2	23	142	95	264	3	4	167	713
SIAM Review	8	5	1	0	18	13	16	6	0	105	172
Transactions of the American Mathematical Society	139	327	200	209	67	61	493	121	489	154	2260
Zeitschrift fur Angewandte Mathematik und Physik	3	6	0	8	12	40	10	3	2	222	306
Total	891	2948	1965	1397	1054	1054	4428	940	2995	3660	21332

THEME FOUR

Perennial Discussions Involving Journals

Observers of the journal world are unlikely to ever go out of business. Not unlike the case of law and lawyers, every point of journal behavior or use is argued voluminously and yet still seems able to be appealed. Librarians feel compelled to define laws and manage collections by them. It's a quest for reassurance. The following papers represent momentary resolutions of some controversies for at least the times for which the articles were written. Andy Warhol said that we were all coming to a point where anyone can be a celebrity for fifteen minutes. I hope the worth of these papers endures somewhat longer than that.

Looking for Tutors and Brokers: Comparing the Expectations of Book and Journal Evaluators

Tony Stankus

Library collections contain information resources in a variety of different formats. Two of the principal physical forms in which libraries collect information are books and journals. In traditional libraries, these comprise the bulk if not the whole of all holdings.

Evaluating books and journals inevitably raises questions. What criteria do evaluators apply, with equal emphasis to both formats? Which qualities seem to be more sought after in one format or another? Perhaps equally important, when do the differences among the literatures of science and technology, the social sciences and the humanities affect what evaluators feel they should see? Are the pitfalls to be avoided in selecting or retaining a given library item the same whether it is a book or a journal? What is the basis for making distinctions?

This author believes that some answers can be found by tabulating and comparing the critical comments made by book and journal reviewers in a leading selection guide, *Choice*[1] a work that also serves as a basis for the leading retrospective evaluation checklist—i.e., *Books for College Libraries*.[2] This approach and these particular guides have insights beyond academic libraries. Bonn reminds us that college libraries face formal and frequent evaluation procedures with general implications for other libraries.[3] This study helps identify basic criteria for those examiners who are evaluating a collection by the direct inspection of recent acquisitions and ongoing subscriptions.

METHODOLOGY OF THE STUDY

One thousand book reviews appearing in *Choice* between February and September 1983, were analyzed for explicit emphasis in praise or complaint, yielding 1996 comments. Two hundred forty journal re-

Reprinted with permission from *Library Trends*, volume 33, number 3, pages 99-104, 1985.

views, appearing between September 1974 and August 1983 were similarly examined in *Choice*'s "Periodicals for College Libraries" column, excepting that greater allowance was made for implied criticisms. This latitude in evaluating comments and the greater time span were necessary because substantially fewer reviews of journals appeared in each issue and the researcher wished to reach a more comparable number of comments – 1044 in all – for this format. While only the most explicit comments were allowed for in reviews of books, a lengthier examination of journal reviews ferreted out the criticisms of journals. Most journal reviews are longer than book reviews, providing more potential material – positive and negative – on journals. The discussions that follow treat remarks in approximate order of their importance, and in the tables, the remarks are organized first by discipline and then according to specific comments made in the reviews. The percentages in parentheses following each comment represent its share of the total number of comments for books or journals in that field (see Tables 1 and 2).

POSITIVE EXPECTATIONS FOR BOTH BOOKS AND JOURNALS

Well-Written, Readable, Accessible and Interesting to Undergraduates

Both book and journal reviewers mention these qualities frequently. They placed first or second in book reviews across all disciplines and were similarly first or third among journal reviews. These criteria are at the core of *Choice*'s philosophy: good materials that will be used by undergraduates. Contents must be clearly presented in terms this level of reader can understand, and done so in such a way that he or she will be attracted and sustain interest.

Features Chapters or Articles With Useful Bibliographies, Bibliographic Essays, etc.

Reviewers tended to regard favorably books or journals which helped readers find additional material on the topic discussed in the work. Further complimentary remarks were made if the bibliographies seemed especially current, complete or featured annotations.

Good Layout, Illustrations, Typography, Binding

A surprising number of comments dealt with the quality of book or journal design and production. This was more understandable in the

TABLE 1
1472 FRANK, POSITIVE COMMENTS IN 1000 BOOK REVIEWS RANKED BY IMPORTANCE IN DISCIPLINARY CATEGORIES

Science & Technology (334 titles)	*Social Sciences (333 titles)*	*Humanities (333 titles)*
Good bibliographies & indexes (20%)	Well-written, readable,33 accessible, interesting (15%)	New slant on old material (16%)
Well-written, readable, accessible, interesting (16%)	Superior analysis, well-documented (13%)	Well-written, readable, accessible, interesting (10%)
Good layout, illus., figures, binding, etc. (14%)	New slant on old material (11%)	Good layout, illus., figures, binding, etc. (8%)
Author's, publisher's credentials, reputation (12%)	Good bibliographies & indexes (9%)	Good bibliographies & indexes (8%)
Comprehensiveness (10%)	Author's, publisher's credentials, reputation (7%)	Highly current, topical (8%)
Logical progression of topics, good examples (9%)	Comprehensiveness (6%)	Superior analysis (7%)
Highly current, topical (4%)	Highly current, topical (5%)	Author's, publisher's credentials, reputation (7%)
Misc. comments (15%)	Better than other works in field (4%)	Best edition of several available (6%)
	Misc. comments (30%)	Multidisciplinary (5%)
		Misc. comments (20%)

Source: *Choice* 20-21(Feb.-Sept. 1983)

case of books and journals in the arts and science technology fields where illustrations are often critical to clear understanding of the text. Nevertheless, reviewers in such humanities subjects as theology and literature also stressed visual details, even though illustrations are rarely crucial in those fields. Their comments tended to show some appreciation for the physical book or journal issue as an art form that should be suitably matched to the well-crafted writing it contained.

Authors, Editors, or Publishers are Famous or Well-Credentialed

Book reviewers almost always gave the current university affiliation and/or academic pedigree of authors, often mentioning their earlier publications. Similarly, journal reviewers tended to mention the name and background of the chief editor at least. In the humanities, particu-

TABLE 2
947 Frank and Implied Positive Comments in 240 Journal Reviews Ranked by Importance in Disciplinary Categories

Science & Technology (76 titles)	*Social Sciences (97 titles)*	*Humanities (67 titles)*
Well-written, readable, accessible, interesting (12%)	Well-written, readable, accessible, interesting (14%)	Editor's, contributor's credentials, reputation (14%)
Affiliated with major Institution or Prof. Soc. (11%)	Features book reviews, biblio. essays, etc. (11%)	Features book reviews, biblio. essays, etc. (8%)
Features book reviews, biblio. essays, etc. (8%)	Editor's, contributor's credentials, reputation (7%)	Wide variety of topics, broad surveys (7%)
Features regular columnists, news items, calendars, etc. (8%)	Features regular columnists, news items, calendars, etc. (7%)	Rigorous refereeing, responsible editing (7%)
Good layout, illus., figures, binding (8%)	Features theme issues (7%)	Multidisciplinary (6%)
Wide variety of topics, broad coverage (8%)	Wide variety of topics, broad coverage (7%)	Reviews of media, concerts, exhibits (6%)
Editor's, contributor's credentials, reputation (8%)	Multidisciplinary (7%)	Good layout, illus., figures, binding (6%)
Rigorous refereeing, responsible editing (7%)	Affiliated with major Institution or Prof. Soc. (7%)	Affiliated with major Institution or Prof. Soc. (6%)
Controversial correspondence replies to criticism (7%)	Serves special interest group or alternative views (5%)	Well-written, readable, accessible, interesting (6%)
Highly current, rapid publication (7%)	Rigorous refereeing, responsible editing (5%)	Features theme issues (5%)
A leader (7%)	Prints summaries of articles from other journals (4%)	Features interviews, biographical articles (5%)
Misc. comments (9%)	Misc. comments (19%)	Misc. comments (24%)

Source: *Choice* 11-20(Sept. 1974-Aug. 1983)

larly in literary small press reviews, it was common to list a string of recognizable contributors as well. Journal reviewers particularly emphasized publishers especially if they were professional or research societies. Book reviewers seem to favor university press productions.

Broad Coverage of Field, Comprehensiveness, Wide Variety of Topics Within Discipline

Book reviewers clearly favored titles that covered all the major points within the announced topic. Journal critics did not expect each issue to cover all the subdivisions of a discipline. Rather, they favorably recommended journals which regularly featured broad overview articles and which, through a variety of topics covered in each issue, would eventually cover the entire field over several issues.

Multidisciplinary Perspectives

Works which featured authors from differing academic or professional backgrounds were most frequently endorsed by book critics looking at materials with a humanities emphasis. To a lesser degree science and technology publications combined with a social science (or ethical) consciousness were also commended with regularity. In social sciences literature, an occasional combination with archaeology or literature received favorable notice.

Timeliness, High Currency

This quality was everywhere esteemed, although it took on different nuances across the disciplines. In the sciences it generally meant, "contains the latest developments." In the social sciences it often meant, "of use in some current controversy." In the humanities it often meant, "in time for a revival of interest in this topic." In some journals, an added meaning concerned quickly printing papers accepted for publication.

Leading Publication, Better Than Others in the Field, Superior Analysis

The notion of comparison and competition recurred in reviews of books in the social sciences and humanities and journals in science and technology. In the social sciences and humanities, where there often is a broad assortment of readable works on a given topic, critics felt obligated to assist librarians with fairly frank comparisons. By contrast, in science and technology book publishing, there may be less similarity among a smaller number of titles directed toward undergraduates and book-to-book comparisons seem less urgent. But science and technology journals provided a contrary example. Often there were several comparable titles in a field, all of them expensive. Economic pressures on serials budgets and the availability of published citation rates prompted reviewers to make comparisons among science and technology journals.

Serves Special Interest Groups or Alternative Viewpoints Well

Both book and journal reviewers seemed well aware that a library containing only totally balanced presentations on topics that are already popular, is itself biased in favor of the status quo. While journal reviewers seemed more readily inclined to recommend purchase of alternative viewpoint titles, book critics were prepared to go along only if a work called attention to its viewpoint with a certain polish and without clumsy distortion.

NEGATIVE EXPECTATIONS FOR BOTH BOOKS AND JOURNALS

Absurdly or Deceptively Biased

Book and journal critics have repeatedly registered disdain over awkwardly argued, biased works, particularly in the social sciences and humanities. Additionally, they generally did not recommend works that had a bias but did not clearly profess it in the front matter – e.g., preface, foreword, introduction – or by subtitling or other prominent methods. In the criticisms for science materials, bias had a different nuance. It meant neglect of one topic or theory for another in what purported to be a comprehensive treatment.

Second-Rate, Duplicated Functions of Better Works in an Already Crowded Field

Book and journal critics were particularly sensitive to titles that attempted to compete with already established works. To a certain degree, the reviews of the later works were almost always more exhaustive. The enumeration of advantages of the new title often included criticism of obsolescence in older books, or mention of some sort of stodginess in journal editorial policies. Weaknesses cited by book reviewers were suspicions that a kind of gutless, no-risk "cashing in on the wave" publishing venture was involved. Journal reviewers might pan a duplicative journal by saying that its papers were likely to have been rejected by the better journal(s) in the field.

Superficial Treatment of Topic

Books and journals in virtually all disciplines appeared to receive poor reviews for too shallow a treatment of their subject. Critics would note in a review that the book or the journal's articles might well be readable, but would not recommend it for a library collection that supported serious instruction or research.

Too Specialized, Too Advanced, Too Narrow a Geographic Focus

The reverse of superficiality—i.e., over-specialization—was also common as a negative comment. There were several variants by discipline. In science and technology fields, one meaning was, "the work is concerned with a subject only rarely dealt with in the undergraduate years." In the social sciences one might find this comment, "the title is dominated by authors from a consortium of lesser-known institutions focusing on problems peculiar to their locale." In the humanities these were elements of both variants when reviewers considered whether regional small press magazines were important, or when reviewers decided whether certain particularly esoteric symposia had enough introductory material to help undergraduates understand them, or enough background to provide them with a context.

Poor Layout, Print, Illustrations; Flimsy Binding, Skimpy Issues

In science, technology and humanities books, and in the journals of all disciplinary groups, a poor quality or overly meager physical product could expect to be criticized. This included details such as binding, even of individual issues. While there was some allowance made for products of underfinanced or inexperienced publishers, *Choice*'s reviewers had a distaste for typescript or camera-ready-copy publications. Interestingly, the 1970s and early 1980s saw many representatives of this speedy and economic, but often unattractive, genre. The advent of more widespread and more sophisticated office word processors with multisized and multistyled character fonts may reduce this aesthetic complaint, while retaining the original advantages in publishers' cost savings and speedy production.

Poor Internal Indexes; Not Yet Indexed by Others

While details of these criticisms understandably differed between books and journals, the central issue was the same—no matter how good the contents are, they cannot be easily and systematically explored without good finding guides. The value of books as ready reference tools is considerably diminished when terms they might define or tables they might offer are not indexed. Flipping through journal issues might provide some serendipitous insights for researchers, but might just as easily cause them to miss the original object of their research through inefficiency and frustration.

Excessive Price

While the frequency with which this complaint was made was surprising low – and possibly *Choice* and "Periodicals for College Libraries" may avoid reviewing extremely costly materials altogether – its occurrence usually was occasioned by a specific grievance. For books, the critics usually attacked the number of pages for the price. With journals there was a kind of vicious circle: there were too few potential specialists at a typical institution to merit the investment in the high subscription rate, which was due to the fewer subscribers over which costs could be spread.

EXPECTED OF BOOKS, BUT NOT FREQUENTLY OF JOURNALS

Logical Progression of Topics, Good Examples

Critics did not seem to expect journal issues to provide step-by-step instructional pieces; however, they noted this as a favorable characteristic of books. Examples and problem sets were also favored, particularly in science and technology fields.

New Slant on an Old Topic

Book critics noted this attribute most frequently when dealing with social science and humanities titles. While some science and technology books and articles in the journals of all disciplines were of similar character, the critics found book-length treatments especially commendable in this category. This receptivity may be due in part to the purposefully disarming "apologia for another book" with which most humanities and social science authors begin their works. Upon reading the better of these, critics seem willing to give authors the benefit of the doubt. Neither authors' justifications nor their works are likely to end. No interpretation ever seems final, nor are all social problems likely to disappear. The last book-length treatment of Shakespeare or unemployment is yet to be written. Evaluators will read each piece and judge it worthy of collection, largely, if it attempts to offer something new.

Handy Compendium

This attribute was rarely ascribed to journals, but was frequently mentioned in book reviews. While compendia may contain chapters or papers by a wide variety of authors on a central subject, the items discussed in connection with this comment typically were anthologies or collections of the writings of a single author. These compendia frequently have introductory or integrating essays, chronological tables, a biographical sketch of the author, and often a bibliography. Critics noted that compendia saved time in searching the literature and provided convenient reference matter, and they paid particularly close attention to just how representative the selection of writings was.

Best Edition of Several Available

While a comparative and competitive perspective was very common in most book and journal reviews, only among books could virtually identical texts be found. Critics found themselves comparing details such as the introduction, commentary, glosses, physical production, and price. (These are similar to the criteria used for compendia.) In the humanities, there might be a further critical examination of whether the version of the text was the earliest, most authentic, the one favored by the author, etc. Another critical inspection occurred when the edition was one of a standard publisher's series. Some mention usually was made of whether this particular volume met the standard of earlier numbers (see Tables 3 and 4).

NEGATIVE COMMENTS MORE COMMONLY MENTIONED WITH BOOKS

Verbosity, Turgid Argumentation

Book critics in all the disciplines savagely attached works with unnecessarily elaborate vocabulary or lines of reasoning that were bizarrely complicated. In many cases, the critics suggested this style cast suspicion on the author's understanding of the topic and ability to reason clearly, rather than indicating the topic was beyond an undergraduate's understanding. Journal critics rarely mentioned the difficulties of overly technical language or argumentation, perhaps conceding that sophistication in the topic was more likely to occur in professional research journals.

Obsolescence

Obsolescence was rarely criticized in reviews of journals, save for the delayed appearance of manuscripts submitted long before publication. Science, technology and social sciences books were closely examined for their currency, not only in facts and interpretations, but in

TABLE 3
524 FRANK, NEGATIVE COMMENTS IN 1,000 BOOK REVIEWS RANKED BY IMPORTANCE IN DISCIPLINARY CATEGORIES

Science & Technology (334 titles)	*Social Sciences (333 titles)*	*Humanities (333 titles)*
Bias, imbalance of topics (25%)	Flawed premises, failed argumentation (22%)	Flawed premises, failed argumentation (17%)
Misleading title, neglect of stated aims (14%)	Bias (12%)	Superficial treatment (13%)
Poor bibliographies & indexes (13%)	Verbosity, turgid argumentation (12%)	Bias (10%)
Superficial treatment (8%)	Superficial treatment (12%)	Superfluous work in already crowded field (10%)
Uneveness of contributions in multicontributor works (8%)	Overspecialized, too much background assumed, too narrow focus (8%)	Uneveness of contributions in multicontributor works (8%)
Obsolesence (8%)	Uneveness of contributions in multicontributor works (8%)	Self-indulgent, self-serving (6%)
Poor layout, illus., figures, binding (5%)	Superfluous work in already crowded field (8%)	Frequent or annoying errors of fact (6%)
Frequent or annoying errors of fact (5%)	Obsolescence (8%)	Poor bibliographies & indexes (5%)
Verbosity, turgid argumentation (5%)	Misleading title, neglect of stated aims (8%)	Poor layout, illus., figures, binding (5%)
Misc. comments (9%)	Misc. comments (2%)	Overspecialized, too much background assumed (4%)
		Misc. comments (16%)

Source: *Choice* 20-21(Feb.-Sept. 1983)

references as well. Obsolescence was usually a damning criticism and the guilty book often was not recommended.

Misleading Title, Neglect of Stated Aims

Book critics were quick to point out cases where the announced goals of the work were hardly dealt with in the text. Apart from concerns about wasting the reader's time or the library's money on an inappropriate title, there seemed to be doubts of the writer's competence to understand the problem or to advance a particular case beyond a mere statement of thesis.

Frequent or Annoying Errors of Fact

Critics felt that recurrent small errors detracted from the professionalism of a book. For example, they complained at the consistent mis-

TABLE 4
97 FRANK AND IMPLIED NEGATIVE COMMENTS IN 240 JOURNAL REVIEWS RANKED BY IMPORTANCE IN DISCIPLINARY CATEGORIES

Science & Technology (76 titles)	*Social Sciences (97 titles)*	*Humanities (67 titles)*
Overspecialized, too advanced (15%)	Bias (23%)	Bias (23%)
Not refereed, loosely edited (15%)	Overspecialized, too advanced (16%)	Too superficial (18%)
Predominantly staff written (11%)	Poor layout, print, illus., binding, etc. (12%)	Predominantly staff written (14%)
Second rate, duplicates better titles (11%)	Predominantly staff written (8%)	Irregular publishing schedule, chronically late (10%)
Poor layout, print, illus., binding, etc. (10%)	Not yet indexed (8%)	Overspecialized, too advanced (9%)
Not yet indexed (9%)	Too superficial (5%)	Second rate, duplicates better titles (9%)
Too superficial (5%)	Price excessive (5%)	Poor layout, print, illus., binding, etc. (9%)
Price excessive (5%)	Irregular publishing schedule, chronically late (5%)	Not yet indexed (8%)
Misc. comments (19%)	Misc. comments(18%)	

Source: *Choice* 11-20(Sept. 1974-Aug. 1983)

spelling of names, or repeated confusion over which of several people with similar names did what deeds on which dates. Repetition of an error was not always necessary to do damage to the writer's credibility. An incorrectly printed table of values could cause confusion for students using the table to work problems. Journals rarely seemed to get this sort of close scrutiny, but perhaps they have a self-checking device in being able to insert corrections in later issues.

Flawed Premises, Failed Argumentation

In *Choice*, only books were examined thoroughly enough to conclude whether or not the extended arguments they contained were valid—that is, in the opinion of the reviewer. When the reviewer disagreed with an author, one of two explanations was generally offered: the thesis was promising, but not convincingly argued; or the argumentation was eloquent, but the author had a poor case to begin with. It should be noted this category of criticism did not invariable end with a negative purchase recommendation. Reviewers seemed to feel that in some cases, lessons could be learned by the reader just in an exploration of the issues involved.

Unevenness of Chapters in Multicontributor Works

While journal critics have come to tolerate a certain variation in the style and length of papers in a journal issue, reviewers of multiauthored books perceive this as a lack of editorial control. This is somewhat unreasonable in light of the current critical favor for multidisciplinary works. It is not at all clear that authors from different traditions can be expected to use the same structure and pattern of argumentation and to bring in their chapters within a two- or three-page variation. However, book critics seem to suggest this is indeed possible within the confines of a single volume—and that a reader deserves no less.

Self-Indulgent, Self-Serving

Book-length works purporting to give "inside information"—including some memoirs and assisted biographies—were closely scrutinized for real substance, factual accuracy and potential importance to their fields. Works which tended to make their participant-author a hero, or which served as a chopping block for the author's enemies, or seemed to be attempts of family or friends to cash in on a favored topic of dubious value, generally were not recommended. According to *Choice*'s editors, many of the more obvious examples of the genre were not even selected for review.

EXPECTED OF JOURNALS BUT NOT FREQUENTLY OF BOOKS

Rigorously Refereed, Responsibly Edited

As a factor of quality, *Choice*'s critics often indicated whether or not a journal's research articles had been examined by experts. During the preliminary reading, these referees will suggest revisions in the texts before they appear, and indeed they will often reject poor material outright, thereby saving the reader's time and insuring a certain reliability in the journal's contents. While books certainly have editors who suggest revisions to authors, and who often reject book-length manuscripts, editors are usually full-time employees of the firm and not hand-picked experts in each field covered by each book. Book editors were rarely mentioned by *Choice*'s critics, and in fact, book editors' work and contributions of an author's colleagues in reading book manuscripts before publication seldom receive much attention outside of the author's preface. In contrast, while anonymous refereeing of individual articles in journals remains the norm, an increasing number of journals publish annual lists of the referees, nominally to thank them. In a real sense, this practice serves to alert the readership to what amounts to an extended editorial board of experts willing to associate themselves with the journal.

Features Current Book Reviews, Bibliographic Essays

While books are valued for their references and bibliographies, only journals are capable of current reviews on a continuing basis. Journals scored well with critics when their reviews were signed, fairly extensive, seriously prepared, evaluative, numerous, dealt with the most recently published titles, and appeared regularly.

Features Regular Columnists, News of the Field, Calendars of Professional Events, etc.

Journals often were expected by *Choice*'s critics to provide some items of general interest in each issue. This is partly a hedge against those times when no research papers appeal to a given reader, or, as is frequently the case with undergraduates, the reader has yet to develop full subject literacy. This task generally is given to permanent staff writers in larger circulation journals, or to contributing editors who turned out signed columns in each issue. These pieces can be monthly overviews of the profession, popularization of hot research topics, columns for teachers of the subject, editorials from the associations' president, news on governmental actions affecting the field, and others. Book reviews, already discussed, were the preeminent feature column noted by *Choice*'s journal critics, but each of the following kinds of columns merit some independent discussion.

Features Current Reviews of Nonprint Media and Entertainment

While there are certainly entire books consisting of reviews of films, concerts and exhibitions, *Choice*'s critics stated that publishing such reviews in journals had advantages of currency and continuity. While most such reviews understandably were in humanities journals, some social science and technology journals were cited for reviews of instructional audiovisual materials. Much as they did with book reviews, the critics tended to differentiate superior quality media reviews on the regularity of their inclusion and on the reviewers' sophistication in the media they reviewed.

Features Controversial Correspondence, Replies to Criticisms, Open Refereeing

Journals of all disciplines which published letters raising issues in their subject area, or more often letters criticizing previously published papers, were viewed as more lively. The effect may well be to make the reader feel part of the academic forum. The letters encourage the reader's impression that a given journal's articles are followed closely, and that their readers care enough, have sufficient credentials and a sense of obligation to offer competent feedback. A more recent trend in some social science journals, with which some of *Choice*'s critics were impressed, is the openly-refereed journal. Here articles are published along with the signed commentary of several reviewers. While this practice goes again the dominant tradition of anonymous review, it offers the advantage of beginning debate and discussion straightaway.

Features Interviews, Bibliographical Articles, or Obituaries

While there are certainly many book-length biographies of major figures, usually the well-established ones in most of the professions, there are many more article-length pieces on contemporary figures. If the interviewer is sharp, and the celebrity is candid, the piece increases a reader's sense of involvement in the field. Particularly in the humanities, interviews of literary figures, artists and performers by journal staff writers or by contributing editors received positive emphasis and special mention.

Features Abstracts, Summaries, or Reprints of Articles From Other Journals

While books that are essentially collections of articles reprinted from journals have been praised as "handy compendia," there is a parallel trend, for journal critics to praise journals that carry short summaries of papers published in other journals. Reviewers founded their praise on three premises: (1) the reader's time is saved; (2) awareness of the professional literature is increased; and (3) perceptions of the journals' involvement with the field are heightened.

Features Theme Issues

Journal criticism is not without contradictions. While a variety of papers and feature columns is still probably the favored approach for most journals, theme-issue journals are becoming increasingly popular. Ironically, accumulating papers on a single subject is the closest a journal comes to serving traditional book functions. Indeed, many journal publishers sell individual theme issues separately. Examples in our own profession include *Library Trends*, *Drexel Library Quarterly* and some Haworth Press titles such as *Science & Technology Libraries*, *Special Collections* and *The Reference Librarian*.

NEGATIVE CRITICISMS LEVELED PRIMARILY AT JOURNALS

Irregular Publishing Schedule, Chronically Late

While this complaint was noted by critics less frequently than expected by this author, when remarked upon it was seen as violating the currency attribute of journals. A certain dishonesty was suspected when there was doubling up of issues as numbers failed to appear. Books, of course, can be published later than their announced dates. But it is not quite as common or as easy to determine how late a book is since its cover rarely features its alleged day or month of issue or the date for which it was originally promised its readers.

Predominantly Written by Staff

Though it is considered praiseworthy that journals have staff written feature departments (just as book authors and editors were expected to be responsible for the entire contents of their works), there was some suspicion of academic journals whose research articles were overwhelmingly staff written. One underlying suspicion was of narrowness or bias of viewpoint. Another criticism questioned the "vanity publication" tinge of such works. A third suggestion was that the journal could not attract papers in sufficient quantity from its field.

WHY ARE EXPECTATIONS DIFFERENT?

Expectations of *Choice*'s reviewers for books and journals are different owing to a contrasting view of the proper functions of each format. The reviewers expect books to be *tutors*. Undergraduates spend an extended, important item of their formative lives with books. The book-as-tutor is expected to take its naive pupils slowly and systematically along a well-planned path, and therefore, the books-as-tutor must be as complete and balanced as possible. It cannot assume that the student will have read much in advance or its reading much concurrently. As is the case with a good tutor, the book will try to introduce the pupil to a new and enlarged view of some piece of the world. It will attempt to show off the best of a range of topics in the field, gathered together to save the student's time and to develop a sense of taste. The book-as-tutor expects the pupil to come back to it from time to time to be refreshed with reintroduction to old concepts in times of uncertainty with words that have been read before. While the book-as-tutor tries to be as up-to-date as possible at the time of its first meeting with the student, its strength is much more in reassurance than currency. The individual book-as-tutor probably will last longer in the memory and affections of its pupils than any other journal's articles.

Choice's reviewers see journals as *brokers*. The journal-as-broker is as much a vendor of pieces of information as anything else. The key to the journal-as-broker is the involvement of the student in the ongoing bustle of the professional world. The ideal journal-as-broker for *Choice*'s reviewers has in-house account representatives who, with their feature columns, vie with experts from field offices who come in more occasionally with their research papers to win the "commission" of students' attention. The editors are viewed as senior partners; for them, the preference of the student for any partner is to the benefit of the whole firm. Further, while the same editor seeks research articles of some durability, the nature of both the field and the publisher's self-interest is seen as dependent on student's valuing the most recent issues at least as much as an older one, and yet recognizing that the forthcoming issues will still need to be seen.

The journal-as-broker expects the student will also be reading other journals; there will have to be competition, issue after issue. The ultimate competition is not just for a continuing subscription; its is for the recruitment of the best of the students to become, themselves, contributors and editors. The identification of a scholar with a journal is held together less by the kind of affection engendered by the book-as-tutor – i.e., "first love" – as it is with repeated, mutually satisfying transactions at a particular brokerage.

Library collections require both tutors and brokers, just as readers want and need the particular qualities each has to offer. Though certain common threads should be present in both forms – i.e., readability, good writing, presence of bibliographies, well-respected authorship, thorough coverage of the field, timeliness, and quality of the physical productions – unique attributes exist that make the sum of the criteria by which they are judged differ considerably. Far from being interchangeable, this author believes books and journals function differently with their readers, each furnishing part of the total learning and information-seeking process integral to college and university settings as well as to other library environments.

NOTES

1. Association of College and Research Libraries. *Choice: Books for College Libraries*. Middletown, Conn.: ACRL, 1964 (This current review journal appears eleven times a year and should not be confused with the retrospective bibliography derived from it and published by the same American Library Association division.)

2. ______, "Introduction," In *Books for College Libraries: A Core Collection of 40,000 Titles*, vol. 1, pp. vii-x, Chicago: ALA, 1975.

3. Bonn, George S. "Evaluation of the Collection." *Library Trends* 22 (Jan. 1974): 265-304.

Handle With Care: Use and Citation Data for Science Journal Management

Tony Stankus
Barbara Rice

ABSTRACT. Science journal managers should exercise care in preparing data for testing correlations between use and citation data. Correlations should be sought only among journals of fairly similar subject specialty, scope, purpose, and language rather than among journals in a broad field, e.g., science overall. Either gross citation ranking or impact factor will usually correlate well with use, except in cases where a journal is either new or characteristically publishes a few papers. In these cases impact factor must be used in comparisons. In order for the comparisons to have statistical validity there should be relatively heavy overall use, an average of 25 potential borrowings per title in the subject specialty being analyzed. The authors present tables showing good correlations when these conditions are met and other tables showing poor correlations are analyzed in terms of unmet conditions.

INTRODUCTION

Studies ranking demonstrated use of science journals at many individual institutions have long been reported as aids in their purchase, cancellation and storage. Collection managers have hoped to find in citation data a compatible and perhaps more broadly based decision making tool, reasoning that the worldwide most cited journals should be the most used; the worldwide least cited journals; least used. If this correlation could be proven it might lessen one uncertainty inherent in use studies; lack of comparability of institutions. However, attempts to clearly demonstrate this have given contradictory results.

Campbell, in a very comprehensive study of science periodicals in

Reprinted from *Collection Management*, volume 4, numbers 1/2, pages 95-110, 1982.

Wolverhampton Polytechnic (England), did a citation analysis of papers, projects, and dissertation of staff and students.[2] Percentage of use by department correlated well with percentage of total citation by department. Broadus, in reviewing the information prior to 1977 about correlations between use and citation analysis in several fields including some sciences, concluded that "there do seem to be parallels between use of materials as indicated by citation patterns and as shown by studies of requests in libraries, especially in relation to the needs of people engaged in research."[1]

However, two recent studies have reported a low correlation between the frequency of use and frequency of citations of science journals. Scales[10] compared data gathered in an analysis of requests to the National Lending Library (Great Britain) with a preliminary version of Journal Citation Reports, *JCR*.[4] Spearman-Rank-Correlation-Coefficients were calculated and found to be .42 for the 50 most used journals and .26 for the 50 most cited. Only 16 titles were common to the lists of 50 most cited and 50 most used. Rice reported insignificant correlation between use in a large science collection with *JCR*.[9] Both studies compared lists of heavily used journals ranked by frequency of use with *JCR*'s ranking by number of citations.

CITATION/USE CORRELATIONS

Meaningful high correlations are not to be reliably expected when journals from different subject fields are grouped and ranked. Garfield advises caution in comparing journals from different disciplines in the introduction to every annual edition of *JCR*, pointing out that citation practices vary from field to field and that fields differ in the obsolescence rate of the literature.[6] In this article on significant journals of science he enlarges on this warning and contrasts journals in three scientific specialties; Botany, Astronomy/Astrophysics, and Mathematics.[7] "The differences in average impact and citation between the three illustrative categories indicate why comparisons between journals in different specialties may be invidious."[7]

Caution must still be exercised, even within specific subject fields. Journals which primarily report research results should not be compared to those which review the published literature or which serve to report summaries of conference talks. The languages of publication should ideally also be the same, particularly for linguistically limited Americans. Schmidt[11] has documented a frequent mix of professed respect but practiced avoidance of her institution's scientists for the

German language scientific literature while Stankus and co-workers[13] have reported the varying degrees and rates at which 37 highly cited or high impact German basic science journals are evolving towards English by way of reply. In most disciplines English language writers use and cite primarily English language materials. If the perceived language of publication is not the language of the user group, except a demonstrated use below that predicted by comparison with citation ranking.

Comparing gross citations in setting up correlations with demonstrated use works well if all the journals in the subject specialty are long established and publish approximately the same large (100+) number of papers annually. If, however, newer journals are included or if some of the journals publish markedly fewer papers impact factors are preferred. Through their dividing of gross citations by number of papers that could be cited, one can see whether low use is due to *either* of the above factors or to genuine, universal, low per-item interest.

Finally, the use-study/citation-data correlation is only valid if there is a relatively heavy use of journals in the particular subject field at the institution studied. this is necessary to provide for statistical validity and to avoid eccentricity. If for example, Dr. A of the "X" department consults Journal One much more than Journal Two we can say something about Dr. A. but little about "X" scientists and Journal One and Two as a whole. If Dr. A and twenty other "X" scientists at the same institution, barring collusion or narrow department-wide subspecialization, consult Journal One much more than Journal Two, we may have something to say about the larger picture as well. Ironically, if the department is in a field of widely divergent sub-specialties, or of a field not tremendously dependent on the journal form of literature, good correlations are not reliably obtained. In short, if the use of the journal literature is already low, low frequency of uses loses meaning in terms of differentially identifying them for cancellation or storage. But, in areas of high institutional activity, low use is reasonably suspect and citation data correlates well, perhaps predictively, in titles that should be eliminated.

EXAMPLES

We now rework the Rice[9] data in light of these conditions. Biochemistry presents a unique opportunity to test the restrictions on comparisons. See Table 1. Both the subject specialty as a whole and the

TABLE I
BIOCHEMISTRY JOURNALS

SUNYA Measured Use		JCR Gross Citations		JCR Impact Factors	
J. Biol. Chem.	202	J. Biol. Chem.	102670	J. Biol. Chem.	6.06
Biochim. Biophys. Acta	195	Biochim. Biophys. Acta	65311	Biochemistry, U.S.	4.91
Biochemistry, U.S.	108	Biochemistry	38027	Eur. J. Biochem.	3.81
Biochem. Biophys. Res. Commun.	70	Biochemical J.	35305	Biochem. Biophys. Res. Commun.	3.55
Arch. Biochem. Biophys.	68	Biochem. Biophys. Res. Commun.	30254	Biochem. J.	3.23
Biochem. J.	61	Eur. J. Biochem.	20452	Biochim. Biophys. Acta	3.71
Eur. J. Biochem.	51	Arch. Biochem. Biophys.	18770	FEBS Lett.	3.00
Analyt. Biochem.	32	FEBS Lett.	16399	Arch. Biochem. Biophys.	2.93
FEBS Lett.	31	Analyt. Biochem.	15131	Hoppe-Seylers Z. Physiol. Chem.	2.46
J. Biochem., Tokyo	23	J. Biochem., Tokyo	6406	Anal. Biochem.	2.30
Can. J. Biochem.	9	Hoppe-Seylers Z. Physiol. Chem.	3842*	J. Biochem., Tokyo	1.74
Hoppe-Seylers Z. Physiol. Chem.	4*	Can. J. Biochem.	3041	Can. J. Biochem.	1.54
Biochimie	3*	Biochimie	1610*	Ital. J. Biochem.	1.15*
Italian J. Biochem.	3*	Acta Biochim. Polonica	349*	Biochimie	1.11*
Acta Biochim. Biophys.	2*	Indian J. Biochem.	310*	Acta Biochimica Polonica	0.73*
Acta Biochim. Polonica	2*	Acta Biochim. Biophys.	220*	Indian J. Biochem.	0.47*
Biochemistry, USSR	1*	Italian J. Biochem.	205*	Acta Biochem. Biophys.	0.40*
Indian J. Biochem.	1*	Biochemistry, USSR	23*	Biochemistry, USSR	0.007*

SUNY A library are rich in biochemistry journals. Garfield reports that biochemists are very heavy publishers in the journal literature and cite it very heavily.[8] There are sufficient general biochemistry journals to construct a group free from sub-specialty journal, e.g., *Journal of Lipids*, review journals, e.g., *CRC Critical Reviews in Biochemistry*, and society meeting summary journals, e.g., *Biochemical Society Transactions*. All of the journals are several years old. While the range of numbers of papers is wide, only *Biochimie*, *Italian Journal of Biochemistry*, *Acta Biochimica et Biophysica*, *Acta Biochimica Polonica*, *Biochemistry USSR*, and the *Indian Journal of Biochemistry* are among the significantly lower article group. While several of these latter journals have some foreign language content, only *Biochimie* has a substantial current non-English content. Taken collectively, the 18 journals circulated 866 times for a statistical group average of 48.

Examination of Table 1 shows that correlations are excellent using both gross citations and impact factors, particularly at the low, cancellation-vulnerable range. Of the seven journals seeing so little use that photocopy provision would be allowable, six also have the low gross citations. (See titles marked by an asterisk.) The same six have low impact as well, indicating that it is likely that universal low interest is the problem, not age nor the fewer articles. The one anomaly is *Hoppe-Seylers* . . . This is partly explained by the actual foreign language history of the journal and partly by lingering impressions of it as such. Recall that unlike the reformatted *European Journal of Biochemistry*, with its English title, *Hoppe-Seylers* . . . as it appears in references probably connotes its past better than its present. In working terms all six of the other low use journals should be recommended for cancellation at this institution.

Cell Biology is presented in Table II. This represented another of the most active subject specialties circulating at SUNYA, a result consonant with Stankus' finding that biochemists publish in that field second only to their own.[12] While the number of journals in this comparison is smaller than for biochemistry, the members of this group are similar in subject specialty, scope, purpose, and language. Most of them are now several years old. *Cell* being an exception at four at the time of this study. While the range in number of papers in the journals is again wide, only *Cytobios* and *Cytologia* are among the very low paper output group. While several of the journals occasionally publish foreign language papers, they are all virtually English language. Taken collectively, the eight journals circulated 228 times for a statistical group average of 28.

Correlations are again excellent with both gross citations and impact

TABLE II
GENERAL CELL BIOLOGY JOURNALS

SUNYA Measured Use		JCR Gross Citations		JCR Impact Factors	
J. Cell Biol.	55	J. Cell Biol.	24156	Cell	12.933
Cell	35	Exp. Cell Res.	13501	J. Cell Biol.	8.102
J. Cell Physiol.	34	Cell	10057	J. Cell Physiol.	3.571
Exp. Cell Res.	27	J. Cell Physiol.	5770	Exp. Cell Res.	3.031
J. Cell Sci.	13	Cell Tissue Res.	3328	J. Cell Sci.	2.77
Cell Tiss. Res.	7	J. Cell Sci.	2951	Cell Tiss. Res.	1.870
Cytologia	6*	Cytologia	531*	Cytobios	.337*
Cytobios	4*	Cytobios	260*	Cytologia	.265*

factor, and again, particularly at the low, cancellation-vulnerable end. Both of the very low use items also have low gross citations. Their poor impact factors suggest that universal, low per item interest is the problem. In working terms, both are recommended for cancellation at this institution. Two other journals are of special interest. *Cell* was a relatively young journal at the time of this study and ranked third in gross citations. Its remarkable impact factor was perhaps a better indicator of its precociously high level of use. *Cell and Tissue Research* showed as a journal of passable interest in this institution and yet had fair gross citations and impact. *Cell and Tissue Research* is the reformatted, originally German language *Zeitschrift fuer Zellforschung und Mikroskopische Anatomie*.

Ecology is represented in Table III. While still a life science, ecology has few immediate ties to the previous two fields. The journals are again alike in subject, scope, and purpose. (*The Journal of Animal Ecology* represents the majority interest in the field and is not a small sub-specialty journal.) All of the journals are at least several years old, and all except *Ecological Monographs* publish about 100 papers annually. It published about 30 longer papers annually. While both *Oecologia* and *Oikos* have a foreign language past, and still some current foreign language activity, all of the group could be said to be predominantly English language. Taken collectively the seven journals circulated 251 times for a statistical group average of 36.

Correlations are again excellent. It is particularly reassuring that when the use data suggested that none of the journals was likely to be cancelled, the citation data correlated in an equally positive fashion. while *Oecologia* and *Oikos* were demonstrated to be marginal, they were not shown to relate as only a small fraction of the lower retainable journals, as was the case with Biochemistry and Cell Biology candidates for discard.

We will now move to cases where conditions are unmet, and correlations can be less clear and even unworkable in operational terms.

Table IV represents Geosciences, a field of some importance at SUNYA whose correlation preconditions nonetheless fail in a number of points. First, 32 journals in the SUNYA collection are not in the SCI database and cannot be studied by our method. Second, while all the journals in our current tables can be readily classified as being Geoscience, they are not all of similar subject and scope. It is not at all clear that *Geochimica et Cosmochimica Acta* and the *International Journal of Rock Mechanics and Mining Science* have the same constituency nor is it likely that *Mineralogical Magazine* and the *Journal of Geophysical Research* have similar scope. Garfield has discussed the

TABLE III
GENERAL ECOLOGY JOURNALS

SUNYA Measured Use		JCR Gross Citations		JCR Impact Factors	
Ecology	105	Ecology	4894	Ecol. Monogr.	3.800
Am. Nat.	67	Am. Nat.	3182	Am. Nat.	3.062
Ecol. Monogr.	28	J. Anim. Ecol.	1775	J. Anim. Ecol.	2.142
J. Ecol.	23	J. Ecol.	1544	Etology	1.606
J. Anim. Ecol.	11	Ecol. Monogr.	1426	Oecologia	1.365
Oecologia	9	Oecologia	1140	J. Ecol.	1.353
Oikos	8	Oikos	873	Oikos	.951

TABLE IV
GEOSCIENCE JOURNALS

SUNYA Measured Use		JCR Gross Citations		JCR Impact Factors	
Geol. Soc. Am. Bull.	97	J. Geophys. Res.	17657	J. Geophys. Res.	7.041
J. Geophys. Res.	77	Geochim. Cosmochim. Acta	5609	Geophys. Res. Lett	3.109*
AAPG Bull.	72	Geol. Soc. Am. Bull.	5515	J. Petrology	2.977
Earth Planet Sci. Lett.	59	Earth Planet Sci. Lett.	3879	Geochim. Cosmochim. Acta	2.942
Can. J. Earth Scis.	28	Am. Mineralog.	3113	Am. J. Sci.	2.804
Tectonophysics	27	Am. J. Sci.	2987	Earth Planet Scis. Lett.	2.260
Mineralog. Mag.	27	Planetary Space Scis.	2361*	Tectonophysics	1.919
Am. J. Sci.	22	Contrib. Mineralog. Petrolog.	2242	Geology	1.912
Geochim. Cosmoschim. Acta	22	J. Geol.	1906	Geol. Soc. Am. Bull.	1.912
Contrib. Mineralog. Petrolog.	18	Econ. Geol.	1858	Contrib. Mineralog. Petrolog.	1.824
Am. Mineralog.	18	Geophys. Res. Lett.	1790*	Quaternary Res.	1.744*
J. Geol.	17	AAPG Bull.	1679	Planetary Space Scis.	1.495*
Tellus	11	Can. J. Earth Scis.	1599	J. Geol.	1.378
Marine Geol.	9	Tectonophysics	1545	Marine Geol.	1.277
Econ. Geol.	7	Tellus	1422	Tellus	1.257
N.Z.J. Geol. Geophys.	6	J. Petrology	1241	Am. Mineralog.	1.253
J. Res. U.S. Geol. Surv.	6	Geology	936	Can. J. Earth Scis.	.980
J. Paleontol.	5	J. Paleomtol.	747	Econ. Geol.	.980
J. Petrology	5	Mineralog. Mag.	711	Sedimentology	.905*
Geol. Mag.	5	Ann. Geophys.	661*	Ann. Geophys.	.817*

TABLE IV (continued)

SUNYA Measured Use		JCR Gross Citations		JCR Impact Factors	
Geology	5	Marine Geol.	625	Int. J. Rock Mech. Mining Sci.	.784*
Planetary Space Scis.	4*	Quaternary Res.	618*	AAPG Bull.	.714
Pure Appl. Geophys.	4*	Pure Appl. Geophys.	536*	Pure Appl. Geophys.	.646*
World Oil	4*	Sedimentology	520*	J. Res. U.S. Geol. Surv.	.581
Engineer Geol.	3*	N.Z.J. Geol. Geophys.	498	N.Z.J. Geol. Geophys.	.537
Sedimentol.	3*	Geol. Mag.	475	Mineralog. Mag.	.520
Arch. Meteorol. Geophys. Bioklimat.	2*	Geotechnique	280*	Norsk Geol. Tidsskr.	.481*
Geophys. Res. Lett.	2*	J. Res. U.S. Geol. Surv.	275	J. Paleontol.	.455
Ann. Geophys.	1*	J. Geomag. Geoelectr.	252*	J. Geomag. Geoelectr.	.377*
Geotechnique	1*	Int. J. Rock Mech. Mining Sci.	182*	Geotechnique	.365*
Int. J. Rock Mech. Mining Sci.	1*	Norsk Geol. Tidsskr.	151*	Geol. Mag.	.330
J. Geomag. Geoelectr.	1*	Arch. Meteorol. Geophys. Bioklimat.	139*	Arch. Meteorol. Geophy. Bioklimat.	.125*
Norsk Geol. Tidsskr.	1*	World Oil	80*	Engineering Geol.	.105*
Quaternary Res.	1*	Engineering Geol.	27*	World Oil	.098*

problems of defining this field for citation analysis in detail.[6] Third, the ages and outputs of the journals vary widely. Some journals are as old as 150 years, others are six years old. Some journals produce 35-40 papers, others several hundred. Fourth, the 33 journals have a group circulation average of only 13.97 only half of our more successful study groups. Of the necessary conditions we have only the almost uniform dominance of English language publication.

Correlations overall are good. Several of the most used journals are also among the more cited and of higher impact factors. There are, however, several embarrassing problems that require lengthy and roundabout explanations. The low use data for *Geophysical Research Letters* and *Planetary and Space Sciences* does not correlate with either their high gross citations or high impact factors. While the age of *Geophysical Research Letters* at the time of the study (it was six), might explain its behavior, *Planetary and Space Sciences* was 21. *Quarternary Research* had a relatively good impact factor yet saw poor demonstrated use. While again this journal was young (10 years), equally young *Geology* and the *Journal of Research of the U.S. Geological Survey* did better. This is particularly puzzling, in light of poor impact factors for the last journal. Perhaps the latter two journals had a wider appeal through a broader subject scope. Yet, the specialized *AAPG Bulletin* saw a tremendous use beyond all of these journals and any citation-based predictions. The uncertainty of the additional analysis that this table required makes it a less reliable tool. While in operational terms it does predict some successful journals, it is less useful at the low use cancellation-vulnerable range. This Geosciences group must build up its record of use through more users or a longer record of use. This larger group should be broken into smaller groups of general or specialized journals of similar subject, scope and function with each group having of itself the high required group use average. We might then more reliably find good correlations between use and citation data. We might then say much more meaningfully, that the *Journal of Geophysical Research* does better in all respects than *Pure and Applied Geophysics* or that the *Journal of Geology* and *Geology* are likely to see similar use based on similar citation data or that *World Oil* can be predicted to see less use that the *AAPG Bulletin*.

Table V represents pure and applied mathematics exclusive of computer science journals. This table is of particular interest since Garfield reports that citations to mathematical literature are not dominated by the journal form of literature.[3] This is reflected in the very low journal use in this field at SUNYA. Thirty-four journals saw 93 uses for a group average of only 2.7. Several of the journals in the group are of distinctly specialized scope, including *Numerische Mathematik*,

TABLE V
PURE & APPLIED MATHEMATICS JOURNALS

SUNYA Measured Use		JCR Gross Citations		JCR Impact Factors	
Ann. Math.	12	Trans. Am. Math. Soc.	2824	Acta Math.	1.469*
Trans. Am. Math. Soc.	8	Ann. Math.	2410	Ann. Math.	1.340
Am. J. Math.	8	Proc. Am. Math. Soc.	1701	Mem. Am. Math. Soc.	1.314*
Proc. Am. Math. Soc.	6	Math. Ann.	1531	Commun. Pure Appl. Math.	1.257
Math. Ann.	5	Bull. Am. Math. Soc.	1247	Invent. Math.	1.185*
Numer. Math.	5	Math. Z.	1247*	Advan. Math.	1.120*
J. Math. Anal. Appl.	4*	J. Math. Anal. Appl.	1238*	SIAM J. Numer. Anal.	.799*
Advan. Math.	3*	Pacific J. Math.	1215*	Am. J. Math.	.750
Duke Math. J.	3*	Am. J. Math.	1155	Duke Math. J.	.734*
Mathematika	3*	Comptes Rendus A Math.	1044*	Numer. Math.	.727
Pacific J. Math.	3*	Commun. Pure Appl.	1018*	SIAM J. Control Optim.	.693
Bull. Am. Math. Soc.	2*	Math. Comput.	842*	Topology	.678*
Comment. Math. Helv.	2*	Duke Math. J.	765*	SIAM J. Appl. Math.	.673*
Comptes Rendus A Math.	2*	SIAM J. Appl. Math.	759*	Math. Comput.	.607*
Indiana U. Math. J.	2*	Numer. Math.	755	Math. Ann.	.576
J. Math. Soc. Jpn.	2*	Acta Math.	753*	Bull. Am. Math. Soc.	.527
Math. Syst. Theory	2*	SIAM J. Control Optim.	687*	Indiana U. Math. J.	.480*
Math. Z.	2*	SIAM J. Numer Anal.	685*	Trans. Am. Math. Soc.	.473
Mem. Am. Math. Soc.	2*	Invent. Math.	685*	Comment. Math. Helv.	.463*

TABLE V (continued)

SUNYA Measured Use		JCR Gross Citations		JCR Impact Factors	
SIAM J. Appl. Math.	2*	Can. J. Math.	669*	Math. Z.	.449*
Topology	2*	Topology	516*	Quart. J. Math.	.447*
Acta Math.	1*	Studia Math.	513*	J. Math. Anal. Appl.	.404*
Arch. Math.	1*	Advan. Math.	442*	Studia Math.	.391*
Can. J. Math.	1*	Arch. Math.	373*	J. Math. Soc. Jpn.	.352*
Commun. Pure Appl. Math.	1*	Comment. Math. Helv.	321*	Math. Syst. Theory	.298*
Invent. Math.	1*	Quart. J. Math.	309*	Mathematika	.298*
Math. Scand.	1*	Indiana U. J. Math.	338*	Comptes Rendus A Math.	.289
Math. Comput.	1*	Math. Scand.	295*	Pacific J. Math.	.257*
Math. USSR	1*	J. Math. Soc. Jpn.	274*	Can. J. Math.	.219*
Monatsh. Math.	1*	Mem. Am. Math. Soc.	246*	Arch. Math.	.212*
Quart.J. Math.	1*	Mathematika	201*	Proc. Am. Math. Soc.	.198
SIAM J. Control Optim.	1*	Math. USSR	158*	Math. Scand	.188*
SIAM J. Numer. Anal.	1*	Math. Syst. Theory	146*	Monatsh. Math.	.088*
Studia Math.	1*	Monatsh. Math.	106*	Math. USSR	.016*

Mathematical Systems Theory, and *Topology*. Some of the journals have a survey or tutorial format that borders on the review journal. Examples include *Acta Mathematica*. While most of these journals have been established for over ten years, the annual outputs vary. Journals like *Acta Mathematica*, the *Annals of Mathematics*, and the *Memoirs of the American Mathematical Society* regularly print less than 50 articles per year while both the *Proceedings* . . . and *Transactions of the American Mathematical Society*, *Journal of Mathematical Analysis and Applications*, the *Pacific Journal of Mathematics*, *Mathematische Annalen*, and the *Comptes Rendus.A. Sciences Mathematiques* are among those who regularly exceed 150 papers a year. Finally, while most of the West German based journals have a substantial English language component, Austrian, East German, and French journals are essentially foreign language vehicles.

Correlations in their inauspicious group are deceptively good when using gross citations and obviously poor when using impact factors. It first appears that gross citations are the best predictors of journal use in this field, but sheer bulk does almost as well. Of the journals with five uses or more and of those with three of four uses the *AMS Transaction and Proceedings*, *Mathematische Annalen*, the *Journal of Mathematical Analysis*, and the *Pacific Journal of Mathematics* are all among the very heaviest producers of articles. While this effect was seen in the Biochemistry journals as well, some of the less voluminous journals also did well. Regardless of bulk in that group, the heaviest cited also had good impact factors tending to assure us that quality per article was also involved. Checking the impact factors in this group, one finds that half of the journals with 3 or more uses do not have large impact factors. Few journals rank high in all three measures in this group—perhaps only the *Annals of Mathematics* is an unambiguous choice. Collection management decisions in this group also tend to be precarious for we might say that a given journal, for example the *Proceedings* . . . saw twice the use of *Advances in Mathematics*. This argument would be persuasive in an active use group like Biochemistry, but the working librarian would be hard pressed to cancel the latter journal on the basis of three less actual uses. We again stress that when overall use is low, differential diagnosis of the lowest users for cancellation is difficult to argue with assurance.

SUMMARY

The collection manager can find correlations between the use of his science journals and citation data if the following conditions are met:

1. Comparisons should be made only among journals of fairly similar subject scope, purpose, and language. If the journals are significantly different in these respects the correlation will be less likely found. Decisions to favor one journal very different from another will be based on a false comparison and misuse of citation data.
2. While using either gross citations or impact factors will usually yield good correlations, the latter measure helps the collection manager decide whether lower than expected use is due to modest article output, young publication history or the kind of genuine low-per-article interest that suggests cancellation or storage.
3. The correlation of the citation data of a subject specialty's journals and their use will reliably appear only if there is heavy journals use, perhaps a group average of 25 potential borrowings per included journal in that specialty at that institution. Otherwise the manager may find his records skewed by eccentricities of few or infrequent borrowers who are not characteristic of those specialists as a whole.

When these conditions are met, the correlations are likely to be clear. The manager can more confidently decide to cancel or store. If some of the conditions cannot be immediately met the manager must seek additional data over a longer period of time so as to have sufficient use to more carefully regroup his journal prior to reexamination. Both situations are portrayed here using actual data from a recent study in the literature.

NOTES

1. Broadus, Robert N., "Citation Analysis and Library Collection Building," in *Advances in Librarianship* 7 (1977), 299-333.

2. Campbell, M. B. M., "A Survey of the Use of Science Periodicals in Wolverhampton Polytechnic Library." *Research in Librarianship* 5 (May 1974): 39-71.

3. Garfield, Euguene, "Highly Cited Works in Mathematics," in *Essays of an Information Scientist* 1 (1977): 504-513.

4. Garfield, Eugene, ed. & compiler, *Science Citation Index, Journal Citation Reports*, Philadelphia: Institute for Scientific Information, 1976- , Annual.

5. *Ibid.*, "Introduction" (each annual volume).

6. Garfield, Eugene, "Journal Citation Studies X. Geology and Geophysics," in *Essays of an Information Scientist* 2 (1977): 102-106.

7. Garfield, Eugene, "Significant Journals of Science," *Nature* 264 (1976): 609-615.

8. Garfield, Euguene, "Trends in Biochemical Literature," *Trends in Biochemical Sciences* 4 (1979): 290-5.

9. Rice, Barbara, "Science Periodical Use Study," *The Serials Librarian* 4 (1979): 35-37.

10. Scales, Pauline A., "Citation Analysis as Indicators of the Use of Serials: A Compari-

son of Ranked Title Lists Produced by Citation Counting and from Use Data," *Journal of Documentation* 32, No. 1 (March 1976): 17-25.

11. Schmidt, Jean Mace, "Translation of Periodical Literature in Plant Pathology," *Special Libraries* 70 (1979): 12-17.

12. Stankus, Tony, "Collecting Biochemistry Serials," *Special Collections* 1 (1981).

13. Stankus, Tony, Schlessinger, Rashelle, and Schlessinger, Bernard, "English Language Trends in German Basic Science Journals: A Potential Collection Tool," *Science & Technology Libraries* 1 (1981).

Publication Quality Indicators for Tenure or Promotion Decisions: What Can the Librarian Ethically Report?

Barbara A. Rice
Tony Stankus

Academic faculties are becoming increasingly aware of the many capabilities of *Science Citation Index*,[1] *Social Sciences Citation Index*,[2] and *Arts & Humanities Citation Index*.[3] These indexes are used for subject searching, for obtaining lists of publications by a given author, for determining centers of certain types of research, for comparative evaluations of academic departments, and for evaluation of peers in tenure and promotion considerations. Although considerable controversy surrounds the use of citation counts for the latter practice, they *are* being used in such evaluations. It is not the purpose of this paper to reexamine or enter into the controversy surrounding the use of citation data in promotion or tenure considerations. The literature on this subject is voluminous. We wish to discuss the impact of online availability of citation data and provide information relating to provision and interpretation of search results by librarians. In addition, we recommend other types of information which the librarian should suggest to patrons in order to supplement citation data, or to be used when citation data is nonexistent or appears incomplete.

ONLINE CITATION SEARCHING

Until quite recently a patron wishing to determine whether or not a given author's works were cited could do a manual search of the appropriate citation index and come up with a tally, or more often, a tally and listing of who was citing the author being evaluated. In order to do

Reprinted with permission from *College and Research Libraries*, volume 44, number 2, pages 173-178, 1985. Copyright, the American Library Association.

an effective search it was necessary to understand how the index worked, and it is likely, although not guaranteed, that the searcher would read the introductory material to learn how to do the search and become aware of some of the difficulties inherent in compiling a listing which are due to the nature of the index. For example, in doing a manual search it is likely that the patron would become aware of the fact that only the first author is listed in the citation index and that, by tracing the citation to the source index, would realize that there might be more than one author of the same name. However, with the advent of online availability of these indexes, this is no longer the case. A patron can bring in a list of references, leave them with a searcher, and return to pick up the list of citations. Although Caldwell and Livingston[4] state that "citation indexes provide a way to determine how highly valued and widely read the research produced by your faculty is," we caution that the process is not as simple as running an online search, as these authors imply.

The librarian performing a citation search has an ethical responsibility to inform the patron of the nature of the citation index being searched, with the inherent limitations this places on the search. The patron should also be provided with information on known citation practices in the evaluation field and references to the literature, which give caveats relating to the application of the references obtained in evaluation procedures.

Before attempting the search, the searcher should discuss the list of references with the patron to ensure that it is complete, and that the patron understands the search process. It is frequently the case that the person gathering the information sends a graduate student to deliver the list and, if required by the library, participate in the search interview or search process. *The librarians should not permit this.* The limitations of the index and search capabilities are difficult to explain and the searcher should not assume that the student will convey all information to the requester.

During the interview the searcher should examine the submitted bibliography carefully to see that references are complete and that actual first authors are given. Cited items are listed only by the first author in the citation indexes. Therefore, simply doing a search to find items citing Jane A. Doe will find only those papers where she is second or third author unless the first author is provided.

Whether or not this is important is discussed by Garfield.[5] It is decidedly important that the requester know whether or not his bibliography is accurate in this respect and, if not, what qualifications this imposes on the search results.

The patron must also be made aware of the scope of the particular citation index being searched and be shown the list of journals covered. Each citation index covers the most heavily cited journals in each field covered, but there are certain academic specialties for which the source journals might not be a very comprehensive list of works citing the author being evaluated. A quick way to check is to see whether the author's own papers are listed in the journals as possible citations. If a majority are not, the searcher should advise the patron of the alternative strategies discussed later in this paper.

Another difficulty sometimes encountered is that the index cannot distinguish between two people having the same last name and first initial. who may be publishing during the same time period. The patron should understand the necessity for examining the search result carefully for entries that seem to be in a field different from the author being evaluated.

COMPARATIVE CITATION PRACTICES IN DIFFERENT FIELDS

As Garfield points out, "It certainly is improper to make comparisons between citation counts generated in different fields."[6] Not only are there differences with respect to the average number of citations in a given field, but there are differences with respect to the type of material cited, e.g., mathematicians cite books more often than chemists. *Science Citation Index* and *Social Sciences Citation Index* primarily examine journal sources for citations.

What then can the searcher give to the patron relating to citation practices in different fields? It is recommended that the user be given a reprint of Garfield's chapter entitled "Perspective on Citation Analysis of Scientists"[7] for a summary of known norms in the sciences. In actuality, limited information is available, but is should encourage the user to consider what norms should be used and what significance any raw number of citations, whether 0 to 5 or 500, means in the field where the information is supplied is to be used. The average annual citation rate for a scientific paper is only 1.7 and many papers published are not cited at all. Endler,[8] in studying Canadian psychologists using *Social Sciences Citation Index*, reports that during 1975, 40 percent of those studied had zero citations and three out of every five had two citations or less. "A disproportionately small number of individuals," Endler stated. A disproportionately large amount of citations and publications is accounted for by a disproportionately small number of individuals. Helmreich[9] also points out that there are large sex differences in citation rates among psychologists and analyzes possible causal factors.

If no norms are known for the candidate's field, it is conceivably possible to construct them using the following technique: the patron supplies a list of departments considered to be of comparable nature (e.g., size, national reputation, student body, etc.) Using the corporate source index of the appropriate citation index, the number of papers from each of these institutions is tallied. Then an average number of papers per faculty member can be obtained by dividing the total number of papers by the number of faculty. This could be done for one year, or preferably, for several years. Such techniques have been used for comparing institutions.[10,11,12] Alternatively, the records of only those faculty from these peer institutions whose specialization matches that of the candidates could be found.

As noted earlier, *Science Citation Index* and *Social Sciences Citation Index* examine predominantly journal sources for citations. Citations appearing in most books are not included, although books cited in the journals scanned are. Citation counts may or may not include citations to book reviews, and what would seem apparent here is that it is not as important to know whether or not there was a review, as it is to know what the review stated as to the quality and importance of the book being reviewed. A librarian should know the major review sources in any field and can assist the patron compiling the information for the promotion or tenure review to ferret out reviews should the candidate's vita include books as well as journals.

The searcher should inform the patron that a library staff member, knowledgeable in the use of citation indexes, is available to discuss the search results and interpret the results and other techniques which should be considered in order to obtain as complete information as possible on citations to the work of the individual being evaluated.

The use of the citation data in promotion and tenure processes has been urged as a quantitative, objective standard of evaluation. Given the little that is known about the norms, it does not seem that citation data is yet a wholly effective tool in this respect. What if no norms are known for the candidate's field? What if the candidate's publications are very recent and have not yet been cited, or cited comparatively little? What then? The librarian, in addition to supplying information on known norms, should suggest other information relating to the journals in which the candidate has published which can be of use in the evaluation process.

Information about the quality of the journals within which the candidate being evaluated has published can easily be supplied by librarians. An evaluator may wish to consider some or all of the following factors in addition to or in lieu of citation information.

- What is the purpose of the journal?
- Who publishes the journal?
- What types of articles does it carry?
- Who are the editors and referees?
- What role do the editors and referees play in the acceptance or publication process?
- What institutions are represented among contributors?
- Who are the individual contributors?

JOURNAL PURPOSE, PUBLISHER, AND TYPES OF PAPERS

Journals cited in the vita may be characterized by purpose, publisher background and specialization, and the nature of the papers being published. There are many for-profit firms, university press, and professional societies which are known to be quality publishers. Most librarians can list publisher of known repute in various academic disciplines. The librarian however, should not report unsubstantiated hearsay, but should instead gather factual information for analysis. This may be types of journals published, e.g., scholarly versus popular, general fields in which the publisher specializes, e.g., scientific, legal, etc., and the number of journals titles published. If the publisher is a society, then information on the society's membership and purpose should be reported.

The type(s) of paper(s) carried is also a consideration in evaluating the nature of the candidate's contribution. For example, is it a review journal or does it consist of original research contributions? Is it an informal news bulletin – an alumni journal, for example? Is the contribution of the candidate a full-length article? Book review? Brief communication? Letter to the editor? Are there special requirements for publication, e.g., membership or alumnus status? While some of this information may be known to the individual requesting the information, it may not all be known, nor may it be known uniformly through the department or by other persons or review bodies which are often involved in the evaluation process, such as a campus-wide promotion and tenure committee or the vice-president or president of the college or university. Sample of specific information which the librarian might compile follow.

1. *The Journal of "A" Studies*, founded in 1948, publishes about 200 eight-to-fifteen page contributed, original research papers each year in the general field indicated by the title. It also publishes monthly society personnel news, an editorial, five to ten book reviews, and job placement notices. It is sponsored by the Society for "A" Research and Treatment, located in New York, which has a membership of 12,000. Membership is open to those with an MD or PhD in an appropriate discipline who demonstrate an interest in the field and can provide references from two established members. Membership is not necessary for acceptance of an article, although members do not have to pay page charges. The candidate is a member and the publications 1 and 5 in this vita represent a research article of standard length for this journal and a standard length, 200-word book review, respectively.

2. *The "B" Review* has been published by the Midwestern University press since 1975. It is the only journal published by them. Each year it publishes approximately 30 twenty-to-forty-five-page surveys of recent developments in law and politics. Articles are written largely by its own students, faculty, and alumni. It appears on a trimester basis with the spring issue listing biographies of honorary-degree recipients the text of commencement speeches, and a directory of recent graduates. The candidate is an alumnus of this institution. His contribution, number 8 on the vita, is a letter to the editor criticizing the choice of an honorary degree recipient and rebutting that recipient's article in a prior issue.

3. *Acta "C" Internationalis* has been published since 1960 by Alexandrian Press, a for-profit scientific, technical, and medical publishing house which currently publishes about 300 journals in New York, Paris, London, and Vienna. *Acta "C" Internationalis* is a bimonthly organic chemistry journal which carries an annual total of approximately 70 twenty-to-twenty-five-page overviews of recent research, approximately 400 eight-to-twelve-page contributed articles, approximately 250 four-to-six-page brief communications, and approximately 300 paragraph abstracts of presentations at professional symposia in the field. Publications 1, 2 and 3 on this candidate's vita are abstracts from the symposia. Item 4 is a brief communication of the results announced in the first abstract, and item 5 is an article of standard length elaborating on the findings of the second and third abstracts.

JOURNAL RANKINGS AND REJECTION RATES

Another possible way of describing the importance of a given journal is to use *Journal Citation Reports*, an annual compilation which is part of *Science Citation Index* and *Social Services Citation Index*, which rank journals in several ranking packages, e.g., total citations and impact factor. The experiences of author Stankus working with use of impact factors to provide information on science journals in promotion and tenure decisions has been that stronger candidates have published in journals with relatively high impact factors.

Rejection rates are a piece of information that is not always readily available, but in some cases can be found by digging through the front matter of journals, or in the annual reports of publishing houses or societies. The information is usually available on request from the editor or publisher.

EDITORS, REFEREES, AND CONTRIBUTORS

Another important consideration in journal quality is the prestige of its editors and referees. While there is no guarantee that all members of an editorial board are actively involved in the journal or that stated refereeing policies are follow, information about the reputations of the editors and referees can be gathered from biographical directories. For example, *American Men and Women of Science* can supply an outline of factual information. A quick literature search can establish the extent of a given editor's or referee's own publication history. Compilations of academic institutional evaluations, e.g., Anderson & Roose's *Rating of Graduate Programs*, can give an idea of the degree of distinction of the program with which the editor or referee is affiliated. Some sample information that might be supplied follows.

1. The editors of *Journal "X"* are Jones, Harvard University; Smith, University of Chicago; and Johnson, University of California, Berkeley. Jones, Smith, and Johnson are all full professors in programs rated by Anderson and Roose as distinguished. Jones and Johnson are members of the National Academy of Sciences. Manuscripts are read by one of the editors plus two outside referees of his choosing.

2. *"Y" Journal* has more than sixty listed editors. A sampling shows that slightly more than half are affiliated with clinical programs

in drug and alcohol abuse, while the remainder are equally divided between highly rated schools of social work or psychology. Manuscripts are sent to the editor in chief who designates three of the editors as referees.

3. *The Yearbook of the "Z" State University Teaching Effectiveness Workshops* is edited by a committee drawn from the chairpersons of the departments of education at each of the university's branches. Workshop faculty and all working teachers who plan to attend furnish an outline of their presentation three months before the meeting for review by all members of the board. Approximately 10 percent are selected for general presentation at the meeting and subsequent printing in full in the yearbook. The remaining are accepted for poster presentations with subsequent printing as one-page summaries.

In addition to evaluating editors, all of whom may have been selected for high repute in their fields, it is also possible to sample contributors. Virtually every author makes some commitment to a journal by having submitted a paper to it. An author's choice of journals lives on in personal biographies which the author (if academic) is aware will be reviewed by tenure or promotion committees, for grant proposals, etc. In the aggregate, academic departments gain a reputation by publishing in the best journals, and the best journals are characterized by repeatedly publishing the work of the best departments. Consequently, librarians can use online techniques to sample departments to see which have contributed to a journal in which the candidate has published.

CONCLUSION

Academic librarians who are asked to supply information for tenure or promotion decisions have an ethical responsibility not only to supply the requested information but to educate the requester in the limitations of any search techniques used (manual or online) and the types of factual information that can be supplied. Librarians should require from requesters that they participate in the search process (especially in the case of online searches) and provide a clear statement of what is being asked for. The authors believe that the issue raised in this article merit serious discussion by academic librarians, which would result in statements of library policy with respect to library participation in provision of information to faculties for promotion or tenure consideration.

NOTES

1. *Science Citation Index* (Philadelphia: Institute for Scientific Information, 1961-).

2. *Social Sciences Citation Index* (Philadelphia: Institute for Scientific Information, 1973-).

3. *Arts and Humanities Citation Index* (Philadelphia: Institute for Scientific Information, 1980-).

4. Jane L. Caldwell and Celia S. Livingston, "On-Line Bibliometrics," *BRS Brief Paper Series*, no. 4.2 (Jan. 1980).

5. Eugene Garfield, "Perspective on Citation Analysis of Scientists" in his *Citation Indexing – Its Theory and Application in Science, Technology and Humanities* (New York: Wiley, 1979).

6. Ibid., p. 248.

7. Ibid.

8. Norman S. Endler, "Beyond Citation Counts: Developing Research Profiles," *Canadian Psychological Review* 19: 152-157 (1978).

9. Robert L. Helmreich and others, "Making It in Academic Psychology: Demographic and Personality Correlates of Attainment," *Journal of Personality and Social Psychology* 39:896-908 (Nov. 1980).

10. David Lewis Smith, Thomas Roche, and William Snizek, "Quality of Graduate Productivity on Sociology as Measured by the Citation Index: A Longitudinal Overview," *Research in Higher Education* 13:343-52 (1980).

11. Norman S. Endler, J. Phillippe Rushton and Henry L. Roediger III. "Productivity and Scholarly Impact (Citations) of British, Canadian and U.S. Departments of Psychology (1975)." *American Psychologist* 33:1064-82 (Dec. 1978).

12. Richard C. Anderson, Francis Narin, and Paul McAllister. "Publication Ratings versus Peer Ratings of Universities," *Journal of the American Society for Information Science* 29:91-103 (March 1978).

One Researcher, One Journal, One Research Paper: Workable Budgeting Schemes at the Science Departmental Level

Tony Stankus
William Littlefield

ABSTRACT. Published allocation plans for books may be inappropriate when dealing with research journals. Reasons can include inordinate complexity and a lack of focus on issues within departments. Librarians may be better able to cope with the more finite matter of subscription distribution based on either apportionment by specialists within the department or by the relative productivity of those specialists. A comparison of the outcomes of these two approaches in 50 U.S. chemistry departments is reported. Warnings are issued about the possible tyranny of a passive majority in a department as well as undue credit awarded for artificially inflated publication counts.

While many published budgetary schemes attempt to be fair, rationally based, and systematically derived, they tend to share one or more of the following drawbacks when it comes to research journal budgeting:[1]

A Bias Toward Books. The bulk of budgetary articles deal with purchasing monographs and have limited applicability to journals.

Giaganticism. These involve the global "big picture" viewpoint. They attempt to assign given shares to virtually every professional school, academic department, or research institute in

William C. Littlefield is Assistant to the Science Librarian at the Science Library, Swords Hall 100, College of the Holy Cross, 1 College Street, Worcester, MA 01610.

the generally large universities for which they are typically designed. Having gone that far, they rarely discuss dividing up the share between specialists or specialty groups within departments.

A Student Enrollment Basis. Most schemes are based in some part on student enrollment at various degree levels. A given large number of students is multiplied by some factor for their being bachelor degree candidates, a perhaps lesser number of master degree candidates is multiplied by an offsetting factor for their more sophisticated needs and so on, up through the doctorate or terminal professional degree. The problem is that faculty members in departments with few students may be required to publish just as much (if not more) as those in departments with many. True, the level of sophistication of the students at higher levels may have some effect on their ability to assist the professor in the laboratory but their numbers at lower levels are unlikely to affect the level of familiarity of the professor with the literature required for him to competently compose papers. There are few journals designated as the place for people who have only a master's degree program to publish. Nor are there "Instructions for Authors" that say: "You are excused from citing important papers in expensive journals if you teach at a bachelor-degree-only school. Nor has it been demonstrated that increasing enrollment should increase a professor's time or need for a given journal, or the ability of his students to read it."

Overly Elaborate Formulas and Models. In an attempt to substitute data for guesswork a growing number of formulae, even more complicated than the example above, have been derived. There are modifications based on whether the student in the equation is a major in a given discipline, or is in a neighboring discipline, or has a basic vs. an applied orientation, and so on. While each of these nuances makes sense individually, it is not clear that the aggregate formula is understandable or applicable.

Powerlessness of the Recipient of Complaints to Effect a Change in an Overall Budget. The working librarians who deal directly with customers and who are the first to hear about unfairness or inadequacy in collection outlays often have no personal authority to simply spend more. Their typical response is to report the disgruntlement to the head librarian. Yet he often cannot produce more money, and can suggest that he lacks special knowledge of the discipline, or does not wish to involve himself in the situation's politics.

The plan presented here seeks to correct some of these biases. It involves:

- An intended bias towards journals.
- An emphasis on dividing up allocations within the much smaller domain of individual departments on the basis of specialists or output of specialists.
- Recognition that the internal urges of the professor or the institutional pressure to publish drives journal use, not student enrollment figures. Reliance on simple arithmetic.
- Recognition that while it may be impossible to change the overall library budget or even to know the overall financial condition of the school, it may be possible to more equitably distribute the known amount of money coming to the department. The idea is one of lighting a single candle in the departmental lounge rather than cursing the darkness in the treasurer's vault.

A BASIC THESIS AND ITS SUPPOSITIONS

Library allotments for research journals for individual departments may be divided up fairly along two lines: by the number of specialists or by number of papers from those specialists. The assumptions and advantages of the first procedure include:

Assumption. The attractive notion that all specialists and specialties are created equal. Each deserves an equal share of the budget.
Ease of Determination. The librarian merely consults a directory or asks the individual to which specialty he wishes to be assigned, and does some division.
Ease of Defense. Disgruntled faculty may be referred to their departmental peers whenever they wish to argue that they or their needs are more valuable.
Flexibility. As long as there are not truly volcanic personnel changes on a regular basis, the arrival and departure of specialty faculty can be readily accommodated.

The second procedure involves:

Assumption. The notion that budgets reward the most productive specialists, who, simplistically, are those who get the most papers published. This involves the less universal notion that all papers are created equal. While this would seem ridiculous in comparing persons from different fields, a certain comparability of publication numbers and practices might be expected within members of the same disciplinary tradition and department.

Ease of Calculation. The librarian keeps accounts of which specialists are publishing and of the number of papers that accrue to each.

Ease of Defense. The disgruntled faculty member may again be referred to his peers if he wishes to argue that his fewer or less frequent papers are more worthy than those of his colleagues.

Flexibility. A librarian could easily adjust journal investment to journal productivity. Indeed this approach is more amenable to periodic review in that changes in the production of papers may occur more often than changes in the composition of the faculty.

A SHARED DISADVANTAGE

Both of these approaches suffer from two liabilities that are treated by some other budgetary schemes. Neither takes into account the fact that the number of journals devoted to given specialties varies with the specialty. Nor is there adjustment for the fact that the journals of some specialties cost more than others. The percentages yielded in either procedure may say more about relative share of budget than the exact number of titles or dollar amounts allotted.

COMPARING RESULTS OF THE TWO APPROACHES IN A LARGE SAMPLE

With a goal of identifying the "middle class" of U.S. chemistry departments, information on 50 institutions at two periods was gathered using the fourth and fifth editions of the American Chemical Society's directory *College Chemistry Faculties*.[2] Thirteen private and 37 public institutions were involved as were 41 states and the District of Columbia. Schools with either blockbuster faculty rolls (40 or more members) or ratings in the top ten institutions were avoided, as possibly atypical. Freestanding subspecialty departments (most often biochemistry, but sometimes polymer science) and wholly independent specialized institutes were not included in these tallies. The hope was to present a composite picture of first, the typical representation of specialists, and second, after an additional step, their comparative article productivity.

Figure One indicates a remarkably consistent finding. Two types of specialists, organic and physical chemists, dominate the total number of chemists, almost always account for the lion's share of departmental staff, and rank first or second in any census of the departments. Moreover, this situation remains stable over time. A check three years later shows changes of no more than plus or minus two percent. This suggests that there is widespread agreement on the specialty composition of most chemistry departments and that a budgeting system for one institution might well satisfy many.

But it might be unwise to immediately opt for the census-of-specialists approach without a look at its census-of-papers counterpart. Output of papers from each department was followed through the "Corporate Index" of Science Citation Index for 1978-1980, roughly covering the output of authors in the directory's fourth edition, and 1981-83, covering that of the fifth.

FIGURE ONE:

WHAT IS THE TYPICAL CENSUS BY SPECIALISTS?

1978-1980

Total Chemists (963)	Ave. Share within Depts.	
	31 Depts. w/Biochemists	19 Depts. w/o Biochemists
Organic 30%	Organic 27%	Organic 34%
Physical 28%	Physical 25%	Physical 32%
Inorganic 17%	Inorganic 17%	Inorganic 20%
Analytical 13%	Biochemists 16%	Analytical 14%
Biochemsts 10%	Analytical 13%	Polymer 1%
Polymer 2%	Polymer 2%	

No. Depts. Numerically Dominated by Given Specialists	Changes in Total Chemists Noted 1981--83 (977)
Organic 47%	Organic -1%
Physical 41%	Physical 0%
Biochemists 6%	Inorganic 0%
Analytical 4%	Analytical +2%
Inorganic 2%	Biochemists 0%
Polymer 0%	Polymer 0%

Figure Two presents the reader with two situations: one reassuring, the other disquieting. At first it appears that since physical and organic chemistry continue their dominance, all is well. Once again they dominate in total numbers, account for the lion's share of papers, and rank first or second in most measures of relative output. Moreover, this situation is also very stable over time, with changes in the next three years varying by plus or minus one percent.

What is disquieting might be detected in the first component of Figure Two. Only two percentage points separate the output of the hitherto dominant organic group from that of the typically undermanned inorganic chemists. The third component in the figure presents an even starker surprise. The papers of inorganic chemists lead as many departments as do those of the organics. This suggests that while there is still good agreement in 30 of 50 of our schools, there is a good chance that inorganic chemists, or even biochemists, are outproducing their more numerous colleagues in the remaining 20 schools. How can this happen?

FIGURE TWO:

WHAT IS THE TYPICAL OUTPUT BY SPECIALISTS?

1978-1980

Total Papers (4,468)	Ave. Share within Depts. 31 Depts. w/Biochemists	Ave. Share within Depts. 19 Depts. w/o Biochemists
Physical 27%	Physical 29%	Physical 33%
Organic 21%	Organic 24%	Organic 27%
Inorganic 19%	Inorganic 18%	Inorganic 19%
Biochemists 16%	Biochemists 16%	Analytical 16%
Analytical 12%	Analytical 10%	Polymer 5%
Polymer 4%	Polymer 3%	

No. Depts. Numerically Dominated by Given Outputs	Changes in Total Papers Noted 1981--83 (5,187)
Physical 36%	Physical -1%
Organic 24%	Organic -1%
Inorganic 24%	Inorganic 0%
Biochemists 14%	Biochemists +1%
Analytical 2%	Analytical 0%
Polymer 0%	Polymer +1%

THE MOST PRODUCTIVE PEOPLE MAY NOT BE THE MOST NUMEROUS

Figure Three presents a sobering insight. It shows how often given specialty groups, when measured within their own departments at their own institutions, either significantly under-produced articles (10% below their representation) or overproduced them (10% above expectations).

One finding is clear. These specialty groups at the top in terms of representation – physical and organic chemists – are ironically those most often vulnerable to charges of underproduction. Of course it can be endlessly argued that these fields *vis-à-vis* the others are "not directly comparable," "accept only longer or more significant papers," "have higher standards," or "are more established and therefore have fewer unsolved problems." And it is undoubtedly true that citation

FIGURE THREE:

WHICH SPECIALTIES CHARACTERISTICALLY FAIL OR EXCEED OUTPUT EXPECTATIONS GIVEN THEIR NUMBERS WITHIN THEIR DEPARTMENTS

Specialty	Depts. with At Least 10% Shortfall	Depts. with At Least 10% Extra	Resulting Score
1978--1980			
Organic	24	2	-22
Physical	22	9	-13
Inorganic	5	18	+13
Analytical	7	6	-1
Biochemists	1	4	-3
Polymer	0	2	+2
1981--1983			
Organic	22	1	-21
Physical	19	8	-11
Inorganic	5	16	+11
Analytical	9	3	-6
Biochemists	1	7	-6
Polymer	0	1	+1

data might be able to resolve some of these claims. But it is beyond the resources of these authors to track citations to 1,100 chemists or 9,655 papers to find out. The answers to the puzzle of frequent underproduction are probably less a matter of technical publishing traditions than some basic sociology of academic life:

- Faculty numbers may be more reflective of course enrollment than research commitment. While the majorities within departments produced the greater number of papers 60% of the time, there are undoubtedly cases where numerous professors are on staff in light of demands for courses, and may not be doing any research at all.
- Majorities tend to sustain their numbers. The response of a majority group of organic chemists whose research output is faltering is not likely to involve disciplining themselves with a firing of one of their number. Rather, when a slot opens, they are positioned to hire yet another, hopefully more productive organic chemist.
- Minorities may be better positioned to avoid research distractions such as committee work, administrative duties, premedical advisory, the chairmanship, etc. They generally do not have the cospecialist votes to get elected. Yet they do have the convenient excuse of fewer peers to substitute for them instructionally or in the lab, should an attempt be made to appoint them.
- An "Avis" effect may be operating with some minority specialists ("Number Two tries harder"). In the battle for departmental resources, including library funds, minority specialists do not have the easy luxury of a census-based entitlement attitude, they are forced to go on the notion that they must produce more if they wish to argue for more.

A WORKABLE MIDDLE PATH

A key to practical implementation of this budgetary scheme is the use of judgment in the tabulation of specialists and their papers. In the personnel sphere it may be wise to discreetly discount those whose publishing careers are essentially over. Recent work[4] suggests that a four-year interval without a paper may be sufficient to declare the death of an active chemistry publishing program. On the other hand, a temporary indulgence may be granted those who are temporarily assigned administrative duties that do not bring with them offsetting access to increased help or materials or a decreased teaching load.

Publication patterns may also be adjusted in at least two, if not three, circumstances. A very substantial allowance should be granted to those who publish overview articles or chapters in reputable review journals or hardbound continuing series (e.g., *Chemical Reviews*, *Annual Review of Biochemistry*, *Advances in Organometallic Chemistry*, etc.). These works require an enormous commitment of time and demand an exceptional degree of familiarity with the literature. They also represent a substantial contribution towards time-saving in literature searching by others, including librarians. In any tally, such review works should be given much more weight than is a single paper.

Conversely, no great budgetary allowance should be made for chemists with many published abstracts of talks given at professional society meetings, when there is a pattern of little or no follow-up with regular articles. Likewise, much book reviewing and even most textbook authoring have limited involvement with the current literature and should be accorded a somewhat lower weight vis-à-vis a continued program of research-quality publications.

One area of controversy is the weight to be given the shorter papers found in "letters" journals. Some critics feel that there is a tendency to publish pieces of what would otherwise be one decent paper in an almost automated manner, and that the resultant inflation of one's vita with these "LPUs" (least publishable units) should not be rewarded. The contrary argument is that this genre and its vehicles represent the modern style of reporting fast-breaking bit-by-bit verification of research facts and that the journals that carry these bits have proven themselves through their high citation rate. These authors are inclined to value the paper by the vehicle that publishes it, consequently papers in *Biochemical and Biophysical Research Communications*, *Tetrahedron Letters*, and *Chemical Physical Letters* are counted much as full-length papers. Short works in lesser-cited letters journals might be devalued somewhat.

SUMMARY

Research journal budgeting should be allocated by the librarian in light of two factors inherent in, or under the control of, the individual departments. One approach is based on the census of specialists present. A general scheme by percentage of specialists is democratic and corresponds to demonstrated research productivity in 60% of the 50 cases examined in the study. Schemes based on productivity tend to reward the most prolific authors. They take into account the fact that representation of specialists may be more strongly affected by differences in the need for teachers brought on by different enrollments rather than by genuine research emphases. To avoid dubious allotments, judgment must be exercised when counting either personnel or papers.

NOTES

1. Jasper G. Schad, "Allocating Materials Budgets in Institutions of Higher Education," *Journal of Academic Librarianship* 3, no. 6 (January 1978): 328-332. Represents an excellent overview with which the authors nonetheless disagree on a number of points. Other notable and more recent budgetary or allocations modeling works, vulnerable to certain criticisms mentioned in this paper, include William E. McGrath, "Multidimensional Mapping of Book Circulation in a University Library," *College and Research Libraries* 44, no. 2 (March 1983): 103-115, and William McPheron, "Quantifying the Allocation of Monograph Funds: An Instance in Practice," *College and Research Libraries* 44, no. 2 (March 1983); 116-127. Apart from the voluminous price "complaint" literature there is little devoted to actual allocation schemes for serials. A good overview is found in Herbert S. White, "Strategies and Alternatives in Dealing with the Serials Management Budget," in Sul H. Lee, ed., *Serials Collection Development. Choices and Strategies* (Ann Arbor, MI: Pierian Press, 1981) p. 27-42.

2. *College Chemistry Faculties*, 4th and 5th editions. (Washington: American Chemical Society, 1977 and 1980) 189 and 197 pp.

3. The "Corporate Index" of *Science Citation Index* lists publications emanating from the sponsors or institutions of the authors of articles. One needs only to know the city and state of a school in order to find a list of most of its scientific output, and even that locational information can be found using the "Geographic Index" feature of the volume. In our counting scheme we awarded papers according to their journal's specialty (e.g., two papers in the *Journal of Physical Chemistry* became two papers credited to the physical chemists). To avoid misassignment we did not credit isolated papers in general chemistry journal to any specialty group. When these papers appeared under the name of an individual who had simultaneously published in specialty journals, they could be credited (e.g.,. two papers in the *Journal of Physical Chemistry* and one in the *Journal of the American Chemical Society* became three papers credited to the physical chemists).

4. Tony Stankus, "Journal Weeding in Relation to Declining Faculty Publishing Activity," *Science & Technology Libraries* 6 (1985), pp. 43-53.

Index